I0626797

MR. LLOYD GEORGE

A STUDY

MR. LLOYD GEORGE

A STUDY

BY

SIR CHARLES MALLET

Author of " A History of the University of Oxford," etc.

LONDON
ERNEST BENN LIMITED

First published in 1930

PRINTED IN GREAT BRITAIN

PREFACE

The object of this essay is to examine, as fairly and frankly as may be, the political record of Mr. Lloyd George. Writing as a member of the Liberal Party, of which Mr. Lloyd George was for many years a distinguished representative, and of which, it appears, he still desires to be the chief, I have approached certain political questions from a standpoint which men of other parties may not share. And I have made no secret of my belief that the best hope for the character and independence of Liberalism in future is to dissociate itself from the political fortunes of Mr. Lloyd George. But many of the issues treated here are national and not party issues, and I hope that I have not lost sight of that larger view. On the personal issue I will only say that I have tried to do justice to remarkable qualities, while criticising speech and action which it seems to me difficult to defend. And I claim that such criticisms as I have expressed rest on evidence which it is not easy to dispose of, and are at least inspired by candour and good faith.

As I wish to take full responsibility for what I have written, I will content myself with offering a general though sincere acknowledgment to the friends and correspondents who have helped me with knowledge or advice.

November 1929.   CHARLES MALLET.

CONTENTS

CHAPTER I

MR. LLOYD GEORGE'S ASCENT TO POWER

CONTENTS

CHAPTER II

MR. LLOYD GEORGE IN THE EARLY YEARS OF WAR

CHAPTER III

MR. LLOYD GEORGE AS A WAR MINISTER

CONTENTS

CHAPTER V

MR. LLOYD GEORGE AS A CONSTRUCTIVE STATESMAN

CONTENTS

CONTENTS

CHAPTER VI

MR. LLOYD GEORGE, POLITICAL FUSION AND POLITICAL FUNDS

CHAPTER VII

MR. LLOYD GEORGE AND THE LIBERAL PARTY

CONTENTS

MR. LLOYD GEORGE:
A STUDY

If a text be needed for this essay, it may be well to remind ourselves at the outset of some words which Lord Grey of Fallodon once used in a political address:

" Watch your motives, be honest with yourselves about your motives. That, I believe, is one of the most important rules for any man to observe in dealing with public affairs."

CHAPTER I

MR. LLOYD GEORGE'S ASCENT TO POWER

I

Mr. Lloyd George has attained a rare celebrity. He has been made the theme of many biographies. He has won warm admiration from followers in many fields. And the chief features of his story are sufficiently well known. Most Liberals look back with special interest to the earlier and more difficult years of his career, when the young Welshman, born in Manchester in 1863, brought up by his mother and a generous and devoted uncle in a humble village home, steeped in traditions of Nonconformity and independence, an adventurous little rebel in boyhood, with gifts of leadership, impulses of mischief, and a great power of winning friends, found his way

at sixteen into a lawyer's office at Portmadoc, began
to train himself to read, to speak, to write, to study
politics, to equip himself consciously or uncon-
sciously for an active political career. Biographers
have told us of his precocity in boyhood, of his readiness to argue upon every subject—especially on
questions of baptism and tithe—of his early defiance
of constituted authorities like the village rector and
the village squire, of the " superb self-assurance,"
the audacity combined with calculating judgment,
which made itself manifest at an early age.   His
Journals, in part published, tell us something of his
hopes and struggles. He was quick to realise the
need of industry and courage if he was to satisfy his
" thirst for renown." In 1880 some spirited articles
over the signature of Brutus in the *North Wales Express* made their mark and brought him into notice.
In 1881, when he paid his first visit to London, and
was disappointed with the appearance of the House
of Commons, a passionate defence of Arabi Pasha
revealed to the debaters of Portmadoc the young
Welshman's love of nationalism and his rare ora-
torical powers. In 1884 he was already hailing Mr.
Joseph Chamberlain as a future leader: " He is a
Radical, and doesn't care who knows it as long as
the people do." Mr. Chamberlain's example proved
a strong influence. Had young Lloyd George found
his way into politics sooner, it is possible that it
might have proved too strong even for his attachment to Home Rule. But in February 1886 a visit
paid by Michael Davitt to Festiniog gave him an

opportunity of expressing his eloquent admiration
for a popular leader who had not feared to show
himself a rebel, and brought him definitely into the
Home Rule camp.

Early in 1885 Lloyd George started in practice as
a lawyer on his own account. Some thought it a
rash enterprise. But he soon drew a following round
him. Men marked him as a sturdy democrat.
They noted the combination of genuine idealism
with practical astuteness and resource. Farmers,
labourers, fishermen, Nonconformists, all friends of
independence, all rebels against vested interests—all
conscious of a grievance, often a just grievance,
against the feudal conditions which still governed
country life in Wales—found the fearless and adventurous young lawyer ready to defend their cause.
He was a fighter from the first: pugnacity is perhaps
his strongest instinct. He fought tithes and burial
laws and fishing restrictions, the claims of the land-
lords, the supremacy of the Church. And to these
fights he brought, not always, it may be, the most
perfect taste or fairness or discretion, but an astonishing confidence and intrepidity of spirit, an astonishing readiness and persuasiveness of speech. His
fame spread far. He missed no chance of increasing
it, of pressing his campaign against feudalism in
Wales. The Local Government Act of 1888 gave
new opportunities to Welsh democracy. The " Boy
Alderman " of the Carnarvon County Council, intent on breaking the power of the parsons and the
squires, began to make himself the leader of some-

thing like a national movement. Problems of Welsh
Disestablishment and Welsh Home Rule entered the
region of practical politics. In March 1890 a bye-
election in the Carnarvon Boroughs brought to a
head this long-simmering revolt. Lloyd George
came forward as a candidate. A village lad he
might be; but the day of the villagers, he told his
followers, had begun to dawn. By a great effort and
a very narrow majority the seat was won. At the
age of twenty-seven the vigorous and successful
young lawyer, still ignorant of the great world which
he was to enter, but already a proved and confident
protagonist in the small world which he had made
his own, found himself a Member of the House of
Commons.

II

It was no easy day for Liberalism when Mr. Lloyd
George entered Parliament. But it was a day which
offered great opportunities in opposition and revolt.
He was not one of those who find the way open at
once to Ministerial circles. Nearly sixteen years of
Parliamentary apprenticeship and of remarkable
Parliamentary achievement were to elapse before
he took his seat on the Treasury Bench. But once
there he remained there uninterruptedly for sixteen
or seventeen years more. Always sensitive to the in-
fluences round him, he may have felt the atmosphere
of the House at first a little chilling. He was slow to
take liberties with it. His maiden speech in June
1890, against compensation for publicans, was easy,

humorous, winning and quick to realise the temper of his audience. The speaker—in those days he was wise enough to take pains in preparing his speeches —confessed that he had succeeded beyond his highest expectations. Great judges joined in expressing their praise. But before long a bolder note was struck. There were attacks on grants for Royalties and Viceroys, reminders of the needs of poorer people, urgent demands for Welsh Disestablishment, pressed, as some Liberals thought, unreasonably hard. Mr. Lloyd George soon became known as a brilliant platform speaker. But to the Liberal Whips he was at first a thorn in the flesh. It was no easy thing in 1893–94 for Liberal leaders to hold their small majority together, to carry through the difficult tasks undertaken by the party as a whole. And there were even Liberals from Wales who found the young Member for Carnarvon too much inclined to fight for sectional interests, too ready to assume the mantle of a Welsh Parnell.

But when the Liberals went into the wilderness these difficulties declined. There was no call then to harass Liberal leaders by insisting on priority for Welsh interests. There was far more to be gained by exposing the errors and failings of Unionist statesmen. In that congenial task all Liberals could unite. And in the opportunities which a Parliamentary Opposition offers Mr. Lloyd George was pre-eminently fitted to excel. He became one of the nimblest of guerilla leaders : in opposition it is not always imperative to be discreet. He fought the Agricultural

Rating Bill of 1896. He fought the Voluntary
Schools Bill of 1897. He fought the closure. He
underwent suspension. But every observer of experience noted his growing mastery of Parliamentary
methods and his unfailing intrepidity and resource.
In days of divided counsels, when a passion for resignation seemed to have overtaken their accustomed
leaders, many Liberals learned to realise the value
of a vigorous and confident fighter, who, however
insignificant his following, was rarely unready to give
the lead desired.

Once, indeed, in those years a greater issue stirred
deeper feelings, touched a loftier height. The policy
which produced the South African War has already
passed into happy oblivion. But the sharp differences of opinion which it roused gave a bitter edge
to party feeling. The tide of excitement which swept
over the country, aggravated by military failures,
made it difficult to oppose the action of the Government without seeming to imperil national unity and
to weaken the support given to our forces in the
field. That difficulty Mr. Lloyd George boldly faced.
Fearless he has always been. But he showed now a
rarer kind of courage. He set himself to stem the
tide. He may have been right or wrong in his con-
tentions. Englishmen, if among the stubbornest, are
also among the most generous of nations, and it is
possible that in retrospect the majority of his
countrymen would range themselves on Mr. Lloyd
George's side. But at the time the opponents of the
war were overwhelmed. Many preferred to be silent.

While the war was going badly, the nation would not listen to arguments against it. It required some quality higher than self-confidence for Mr. Lloyd George to face hostile audiences at Glasgow or at Birmingham, to fling himself for the first time against the current of opinion in his native Wales. He enjoyed fighting, no doubt. But he risked not only unpopularity and violence. He risked his professional future and his means of support. He saw his practice disappearing, his household broken up. He was burned in effigy in his own Boroughs. He had to strain every nerve to keep his seat. He came through in the end, triumphant and ennobled, for courage of that quality to some extent ennobles men. He had won the admiration of a multitude of Liberals whom Parliamentary dexterity alone would never touch. Had he learned from that searching experience the value of faithful idealism in public life? Or had he learned to ask himself the question whether such sacrifices were in the end worth making, whether it might not be wiser for a man who aimed at political ascendency to swim with the tide of popular applause?

Fame had come to him now and a place in Parliament hardly second to that occupied by the Liberal chiefs. Mr. Chamberlain had no livelier opponent. It is amusing to find Mr. Lloyd George in these days insisting on Mr. Chamberlain's " strong, forcible, but rather savage personality," and dismissing him as too impulsive and impatient to be considered a great statesman. Among Conservatives

there were critics who compared the two com-
batants freely with each other, in their self-assertiveness, their incisive oratory, their power of making
themselves storm-centres and concentrating attention on their plans. The comparison may have been
just or not, but in the fight against Mr. Chamberlain's policy, and even more in the fight against Mr.
Balfour's Education Bill, Mr. Lloyd George again
proved his great Parliamentary powers. In the Education controversy he won not only the applause of
his colleagues, but the undisguised appreciation of
the Unionist Leader. Mr. Balfour rarely failed to see
the weaker points of any cause which he defended,
or the stronger points of those to whom he was
opposed. Mr. Lloyd George carried the fight into
the Welsh counties and rallied Welsh Nonconformity, Welsh nationality, again to his support. On
Free Trade his speeches were as winning and acute,
if the note was a little more uncertain. Economics
never appealed to him so powerfully as the idea of
asserting the rights of democracy and improving the
lot of the poor. But long before the fall of the
Unionist Administration it was evident that in any
Liberal Government Mr. Lloyd George would be
entitled to a leading place. When the new Parliament met in 1906, the Board of Trade, where Mr.
Gladstone and Mr. Chamberlain had first made
their names as great administrators, was watching
another notable figure start on his Ministerial
career.

III

It was in that new Parliament that I first found an opportunity of studying Parliamentary leaders from inside the House. Mr. Balfour's singular method of eluding the fiscal problem set him by his formidable colleague had paralysed and for a time ruined the hopes of the Unionist Party. The Liberals, reinvigorated by their opponents' errors, and reunited by the settlement of the conflict in South Africa, had returned in overwhelming numbers. If Mr. Lloyd George had done much to make the Education question a victorious issue, Mr. Asquith had rendered even more conspicuous service by his admirable exposition of Free Trade. Men who for some years past had owned a very uncertain allegiance to Liberalism found themselves returned as Free Traders to Parliament, to swell the great heterogeneous majority at Sir Henry Campbell-Bannerman's back. The Liberal Government was already formed, and it was not easy for new-comers on the crowded benches behind it to find opportunities of making themselves felt or heard. Scores if not hundreds of new Members were waiting to deliver maiden speeches. Even noted lawyers like John Simon or Stanley Buckmaster found it strangely difficult to catch the Speaker's eye. Mr. Lowther, most imperturbable of Speakers, might be detected trying to familiarise himself with the names of innumerable novices by the help of illustrated Parliamentary guides; and the novices on their side were no less eager to make their appearance familiar to the Speaker, whose recognition was the first step on the path to fame.

My own recollections now include six Speakers, beginning with Mr. Brand, for in early days I attended debates as a visitor with an even keener interest than I felt as a Member of the House. I might almost add a seventh, Lord Eversley, with whose kindred I had some slight connection, who left the Chair in 1857, but lived on, like his well-remembered nephew, to a very ripe and honourable old age. Almost every Speaker in turn wins high appreciation. It is perhaps not so difficult as has sometimes been imagined to fill that exalted Chair. For, unlike the Chairman of Committees, the Speaker cannot in effect be challenged. His rulings, even if they should afterwards prove to be founded in error, are practically certain to be supported at the moment by the great majority of the House. Of those that I remember in the Chair Mr. Peel, I think, excelled in majesty, Mr. Lowther in his cool, commanding humour, his sure and quiet mastery of every situation. Mr. Whitley may have had a task in some respects more difficult. But his triumph was not less complete. To a fairness so transparent as to be almost irresistible he added a persuasive patience not always needed before. His reward was the affection as well as the respect of his subjects. And no one doubts that Mr. Whitley's successors, whatever changes overtake democracy, will sustain the traditions which their predecessors have bequeathed.

The Ministerial majority of 1906 was overwhelming when united. But it had diversities and cross-currents in it. The Labour Party had just emerged as a separate if not yet formidable power. They voted almost always with the Liberals. Even had they voted against them, their opposition alone could have had no serious effect. But there was from the first in the Liberal ranks a substantial number of Members who on questions of social legislation or in matters of military expenditure were anxious, even over-anxious, to show their sympathy with Labour views. Stronger in sentiment perhaps than in economic training, they formed an element of weakness in the vast Ministerial majority. They could generally be brought into line by Sir Henry Campbell-Bannerman, and rather less easily by Mr. Asquith. And they were supposed to have special affinities with the opinions and plans of Mr. Lloyd George. The Conservatives, few in numbers and powerless in the lobbies, contrived nevertheless to assert themselves with assurance and effect. And the young lions of the Opposition, encouraged by their Whips to speak on every opportunity, while the budding orators on the Speaker's right sat by reluctantly repressed, men like Robert Cecil, F. E. Smith, George Cave and many another, made themselves quickly conspicuous and renowned. The present leader of the Conservative Party, who entered the House in 1908, was not yet conspicuous among them. But Mr. Bonar Law was recognised already as one of the ablest and adroitest of debaters, and Stanley

Baldwin was destined to owe much to Mr. Bonar
Law. To a new-comer the chief attraction of the
House, apart from the interest of debates and the
charm of new friends and new experiences, was its
atmosphere of good feeling and good manners. Men
wished to seem at their best, and generally were at
their best, in it. Bad taste and insincerity were at
once detected. Egotism and self-assurance were
forced to keep within limits. Players who needed
teaching were taught to play the game. The House
of Commons has long ceased to be, if it ever was, the
first Club in London. But it is probable that its
obstinate tradition of good breeding will be strong
enough to conquer any vicissitudes of chance or
time.

Still it must be admitted that the Parliament of
1906 was in many respects a dull one. The Liberal
majority was too large: there could be little excitement over divisions. The deep passions roused by
the Boer War had died away. The keen struggle over
Home Rule was for the moment in abeyance,
though ageing and illustrious figures on the Irish
benches bore witness still to that unsatisfied demand.
Nonconformity had proved its strength. Free Trade
had triumphed. And though the problem of re-
ligious education remained, and Mr. Birrell's brilliant conduct of his Education Bill aroused strong
interest, there were no issues before us so absorbing
as the great issues of Mr. Gladstone's or Mr. Chamberlain's day. The passing of those rich personalities
left the whole world of politics poorer. With Mr.

Gladstone a glory had departed. Few men who had served under him could feel quite the same zest in public life again. And Mr. Chamberlain's decline from power had taken both colour and sting from political conflict. In the Parliament of 1906 he rarely appeared. He was not popular in that House, though he never failed to be impressive. Mr. Herbert Paul's well-remembered attack on him—a masterpiece of polished vituperation—awoke fierce sympathy in the majority of Members. And when Mr. Chamberlain spoke he seemed to some to survey the ranks of his opponents with a bitter and watchful hostility, which did not soften such resentments as remained. His speech on the Education Bill on May 9, 1906, with its wide outlook, its frank independence, and the sense of concentrated power which it conveyed, was his most remarkable contribution to debate. It was listened to on the Liberal benches with more sympathy than the speaker perhaps realised, with more, one almost thought, than he seemed willing to accept. But Mr. Chamberlain, whose genuine kindliness will not be forgotten by Liberals who knew something of it, as I once did in earlier days, passed only too soon from the House of Commons, and the strongest force in Parliament passed with him out of public life.

It was interesting in those years to watch Mr. Balfour, whose reputation had suffered in the years which preceded the Conservative *débacle*, gradually recovering his ascendency, not only with his own party, but with the Opposition. There were moments at first when Mr. Balfour's recurrence to arguments on the fiscal problem, which seemed to Free Traders ambiguous and evasive, rendered blunt comments like Sir Henry Campbell-Bannerman's " Enough of this foolery " highly acceptable to the House. Between the Prime Minister and the Leader of the Opposition there were to the last differences of temperament which no exercise of mutual tolerance could bridge. But as time passed, and as the Liberal majority began to realise the strength behind the superficial weakness, the resource, the tenacity, the breadth of view and skill in argument which accompanied tactics sometimes difficult to understand, Mr. Balfour quietly reconquered the House. His speaking there, it always seemed to me, depended more than with most men on physical conditions. When in good health he had few equals in urbanity and charm. When below par physically he appeared less happy and assured. In this inequality he suffered at times from comparison with Mr. Asquith, who in Parliament was hardly ever unequal to himself. I do not remember any occasion when Mr. Asquith in the House of Commons fell below his own high level. On the platform, it is true, in his latter years especially, as the habit of studied and deliberate speech grew on him, Mr. Asquith did not move his audience so readily as many speakers of inferior note. But his mastery in Parliament was to the end unquestioned. The admirable form, the happy, stately phrasing, the terse and cogent argument, the perfect temper, never failed. Humour and

irony were always at his call, and a shrewd eye for
the weak points of an opponent. No man excelled
more surely, whether in exposition, in elegy or in
debate.

Among other famous orators and speakers Mr.
Lloyd George was in those days less sure in the
House of Commons. His special field of conquest
was the platform. His level varied. But at his best
he was completely master of any audience to which
he spoke. Mr. Birrell both in the House and on the
platform had qualities which made him irresistible,
and by the end of 1906 his reputation with his party
had reached its highest point. Sir Edward Grey had
added in office a note of quiet authority to speeches
which always held and pleased the House. Younger
Members, too, drew listeners readily. Winston
Churchill's force and brilliancy, Charles Master-
man's quickness in winning the favour of his
audience, John Simon's rare gifts of intellect and
argument stood by no means alone. Of the powers
of speech possessed by Liberal lawyers there were in
those years many notable examples. Two distinguished advocates, who literally gave their lives in
politics, will be long remembered by their friends.
Lawson Walton, with an almost perfect voice and
manner, was one of the most finished speakers
heard in that Parliament. Robson, a delightful debater, never recovered from the work imposed on
him by the Budget of 1909. Between the parties
Harold Cox held sway. And outside the Liberal and
Conservative ranks, among speakers from the Irish

and the Labour benches, there were at least two
voices which commanded every ear. Rarely as Mr.
Healy spoke, the old fires were there, the old fierceness, irony and humour, the old power of holding
and of moving men. And Ramsay MacDonald,
young, eloquent, assured, appealing, and not yet
tormented by the necessity of proving himself in
some way different from the Liberals in whose
Lobby he was found, was making speeches which
seemed to make him admirably suited for a post in
the Cabinet which Sir Henry Campbell-Bannerman
led.

IV

The first two years of the Liberal Government, one
of its most eminent members has told us, were " peculiarly free from personal differences and restlessness." Mr. Lloyd George was winning golden
opinions at the Board of Trade. The demagogue, as
some opponents thought him, was proving in office,
as Mr. Chamberlain had proved before, his practical shrewdness, his adaptability and resource. Mr.
Lloyd George's energy and open-mindedness, his
persuasive methods, his readiness to consult and
draw together men of different views and interests,
his adroitness in defending his proposals in Parliament, his sensitiveness to opinion, his quick eye for a
deal, all helped to make his administration of his first
Department a remarkable success. The legislation
of 1907–8, the Merchant Shipping Act, the Patents
Act and the Port of London Act, bore witness to the

new Minister's activity. And his skilful intervention to avert a strike of railway workers was widely recognised as a great public service. When Mr. Asquith succeeded Sir Henry Campbell-Bannerman as Prime Minister, and Mr. Morley declined to become Chancellor of the Exchequer, the Liberal Party welcomed with sympathy and interest Mr. Lloyd George's appointment to that post. His willingness to serve under Mr. Asquith was at that date, no doubt, perfectly sincere. But, as his opportunities widened, his ambitions, it may be, widened too. And close observers, who were not unkindly critics, felt, as time passed, that his attitude towards his colleagues altered, that his restlessness became more evident, that the temptation to play for his own hand increased. One of Mr. Lloyd George's most enthusiastic biographers has told us that he judges men by their usefulness in furthering his policy, and that " no consideration of private friendship is allowed to hamper his course " in that respect.

At the Exchequer Mr. Lloyd George's work was not so successful as at the Board of Trade. The truth is, he did not always master very thoroughly the economic or financial problems with which he had to deal. There are stories, well authenticated, of Treasury officials who saw with dismay important papers tossed aside, while the Minister invited them to talk to him instead. He was so active in collecting information, so alert to pick the brains of others, so justly confident of his ability to make the most of all that he was told, that he hardly realised how much a

Minister may gain by an appetite for reading such
as Mr. Churchill's, to say nothing of the trained intellect and determined application of a Gladstone or
a Peel. And thus, while plunging with courage and
enthusiasm into great projects for improving social
conditions, he never fully understood the possible
consequences of his own proposals, or the complexity
of the conditions which he had light-heartedly and
gallantly undertaken to transform. The vast number of agreed amendments on the Report Stage of
the National Insurance Bill [1] is an indication of the
" raw edges " which Mr. Lloyd George's legislative
proposals generally revealed. At the Treasury he
was in the wrong place. His mind seethed with
plans for spending public money, plans difficult
to reconcile with the tradition which made the
Treasury the watch-dog of finance. The plans in
themselves were benevolent and large, and inspired
by a real wish to benefit humanity. But benevo-
lence without exact knowledge is apt to be the curse
of the social reformer. If every philanthropist had
to be trained in economics, how much solider the
progress of the world might be!

Treasury traditions were not allowed to daunt the
fighting spirit of the new Chancellor. Mr. Lloyd
George was soon again in the forefront of the battle
wherever the battle of Liberalism was waged. The
Budget of 1909, with its large, ambitious projects,
was not in all respects a satisfactory performance,

---

[1] 480 is the number alleged.

and it was received at first with some degree of coolness. But, helped by the mistakes of his opponents,
Mr. Lloyd George managed to convert it into a great
popular success. His bold challenge to vested interests, the super-tax for rich men, the high licences for
brewers, and above all the attempt to secure for the
public some part of the unearned increment of land,
gradually became a rallying-cry for the forces of
democracy. The fierceness with which these proposals were attacked roused enthusiasm among
their supporters. An intensive campaign followed in
the country. The Budget League outdid all rivals in
advertisement. "We spent without counting the
cost," says one of Mr. Lloyd George's biographers—
a confession which perhaps one would rather not
associate with the Chancellor of the Exchequer. And
the Chancellor himself spared no effort to carry his
schemes through. He made his Budget an issue between rich and poor. If sometimes, as at Limehouse,
he used defiant phrases, the defiance was calculated
to strike resounding chords. And on many platforms
he defended his policy with remarkable persuasiveness and address. So cautious an opponent as Sir
William Anson thought one of Mr. Lloyd George's
speeches in this campaign the finest example of platform oratory in that generation. And I well remember a meeting at Plymouth in January 1910, when
he spoke to an audience of over nine thousand
people—men closely packed, for " suffragette " outrages had rendered difficult the admission of women.
The vast audience could not all see the speaker; so

he mounted on a kitchen chair, and stood there for an hour speaking, with a Blue-book under one arm. His voice had suffered a little in the Election campaign; but he made himself heard without effort. "What shall I talk about?" he had asked me; and I had answered, "Taxing the foreigner is the one cry here." He took that phrase for his text and enlarged upon it, with deviations, it is true, to subsidiary topics. But he argued it with winning simplicity and charm; and he linked it up with one of those eloquent pleas for generous and sympathetic treatment of the unfortunate and needy, which in speaking were so often the secret of his power. That Election was won, as Elections generally are, less by our merits than by the mistakes of our opponents. The House of Lords, misled by violent partisanship, had risked its future to defy the Liberal majority in the House of Commons, and found itself committed to a struggle for the retention of powers which in the Liberal view it had abused. And the passage of the Parliament Bill was rendered practically certain, under Mr. Asquith's cool and steady leadership, by a second Election before the end of 1910.

But during that eventful year Mr. Lloyd George's action was curiously perplexing. He had supplied most of the fuel for the conflict. But the reduction of the Liberal majority in January, though almost inevitable in any Election after 1906, may have made him doubtful about the issue of the fight, and for a time he seems to have hesitated as to the wisdom of persisting with the Bill to limit the veto of the House of Lords.[1] The theory which would represent Mr. George as a man of undeviating purpose, seeing his object always steadily before him and marching towards it with unfaltering step, is of course a pure illusion. He is a man essentially of variable temperament, naturally self-confident and full of fight, often bold and vehement to the point of rashness, but often recalled to prudence by the possibility of defeat. The year 1909 had revealed his energy in attack, but had shown him perhaps that the walls of Jericho would not fall at the first blast of the trumpet. The year 1910 revealed his suppleness in negotiation, his first overtures for compromise or coalition with his opponents. In 1909 he had been the Radical protagonist, assailing liquor, land, capitalism, every stronghold of the Unionist Party. In 1910, in the months following King Edward's death, he was the prime mover in a series of negotiations, which aimed at sinking party differences altogether and settling every point at issue by an all-round scheme of give and take.

Mr. Asquith was of course a member of the secret Conference which assembled, and he defended it steadily in the House of Commons. But the spirit behind it was that of Mr. Lloyd George, with his infinite belief in the possibility of deals. No set views about Ireland or Tariffs or the House of Lords, no stubbornness in refusing to compromise opinions,

[1] Mr. Harold Spender has stated this plainly (*David Lloyd George*, 1919, p. 199). Alternative proposals for the reform of the House of Lords were preferred by some prominent Liberal leaders.

were to interfere with a comprehensive plan. Mr.
Balfour, always appreciative of Mr. George's political adroitness, and naturally inclined to look with
favour on any form of nimbleness or elasticity of
mind, was disposed to encourage the Chancellor of
the Exchequer and to give him all the rope that he
desired. The negotiations dragged on. The mystery
deepened. Outspoken politicians in all parties began
to show impatience at the secrecy imposed and at
the rumours which escaped. Protests were made
against a prolonged political fog. Mr. Asquith was
adjured to bring out of the Conference " a Liberal
Party standing on a Liberal foundation, and not a
coalition or a group of opportunists." Mr. Balfour's
followers and Mr. Redmond's became equally restless and uneasy. Politicians in all camps found it
necessary to remind their leaders that solid political
beliefs existed which no scheme of bargaining could
destroy. In the end Mr. Lloyd George's efforts for a
general understanding failed. A veil was drawn over
the whole transaction. And in the Election which
followed the Chancellor of the Exchequer vindicated
afresh his right to be regarded as the most redoubt-
able of uncompromising party men.

The dream of a Coalition passed for a time. Party
feeling increased in intensity. Home Rule drew
nearer, and the more turbulent spirits of the Conservative Party prepared themselves ostensibly for
Civil War. But Mr. Lloyd George persevered with
his large plans. The Budgets of 1910, 1911, 1912 and
1913—Mr. Lloyd George has presented no less than

eight Budgets to the House of Commons—though
far less ambitious and contentious than the
" People's Budget " of 1909, were inspired by the
same desire to make finance an engine of social improvement, and showed the same inclination to disregard old doctrines of retrenchment and to make
the Treasury one of the spending departments of the
State. But they introduced no startling changes in
finance. National expenditure reached the " very
gigantic " figure of £195 millions. But it was evident
that the country could stand it. Unemployment was
at its lowest, trade, production and profits were at
their best. The Budget of May 1914 reflected the
same astonishing prosperity. And it contained bold
and far-reaching proposals for remodelling local
taxation, which were not altogether happily drafted
and which had ultimately to be withdrawn. But
meanwhile the Chancellor of the Exchequer continued to press forward his important schemes. A
complete valuation of the land was undertaken. In
1911 Mr. Lloyd George carried through Parliament
a great measure of National Health Insurance,
founded in genuine social enthusiasm and handled
in the House of Commons with his accustomed skill.
But the project showed many signs of insufficient
preparation, and it proved for the moment disastrous to Liberals at bye-elections. The same year
saw another promising and useful plan adopted, a
scheme for insuring against unemployment the
workers engaged in certain trades. Projects of
national development, and especially of road de-

velopment—projects at first perhaps a little hazy but both ambitious and far-sighted—had taken shape already in the legislation of 1909. And after 1911 Mr. Lloyd George began to turn his attention to plans for developing another land campaign. That project he has since revived. But it must be confessed that in the interval he has damped the spirits of land crusaders by throwing over, with little appearance of regret, nearly all that remained of the land taxes of his most famous Budget. If it be true, as stated in June 1928 by a brilliant political antagonist who has often been a participant in his schemes, that the increment value duty, reversion duty and undeveloped land duty together yielded in eleven years only £1,300,000,[1] their parent may perhaps be forgiven for displaying a certain indifference to the fate of his offspring. But those who believe, with an earlier Mr. Churchill, that the endeavour to secure for public uses some part of the unearned increment of private land is neither impracticable nor unfair, were glad to see that principle at any rate raised from the grave to which its author had consigned it, and reaffirmed later in the publications of Mr. Lloyd George's Land and Nation League.

The year 1914 found Mr. Lloyd George in a position of very real authority and power. He had a great name in Parliament, a greater name still in the country. If he was sometimes fiercely attacked—

[1] See Mr. Winston Churchill's speech reported in *The Times* of June 6, 1928. The fourth new tax, the mineral rights duty, substituted for the original proposal to tax ungotten minerals, proved more productive.

and the criticisms passed on him in the so-called
Marconi scandal seemed, even to many Liberals who
regretted his action, to be magnified and envenomed
by party feeling [1]—he was also very warmly and
widely acclaimed. If candid friends and even com-
patriots admitted a strong element of egotism in his
nature and a certain element of " gammon " in his
speeches, the public at large did not resent, perhaps
hardly perceived, these traits. In 1884 he had hailed
Mr. Chamberlain as " the future leader of the
people," and thirty years later he seemed as likely
as Mr. Chamberlain had ever been to step into that
place. Like Mr. Chamberlain, he had become the
spokesman of Nonconformist and democratic feeling.
Like Mr. Chamberlain, he was a popular orator with
a special stronghold of his own—Wales was almost
as devoted as Birmingham—and with a wide following in the constituencies beyond. Like Mr. Chamberlain, he was alert, self-confident, indefatigable,
full of new schemes, keenly alive to electioneering
tactics, a good friend to those who attached themselves to his interests, but not unduly hampered by
the claims of colleagues or by a sense of loyalty to
his official chief. Like Mr. Chamberlain, pledged to
peace and retrenchment, he had shown himself as
quick as any Imperialist to defend the rights and
obligations of Great Britain, and as quick as any
Socialist to throw over economic maxims which

---

[1] I shared this opinion. Mr. Asquith took a grave view
of the offence, but was characteristically generous to the
offenders.

conflicted with his political designs. And like Mr. Chamberlain, he was, in the view of many Liberals who observed him closely, and of some colleagues who had stood by him with staunch sympathy in the difficult days of his career, a little too ready to push his own views and his own ambitions, a little too impatient to grasp the first place in controlling the destinies of the Liberal Party.

CHAPTER II

MR. LLOYD GEORGE IN THE EARLY YEARS OF WAR

It is difficult even now, when our knowledge of the facts is growing clearer, to measure with justice the greatness or the littleness of many prominent actors in the tragedy of the War. Few Liberals will blame Mr. Lloyd George for his reluctance to enter into it in July 1914. He had, it is true, startled some of his friends in 1911 by his strong warning to Germany of the dangers which her policy in Morocco might provoke. But he had always been a lover of peace. He had repeatedly advocated a reduction of armaments. And in an interview published as late as New Year's Day 1914 he had urged that the moment had come to overhaul our naval and military expenditure, largely on the ground that our relations with Germany, thanks to the " wise and patient diplomacy of Sir Edward Grey," were " infinitely more friendly " than they had been for years. His forecasts may have been at fault, but his unwillingness to go to war was genuine. His doubts were shared to the last by several of his colleagues. And it was only the pressure of circumstances, the call to defend Belgium against invasion, and Mr. Asquith's steadiness and patience, which finally brought all but two members of the Cabinet to the conclusion that it was not possible for us to keep out of war.

I

As Chancellor of the Exchequer Mr. Lloyd George was of course primarily concerned in the financial measures taken to maintain confidence and prevent panic in the City; and if he lacked the special knowledge or experience to give a lead on difficult economic problems, his quickness and resource and his readiness to take counsel with others proved very useful to the common cause. It is easy to criticise in retrospect expedients resorted to in difficult times, and the Moratorium proclaimed in August 1914 may have been in some respects open to objection. But the Emergency Measures taken by the Government were undoubtedly successful in restoring confidence among the banks and in tiding over the most difficult days of the crisis. Among the resources of British War Finance the Government's readiness to borrow as compared with its reluctance to tax, some of the forms of borrowing adopted, the high rates of interest offered, and the repeated extensions of bank credit, contained features open to criticism, and entailed some consequences probably prejudicial in the long run to the public interest. A Minister of rare financial genius might perhaps have avoided some mistakes. But it would not be fair to hold Mr. Lloyd George entirely responsible for those which were made. He realised from the first the special nature of the British contribution to the Allied cause. And he was a past master of all the arts of publicity employed so successfully later to popularise some of the loans. But he has been widely and not unjustly criticised for his failure in 1915 to impose heavy additional taxation; and it must be admitted that the reasons which he gave in that year for refusing to do so showed no adequate appreciation of the length and severity of the struggle ahead. It may be that he was already too much absorbed in the question of munitions to give the time needed to problems of finance.

Both in 1914 and in 1915, however, Mr. Lloyd George did propose large increases of taxation on the liquor interest, which he was not wholly successful in carrying through; and he combined with these proposals still larger schemes for buying up the drink traffic, which there was little chance of passing through Parliament, and which failed to win assent from many of his colleagues. There are passages in Mr. Asquith's Diary in the spring of 1915 which throw a vivid light on these activities, and on the sharp divisions of opinion which an overburdened Prime Minister had almost daily to compose.

"March 31, 1915.—No sooner had I settled the row between L.G. and McKenna and all but settled the earlier row between Lloyd George and K. than this versatile and volatile personage goes off at a tangent on the question of drink. His mind apparently oscillates from hour to hour between the two poles of absurdity, cutting off all drink from the working man —which would lead to something like a universal strike—or buying out the whole liquor trade of the country and replacing it by a huge State monopoly."

On April 1 Mr. Lloyd George and Mr. McKenna
were momentarily in the happiest accord, urging on
the Prime Minister a scheme for purchase at a cost
of two hundred and fifty millions. On April 8 Mr.
Lloyd George was " engaged in his usual process of
roping in everybody, Opposition leaders, Labour,
temperance men, etc.," and was persuaded that he
would get them all in. On April 15 nationalisation
was losing ground, but a substitute more limited in
character had been proposed, and Mr. Lloyd George
was to the fore with fresh approaches to brewers,
teetotallers and "the whole motley crowd of interests."
On April 19 the great schemes for purchase and for
prohibition gave way to more modest and practicable designs. But if these ambitious plans can be
made to wear a certain aspect of absurdity, and if a
love of large schemes imperfectly considered has
always been one of Mr. Lloyd George's weaknesses
in public life, it should not be forgotten that the
object behind them, the control and diminution of
the temptations to drink, was honourable to the
Minister who kept it in view. The action of the
Board of Control which he subsequently established,
restricting the facilities for buying drink in munition
areas, not only made converts to the policy of
purchase, but proved of undoubted value to the
State. And the candour and courage with which he
urged the need for self-control upon munition
workers and the duty of self-discipline upon the
nation as a whole, had their reward in the results
which they obtained. One cannot but wish that

Mr. Lloyd George's whole time had been occupied in labours as disinterested as these.

It has been stated that Mr. Lloyd George did not in the early months of the War take an active part in its direction. The Heads of the War Office and Admiralty were of course most prominent in executive action, and they, with the Prime Minister, were mainly and properly responsible for the daily conduct of operations. But for any serious decision in policy or strategy the War Council and its expert advisers were summoned, and its conclusions, formulated in writing, were circulated to the Departments in cases of urgency on the same day. Of this War Council Mr. Lloyd George was one of the earliest and most important members, and it is quite clear that he was from the first an active participant in almost all decisions of moment. He had, no doubt, his variations of opinion. In October 1914 he was pressing almost to the point of resignation differences with Lord Kitchener over recruiting in Wales. In November he had become " an enthusiastic Kitchenerite "—a conversion not destined to endure. In January 1915 he was already urging the schemes for large operations in the Balkans based on Salonica, to which he returned so often and with such unhappy consequences later on. Sir William Robertson tells us that Mr. Lloyd George's New Year Memorandum actually proposed that the entire Expeditionary Force, except a general reserve, should be withdrawn from France and sent to the Balkans.[1] In February

[1] See *Soldiers and Statesmen, 1914–1918*, Vol. I, p. 82.

he was persuading Sir John French to agree to the
despatch of troops to help the Serbians, was visiting
Paris and reporting to his colleagues on the weakness of the French Government, suggesting that he
himself should be sent as an extraordinary ambassador to Russia and the Balkan States, actively discussing with the Prime Minister every aspect of the
difficult situation which we had to face. There were
very few occasions of importance on which his voice
was not distinctly heard. " Our two rhetoricians,
Lloyd George and Winston," their chief confides to
his Diary, " have good brains of different types. But
they can only think talking." The rhetoric, when
reduced to reality, could, no doubt, often be turned
to practical account. But any suggestion that Mr.
Lloyd George could be relieved of responsibility for
the measures of his colleagues in the early days of the
War would be neither well-founded nor fair.

II

All the world, however, has been glad to pay him
homage for the vigour and resourcefulness which he
brought to bear upon the problem of munitions, for
his share in the immense task of providing for the
needs of our ever-growing armies in the field. But
here again some false claims have to be corrected
and some false impressions removed. It is no secret
that the defects which accompanied Lord Kitchener's great qualities became, as the War went on,
a source of trial to his colleagues. Mr. Asquith, it
seems, understood him better than most, and to the

last Lord Kitchener relied on Mr. Asquith's help and sympathy and patience with a certainty which is a fine tribute to the characters of both. But many people entitled to judge thought that Lord Kitchener's refusal to build his new armies on the basis of the Territorial Force was a serious military error, and many people found that his self-confidence, his tenacity and a certain secretiveness in counsel made it difficult for him to work with other men. Lord Kitchener tried to do single-handed far more than any single man could wisely undertake. Delays and difficulties inevitably resulted at a time when the whole machinery of the War Office was being subjected to an unexampled strain. And Lord Kitchener's colleagues were justified in insisting that some part of his multifarious duties should be transferred to other hands. But, quite apart from possible errors at the War Office, the sudden demands on our resources were such as no existing system of supply could stand; and the unpunctuality in executing orders, the comparative failure of armament firms and contractors, and the hindrances due to Trade Union customs and restrictions soon aggravated a situation already formidable enough.

These difficulties were vigorously faced. As early as September 1914 it became necessary to take active steps to strengthen and re-organise the whole system of Army Contracts.[1] In October Mr. Asquith

[1] These steps included the appointment of men like Sir G. Gibb, Mr. Wintour, who became Director of Army Contracts in September, Mr. George Booth and others. Sir G. Gibb was made an additional Member of the Army Council in December 1914.

4

appointed a strong Cabinet Committee, of which
Lord Kitchener, Lord Haldane, Mr. Lloyd George
and Mr. Runciman were members,[1] which set to
work with energy to help the War Office in multiplying orders and enlarging supplies. Mr. Lloyd
George found fresh opportunities of driving home
the point on which Mr. Asquith was already insisting, the grave deficiency in guns and ammunition,
and the need of working day and night to make it
good. In November Lord Moulton, engaged at
Lord Kitchener's instance, was at work with his
Committee on the supply of high explosives, and a
new Explosives Supply Department was beginning
to grow up. By the end of 1914 Lord Moulton's
organisation had become a branch of the War
Office, and his programme for developing the
necessary supplies of raw material embraced every
gas works and coke distillery in the country.

" In January 1915 he was able to promise by the following
March supplies of explosives not only adequate to our own
resources in shells, but sufficient to afford substantial help to
our Allies." [2]

And this great Explosives Department, under a
lawyer who was also a chemist of genius, and who
as an administrator " thought in tons while others

[1] And also Mr. Churchill, Mr. McKenna and Lord Lucas.
They met six times from October 12, 1914, to January 1, 1915.
(See the *History of Ministry of Munitions*, Vol. I.) The Board of
Trade under Mr. Runciman gave valuable help in labour
problems, especially in the early months of 1915.
[2] See the *Life of Lord Moulton*, pp. 186-7.

thought in pounds," rendered for four years valuable service to the State. Taken over by the Ministry of Munitions in June 1915, and steadily expanded under Lord Moulton's direction, it was responsible for some of the most important triumphs which the Ministry of Munitions achieved, and it is to Lord Moulton's power and energy that those triumphs were principally due.

The shortage of ammunition in the early days was easy to explain. It was due to three main causes, to our small establishment of artillery in time of peace, to the intense and unexpected nature of the fighting, and to the difficulty experienced by contractors in carrying through the orders given. It may well be that few minds at first fully grasped the need of expanding manufacturing capacity on a sufficiently vast scale. But neither in the placing of orders by the War Office nor in the execution of orders by the contractors was there, it seems, much ground for complaining of backwardness or slackness or red tape. From October 1914 onwards orders were multiplied to an extent which, had they been executed by the time stipulated, would, it is alleged, have trebled or quadrupled the amount of ammunition actually available in July 1915.[1] But it was not a question of giving orders only. It was a question of seeing that they were carried out. And it was, even more, a question of securing the labour and the materials required. Much of the material and

[1] See an interesting letter from the managing director of one of the contracting firms in the *Morning Post* of July 8, 1915.

machinery needed to make fuses and shells had to come from America, and the docks and railways were so congested that transit from New York to London often took sixty days instead of twenty, and even transit from Liverpool to London sometimes occupied five weeks. The difficulty of getting the skilled labour needed for purposes of manufacture was being increased every day by successful recruiting. The public realised the need of men for the armies far more readily than they realised the need of men for the machines. And the sudden enormous demand for gauges of extreme and delicate accuracy —in some fuses nearly two hundred gauges were used—was of course far more than existing firms could supply. All through the winter of 1914–15 vigorous efforts were made at the War Office to cope with the grave difficulties of the position, to make up for the almost inevitable shortcomings, to grapple with the complicated labour problem, to inaugurate a new system equal to the nation's extraordinary needs. By the summer of 1915 the causes of delay had been to a great extent overcome, and the War Office deserves great credit for its efforts, even if additional driving-power was needed to carry them through.

" Small arms and ammunition was ordered by the hundred millions, shells and all their adjuncts in millions, rifles, guns and their equipment in enormous numbers. Every workshop capable of the work in the United Kingdom, in the United States, in Canada, was filled; India was called upon; Japan also helped. Many of the orders were ' continuation orders,' which meant *carte blanche* to make as much as possible."

The attempts afterwards made to represent these efforts as an abject failure were unfair.[1] Mr. Lloyd George, with his great energy, and with the special powers conferred on him by legislation, was able to secure phenomenal results. But in the struggle with early difficulties, and in the combined effort made to overcome them, others too may claim an honourable part.

One temperate and authoritative military critic,[2] speaking as an eye-witness and drawing on many years' experience of the subject, has pointed out the way in which the Ministry of Munitions has been given credit for important new departures which its predecessors had really made. The rapid multiplication of factories, the enlistment of thousands of women, the setting up of local munition committees, the co-operative schemes to utilise the services of private firms, the institution of regular weekly reports to check and quicken the progress of contractors, the costing system which the Ministry of Munitions adopted and expanded, the factory where a " steel pole " introduced at one end of a machine emerged as nine shells at the other, the acres of buildings where girls worked on fuses and cartridge-making, the orders which kept tool-makers in America as well as in Britain busy day and night, the enterprise which secured the help of Messrs.

[1] See, for instance, the speech made by Sir H. Dalziel in the House of Commons on July 1, 1915.

[2] Major-General R. Mahon, to whose article on " Munitions and Mr. Lloyd George " in the *Edinburgh Review* for October 1919 I am indebted for some of these facts and quotations.

Morgan to make contracts and co-ordinate prices in the United States, the magnificent work done by the first Shell Committee in Canada, where hundreds of firms, started without a penny of Government subsidy, were manufacturing components before the Ministry of Munitions was heard of—work inadequately recognised by Mr. Lloyd George—these and many other activities were instituted by the War Office among all the trials and confusions of the early months of the War; and the worst of the early difficulties had been surmounted when they were taken over by the new Department. It would be unjust not to realise the immensity of the task which the War Office had had to face, and not to remember that Mr. Lloyd George and his helpers took over a going concern. The Minister of Munitions inherited an established and growing organisation.[1] He used it, developed it, expanded it, with his own remarkable activity and power. But he was only speaking the bare truth when he referred in the House of Commons on April 21, 1915, to the "marvellous" and "prodigious" things which had been already done.

Lord Oxford's summary of that achievement will be accepted now without dispute:

" The armies in the field had been multiplied between four and five times; the supply of munitions nineteenfold. Between two thousand and three thousand firms, not previously so em-

---

[1] To suggest, as Mr. Montagu did in the House of Commons on August 15, 1916, that Mr. Lloyd George created his Department " out of nothing " is a grave mistake.

ployed, had been brought into the industry. The multiplication of factories, the diversion and dilution of labour, the more extensive employment of women, had been pressed upon all the departments by Lord Kitchener in the spring of 1915 with constant and ever-increasing urgency. . . . By the end of April 1915 we were, despite heart-rending delays in delivery by contractors, producing in three days the amount of ammunition produced before the War in a whole year. Never was there a case in which the charge of apathy or lethargy was worse founded." [1]

One may wish that Mr. Lloyd George had continued to remind his followers of the debt due to their forerunners in their formidable task. But it is right at the same time to remember that in the matter of munitions Mr. Lloyd George was from the first an active and stimulating force, and that he did very valuable work in rousing public opinion, employers, workmen, every class and interest, to the need of effort and co-operation on an unprecedented scale. In February 1915 he told an audience at Bangor that we were engaged in an engineers' war. In March he announced that the Government had determined to organise the whole engineering community. In the same month he took the leading part in the meetings with Trade Union leaders summoned to deal with restrictions practised by the Unions, with the dilution of labour, the employment of women, and with other difficult problems over which the War Office and the Board of Trade were struggling. In April he was at work as Chairman of a new Cabinet Committee on Munitions. In May he was complaining

[1] See Lord Oxford's *Memories and Reflections*, Vol. II, pp. 76–7.

strongly of the shortcomings of the War Office, and of the failure to pass on to him information which he ought to have. That month, on the formation of the first Coalition Government, he became definitely Minister of Munitions. And in June there began to develop under his energetic leadership the " mammoth department," which was to intensify and redouble the work already in hand, and which ere long controlled thousands of factories, employed millions of workers, and spent with undisguised lightheartedness hundreds of millions of the public funds.[1]

War is certainly no time for meticulous economies or for submitting to the tyrannies of red tape. And Mr. Lloyd George's open-handed freedom from tradition, his fearless assumption of responsibility, his compelling energy and powers of drive, deserved and received the fullest recognition and secured astonishing results. Backed, as they were, by every class of the community—business men, experts, employers and wage-earners—they rendered in time of necessity a signal service to the State. Mr. Lloyd George was seen at his best in his appreciation of the vast scope of the problem to be tackled, in his persistent endeavours to carry the Trade Unions with him, in his wide schemes for promoting the social welfare of his workers, in the courageous and inspiring tones in which he asked for effort and sacrifice from all. Sentences still ring in the memory from

[1] See the first two volumes of the *History of the Ministry of Munitions*. They give information, which may yet need some supplementing, about these early days, and do full justice to the activities of Mr. Lloyd George.

speeches which he delivered at this period, rhetoric it may be, but rhetoric finely calculated to fire the imagination and to touch the hearts of men. But it must be admitted that the history of the Munitions Department revealed before long the weakness of Mr. Lloyd George's methods as well as their strength; in his combination of grandiose designs with a lack of care in thinking out their conse-quences; in his habit of empowering this man or that man to go ahead with uncontrolled authority, until some other individual, also summarily vested with uncontrolled authority, got in his way; in the con-fusion caused by these ill-co-ordinated efforts; in the inexcusable wastefulness permitted; in the needless running up of prices; in the extravagant wages paid to large numbers of sheltered workers who did not need to be bribed to do their duty, and whose profitable security was inevitably contrasted with the position of those who sacrificed not wages only, but their whole prospects, their homes, their families, their lives in war. One of the most significant facts recorded in the history of the Ministry [1] is that Dr. Addison, Mr. Lloyd George's successor there and himself a magnificent spender, was able, when he tried to overhaul its expenditure, to recover some £39,000,000, out of many millions temporarily lost through " confusions and deficiencies " under the administration of Mr. Lloyd George.[1] The Ministry of Munitions was not alone in wasting public money, or in offering possible " hidy-holes " to men needed

[1] See the *History of the Ministry of Munitions*, Vol. II, p. 71.

at the Front. But Mr. Lloyd George's authority may
have been too often used to shelter the shortcomings
of a Department whose reputation had become a
part of his own.

III

One further consideration should be added here if
fairness is desired. Mr. Lloyd George has told us
how gravely and forcibly Mr. Asquith impressed
upon him the necessity of multiplying guns and
ammunition, machine-guns especially, upon the
largest scale. Yet at an early date the Prime
Minister's efforts were made the subject of mis-
representation and attack. Of Sir John French's
share in this episode, and of his share in some of the
political intrigues which followed, it is difficult to
speak with the respect one would desire to show. Sir
John French was a cavalry leader of repute, vigorous, high-spirited, generally popular, and endowed
with a fund of genial and persistent optimism which
had its value on a hard-fought field. But it is now
evident that in some respects he lacked both steadiness and weight, and that Lord Kitchener was right
in thinking that he had not the full equipment of
knowledge or training which a great soldier con-
fronted with grave circumstances requires. French
had a grim task to face abroad, and he faced it for
the most part with resourcefulness and courage. But
the strain and trials of the first few weeks proved at
one moment almost more than he could bear. His
resolve at the end of August 1914 to retire beyond

the Seine was not only unfortunate in judgment: it might, if permitted, have proved disastrous in result. It was overruled by the firmness of the Government and by the despatch of Lord Kitchener at a moment's notice to France. That intervention, and perhaps his own consciousness of a momentary failure, Sir John French found it hard to forgive. But his buoyant spirits soon rebounded. Early in September 1914 he was confiding to Mr. Churchill that, if his army could be multiplied by six, he would be at Berlin in six weeks without the help of his Allies. Three weeks later he was light-heartedly proposing an outflanking march across Belgium to Cologne. "He thinks he could do it in a week or nine days," commented the Prime Minister, with unconscious irony, and Lord Kitchener is said to have heartily approved of the scheme. By December this plan was perforce abandoned. But Sir John would hear nothing of Lord Kitchener's pessimism. He was convinced that the Germans had already lost their best troops and officers, and that their men on the Western Front were only forced into action by battle police! [1] In January 1915, in spite of constant friction with Lord Kitchener—"the two Field Marshals," Mr. Asquith once noted, "are an extraordinarily disparate couple, and not born or moulded to work easily together"—the Commander-in-Chief was "as optimistic as ever." In February he was certain that the Germans would

[1] For these opinions see Lord Oxford's *Memories and Reflections*, Vol. II, pp. 32, 34, 49, 50, 62, 67.

never break through in France, or overpower Russia, or annihilate Serbia, and was full of the news that General Joffre was preparing apparatus for bridging the Rhine. In March his optimism was still undaunted, his confidence still undiminished, and his judgment still markedly unsound.

Yet this high-placed and highly-trusted officer, treated from first to last by Mr. Asquith with a persistent kindness not denied, allowed his impatience or his personal feelings to make him a leading figure in political action of which any responsible General ought to have kept clear. The truth about the Shells controversy is now sufficiently well known. But in a matter where it is just possible—if it were ever profitable to set up civilian against military opinion—that the civilians might find as much ground for criticising the soldiers as the soldiers for criticising the civilians, it may be worth while to quote a military expert's view.

"High-explosive shells," writes Major-General Mahon, "had long constituted the major part of the equipment of all our artillery, excepting only the light field guns (13- and 18-pounder Q.F.). It had been deliberately left out of their equipment after extended trials (which took place long before the war) for reasons which seemed good to the army authorities. The demand for high-explosive projectiles for these guns did not, according to my information, arise until October 1914, and then the matter was put in hand at once. The reason for the demand was two-fold: first, that insufficient artillery of the field howitzer type, and of medium and heavy types of guns and howitzers other than field, existed in the country before the war; and secondly, that as a result of trench warfare an entirely new situation had arisen."

The General explains that a high-explosive shell on the scale of the 18-pounder was "an exceedingly difficult one to make," not only for technical reasons of fuse and detonation, but in the purely physical matter of making the shell of hard steel itself.

" I have seen scores of machines knocked to pieces in its operations. I would even venture to assert that nine-tenths of the machines originally put to work on it broke down and had to be replaced by heavier tools. There was no avoidable delay in getting it made, and the out-turn began to flow in January 1915." [1]

Other high-explosive shells of existing patterns were pushed along at the same time, subject of course to the difficulties and delays which affected the supply of all forms of ammunition. But it would be obviously unreasonable to blame the War Office for not having made high-explosive shells of the new pattern before the need for them was understood. The development of trench war had not been foreseen by any commander, and certainly not by Sir John French. The artillery officers and the commanders in the field were not at first by any means unanimous as to the desirability of making this new pattern of shell. They even declined the earliest proposals which the War office put forward on the subject. And in these circumstances it would be wrong not to recognise the debt due both to the Government and to the War Office for the results achieved in speeding up the supply of all munitions during the first six or seven months of the War. [2]

[1] *Edinburgh Review* for October 1919, pp. 225–6.
[2] The first volume of the *History of the Ministry of Munitions* should be consulted on this subject—though written from a rather different point of view.

On March 15, 1915, just after the Battle of Neuve Chapelle, where as much artillery ammunition was, it is said, expended as was used by our armies during the whole of the Boer War, Lord Kitchener appeared in the House of Lords and made a solemn and reasoned appeal to employers and workmen :

" The supply of war material at the present moment and for the next two or three months is causing me very serious anxiety, and I wish all engaged in the manufacture and supply of these stores to realise that it is absolutely essential, not only that the arrears in the deliveries of our munitions of war should be wiped off, but that the output of every round of ammunition is of the utmost importance and has a large influence on our operations in the field."

On April 14 he wrote to the Prime Minister that Sir John French, whom he had just seen, had assured him that " with the present supply of ammunition he will have as much as his troops will be able to use during the next forward movement." Mr. Asquith, who had taken great pains to ascertain the facts, had French's assurance freshly before him when he spoke at Newcastle on April 20. But he did not the less impress upon his hearers the vital need of sparing no effort to get the supplies increased. He told them that " a large and rapid increase in the output of muni- tions " was " one of the first necessities of the State." He implored them in the name of King and country " to deliver the goods." His appeal to the workers of Newcastle met with a fine and immediate re- sponse. And the attempt soon after made to repre- sent him as concealing the truth, and lulling the country into a false sense of security, can only be regarded as one of the more ignoble of the many errors or intrigues of the War. Twelve days later, on the eve of Festubert, Sir John French again reassured Lord Kitchener: " The ammunition will be all right." And yet within two weeks of this he was priming *The Times* correspondent with material for attacks upon the Government for their inexcusable apathy, and was sending over Captain Guest, a Liberal Member of Parliament, to lay his complaints before the Conservative leaders and Mr. Lloyd George. Mr. Asquith put the attacks aside and steadily refused to think evil of a colleague. Lord Kitchener was for practical purposes as unmoved as Mr. Asquith. But he allowed himself to say, " I am deadly sick of this system of intrigue."

Four years later, when Lord French's responsibility as a soldier had lessened and his partisanship had apparently increased, he published, first as newspaper articles and afterwards in the form of a volume,[1] some ill-considered and unsubstantiated criticisms on individuals and events. It is not necessary to dwell upon them, because they cannot always be reconciled with other statements made by the same author, or with the best traditions of the great Service to which he belonged. But it may be well to place beside them the testimony of French's own Chief of the Staff to the full and loyal support which both Lord Kitchener and Mr. Asquith gave to the Commander-in-Chief in France,[2] and two significant

[1] *1914.*
[2] See *Soldiers and Statesmen*, Vol. I, p. 71.

utterances by Lord French himself. One is the summary of his relations with Lord Kitchener which he offered in the House of Lords on June 20, 1916:

" I am anxious to place on record that no effort was ever spared by him to supply all our demands. I knew well the difficulties which lay in his way. . . . Such divergence of opinion as occurred in no way interfered with the national interests nor did it ever shake my confidence in Lord Kitchener's will, power and ability to provide us with everything that we required."

The other is the letter which he wrote to Mr. Asquith on May 20, 1915:

" MY DEAR PRIME MINISTER—
    " For two days I have been hesitating to add one iota to the troubles and anxieties which must weigh upon you just now. You have, however, shown me so much true, generous kindness throughout this trying campaign that I venture at this critical juncture to convey to you what is in my inmost thoughts. I am sure in the whole history of war no General in the field has ever been helped in a difficult task by the head of his Government as I have been supported and strengthened by your unfailing sympathy and encouragement."

I should not have dwelt so long upon Lord French's opinions, had not his services been so conspicuously rewarded by Mr. Lloyd George.[1]

IV

Apart from the question of munitions, Mr. Lloyd George's two chief contributions in early days to the

[1] See for these facts, among other authorities, *The Great Shell Story*, Lord Oxford's *Memories and Reflections*, Vol. II, pp. 76–80, and Sir G. Arthur's *Life of Lord Kitchener*, Vol. III, p. 272 *seq*.

conduct of the War were his steady demand for
adventures in the Balkans and his participation in
the rumours and manœuvres which led to the break-
up of the Government of which he formed a part.
He was quick to criticise—and there was strong
ground for criticising—the unsuccessful fighting, the
great loss of life, in France. And he was quick—far
too quick—to make up his mind that it was useless
to continue attacks upon the Germans there. But he
had not always sufficient knowledge or steadiness of
purpose to impress military men who knew their
business; and his irruptions into military counsels,
original and stimulating as they might sometimes be,
proved often more embarrassing than helpful to
those responsible for the war policy of the Allies. It
was not till the first Coalition Government was
formed in May 1915 that Mr. Lloyd George was
definitely appointed Minister of Munitions, and that
the full extent of his energies in that department was
gradually revealed. But the creation of the first
Coalition was largely Mr. Lloyd George's work; and
it would be difficult to deny that his readiness to discuss the shortcomings of the Liberal Government
with Tory journalists and Tory politicians contributed powerfully to that political change. In March
1915 the Prime Minister had drawn Mr. Lloyd
George's attention to unfriendly articles in the
Press, the inspiration of which many people had
attributed to him, and there had followed the
curious little scene which Mr. Asquith described in
his Diary—Mr. Lloyd George's passionate assurance

of all that he owed to the Prime Minister's kindness, and of the impossibility of his harbouring disloyal thoughts against his chief.

" His eyes were wet with tears, and I am sure that, with all his Celtic capacity for impulsive and momentary fervour, he was quite sincere. Of course I assured him that I had never for a moment doubted him, which is quite true, and he warmly wrung my hand and abruptly left the room."

But in May the clamour against the Government rose high. The long and weary strain in France, the angry controversy over shells, the serious disappointments of the Dardanelles campaign, and above all the crisis produced by Lord Fisher's abrupt resignation and by Mr. Lloyd George's threat to resign unless a Coalition Government were formed,[1] precipitated a decision which, it seems, Mr. Asquith already had in contemplation. It was one of the gravest political decisions of the War. Looking back on events, Mr. Winston Churchill, at the time a believer in the policy of Coalition, and certainly its supporter afterwards, has pointed out how severely the reputation of the Liberal Government suffered from the refusal to defend it in the House of Commons, and how seriously Mr. Asquith's action was embarrassed by his new colleagues. Mr. Churchill is confident that, had the Prime Minister laid his case before Parliament in a secret session, he would

[1] See the precise statements on this point of Mr. Churchill (*The World Crisis, 1915*, p. 365) and of Colonel Repington (*The First World War*, Vol. I, p. 39).

have carried Parliament and public opinion with him.

" I am certain that, had he fought, he would have won."

And he would have been spared " that interlude of distrustful colleagues, of divided or more often mutually paralysing counsels " which a Coalition too frequently involves. But it was characteristic of Mr. Asquith that he never would consent in a national emergency to fight for his own hand. The immediate results of the Coalition were not to quicken executive action, but to increase the opportunities for delay. " At least five or six opinions prevailed on every great topic." At least a dozen influential people had to be consulted on important questions, in place of the small group of Ministers who had decided them before.

" From the moment of the formation of the Coalition power was dispersed and counsels were divided."

It will not be denied that there had been serious divisions of opinion in the Cabinet when it consisted of Liberals alone. But it must be admitted that the creation of this disunited Coalition was so far Mr. Lloyd George's principal specific for improving the direction of the War.

This is not the place to linger on the story of that Government, replaced, on Mr. Lloyd George's initiative, by a second Coalition in December 1916. Mr. Lloyd George was for a time absorbed in organising and expanding the Munitions Department.

But he remained Deputy Leader of the House of Commons. His influence was always of the first importance. He never ceased to deplore the great unsuccessful battles, the cruel losses on the Western Front. He never ceased to hanker for operations in the East: " wild-cat schemes " they seemed to some military critics, who commented acidly in 1916 on the 300,000 men at Salonika, " standing there doing nothing, looking at the skies." And he must share to the full the responsibility for the resolutions which the Government took. There is no indication that at any critical moment he showed the exceptional insight or decision which might have converted failure into success. And if charges of misdirection and instability of purpose are to be brought against those with whom he acted, it is impossible to hold that he alone was quite devoid of blame.

In one form of activity, however, it is evident that Mr. Lloyd George allowed himself too large a part. Every man has the defects of his qualities, and there are defects to which an expansive and sympathetic nature is peculiarly prone. Mr. Lloyd George could rarely avoid exchanging opinions and confidences with people who interested him, whether opponents or friends, especially with people who could influence the Press. From his early days as a Minister he had been accustomed to treat political secrets with unusual freedom. The witty retort which one of his colleagues long before the War made to a critic who complained of a leak in the Cabinet—" Can you wonder? It's his national emblem "—illustrates an opinion which had some foundation in fact. And in the atmosphere of criticism and gossip, of rumour and innuendo, which pervaded some sections of London Society during the War, these inclinations found a ready vent. In April 1915 Mr. Asquith had had to compose a very serious difference of opinion which arose from Mr. Lloyd George's accidental disclosure to members of the Munitions Committee of figures which Lord Kitchener had given in confidence to the Cabinet. Mr. Lloyd George may in that case have had a good defence. Lord Kitchener's view may have been too narrow. It is clear that Mr. Lloyd George would never willingly give away a secret of importance to the State. But it is probably true that his colleagues never felt quite sure that they could rely on his discretion in matters requiring reticence or reserve. And in matters where his own interests rather than those of the State were uppermost, his indiscretions sometimes wore a more calculated air. As the Coalition Government, to a large extent his own contrivance, struggled on, it became evident that Mr. Lloyd George viewed the actions of his colleagues with a detachment difficult to defend. Everyone who had complaints to make against the Government appeared to think that he could count on Mr. Lloyd George for a sympathetic hearing. Newspaper-owners and newspaper-writers who for years past had been bitterly attacking Liberal Ministers—for party feeling recently had run very high—seemed to find in Mr. Lloyd George a confidant. To be open-minded and accessible is

often an admirable thing. But it was disquieting to
find Mr. Lloyd George so eager to get into touch
with the most outspoken assailants of the Cabinet of
which he was a member, so ready to take them into
counsel, to indicate his appreciation of their point of
view. No one can read the records which have since
been published and not realise that this was always
going on.[1]

V

This strangely detached if not disloyal attitude became still more noticeable after Midsummer 1916,
when Mr. Lloyd George had become Minister of
War. Even his warm supporters have found little in
his administration of the War Office to admire. It
was a critical time in the War, but Mr. Lloyd George
never seemed to get into cordial touch with his new
Department. He brought in a few business men:
Lord Rothermere was put in charge of the Army
Clothing Department and Sir Eric Geddes of railway services in France. He displayed from the first
a tendency to consult subordinates, which might
be a little trying to the Departmental mind, but was,
no doubt, a proof of his desire to get at the facts for
himself. But he showed little of Lord Haldane's
patience and ability in winning the confidence of the
soldiers under him, little of the mastery of departmental business which made Mr. Churchill at the

[1] See, for instance, Repington's *First World War* (Vol. I,
pp. 45–6, 52–4, 283–6, 341, 371–4, etc.). Colonel Repington's
gossip should, no doubt, be read with caution, but I see no
reason for rejecting the statements made here.

Admiralty in some respects a great administrative chief. Mr. Lloyd George had his own views on military strategy, and not much regard for those who differed from them. If he listened to his professional advisers, he listened sometimes with a grudging reluctance, which increased in proportion as their advice differed from his preconceived ideas. And apart from pressing military problems, his short term as War Secretary was profoundly unsatisfactory, because he was all the time preoccupied, and known to be preoccupied, with political intrigues. There were public appearances of course, statements made perhaps with one eye on the *Daily Mail*, popular in sentiment if not always dignified in language, advocating a fight to a finish and a knock-out blow.[1] There were outbursts in private, more in keeping with his early sentiments, against the " military Moloch " to whom everyone was asked to bow the knee. And there were all the while the same expansive confidences to men who were known to be hostile to his colleagues. Mr. Lloyd George talked with singular freedom of " the Duma," the Cabinet which he belonged to. He did not conceal from outsiders his poor opinion of British Generals and British Statesmen. It did not seem to occur to him that, so long as Generals were retained in command, it was his duty as Secretary of State for War to support them, or that, so long as he remained a member of the Cabinet, it was his duty to be loyal to decisions in which he shared.

[1] See, for instance, *The Times* of September 29, 1916.

With Sir William Robertson, the Chief of the Imperial General Staff since December 1915, the new War Secretary's relations were at first sufficiently friendly. He felt sure that they would work together " in complete harmony." He was convinced—so he said—that Sir Douglas Haig in France was " playing absolutely the right game " and doing his job " in absolutely the right way." [1] And though Robertson was known to be strongly opposed to the operations undertaken in the East of Europe, he was assured that the War Secretary had no intention of altering or diminishing the large powers which the Chief of the Imperial General Staff enjoyed. But the two men were not of a nature to agree, the soldier intent only on the military problem, the politician intent above all on having popular opinion at his back; the one relying on his experience, the other on his imagination; the one as uncompromising perhaps as he was straightforward in counsel, the other as supple as he was resourceful in devices for getting his own way. Sir William Robertson found that his military recommendations were frequently opposed by the Minister at the War Committee of the Cabinet, that he could not in cases of difficulty depend on the support of the Secretary of State. The " complete harmony " developed before long into constant friction; and only Mr. Lloyd George's fear of being attacked in the Press for interfering with the soldiers postponed for a time the inevitable breach. Robertson's

[1] This was towards the end of August 1916. See Robertson's *Soldiers and Statesmen, 1914–1918*, Vol. I, pp. 271–2.

summary of Mr. Lloyd George's administration as War Secretary is impressive because, while bearing out the estimates of others, it is written, as his whole book is written, with moderation and restraint.[1] In those months, says Sir William, the War Secretary

" was connected with no measure having any special influence on the course of the war. . . . He placed before the Cabinet a recommendation of the Military Members of the Army Council for extending and simplifying the principle of National Service, and gave to it his full support. But on becoming Prime Minister, about a fortnight later, he dropped it, and declined to carry it into effect until the German offensive of March 1918 compelled him to do so. He displayed but little sympathy towards the various Commanders-in-Chief, with the exception of General Maude, the only General who could yet produce a decisive victory, and he listened with sceptical impatience to my explanations of the difficulties with which these officers had to contend. He preferred his own strategical ideas to those of the General Staff; and of administrative work, which seemed to bore him, he left as much as possible to be done by the Under-Secretary of State, Lord Derby. He was, in fact, so much occupied with political activities, especially during the two or three weeks which preceded Mr. Asquith's resignation, as to devote considerably less than undivided attention to the affairs of the Army."

It is not necessary to follow that point further now. But one question raised by Sir William Robertson played a large part in the controversies of the time. The need for more men in the field, and the necessity of compulsion to get them, which military critics insisted on, with more knowledge perhaps than some of the politicians and press-men who echoed their demands, grew more urgent as the losses of our troops increased; and the best way of

---

[1] See *Soldiers and Statesmen, 1914–1918,* Vol. I, p. 179

meeting this need, without sacrificing other essential interests, was a perplexing problem for every Cabinet in turn. Mr. Lloyd George was quick to realise the value of national and universal service. He was prepared to recommend compulsion for workers at home as well as for soldiers in the field. But he was quick also to see, as Lord Kitchener saw, and Mr. Asquith and Mr. Balfour and the Labour leaders, the extraordinary success of the voluntary movement—3,000,000 men voted for the Army and 350,000 for the Navy in less than a year [1]—and the danger of trying to enforce conscription without something in the nature of general assent. In June 1915 Mr. Lloyd George was publicly, but rather guardedly, advocating the idea of compulsory service:

" It has been the greatest weapon in the hands of Democracy, many a time for the winning and preservation of Freedom. All the same, it would be a great mistake to resort to it unless it be absolutely necessary." [2]

As the summer went on he was bolder in supporting the idea. In October he was said to be fighting " like a tiger " for more men for the Army, where the wastage was alarming. Yet the soldiers complained that a million and a half of men had secured exemption in Government employment, mainly under the Ministry of Munitions, and that the drafts

[1] See the statement of the Under-Secretary of State for War in the House of Commons, July 28, 1915. I take it, they had been not only voted but secured.

[2] See *The Times* for June 4, 1915—Mr. Lloyd George at Manchester.

for Salonica were seriously weakening the supply of reinforcements for France. Fresh efforts to stimulate recruiting followed, in which Lord Derby and the Labour Party took an honourable share, and fresh efforts also to introduce conscription, in which Mr. Lloyd George's influence was strongly felt. It was known that the differences of opinion on this point both inside and outside the Cabinet were grave. At last Mr. Asquith's tact and judgment secured virtual agreement. A Military Service Bill accepting the principle of compulsion was carried through Parliament with little resistance in May 1916. The King, while dwelling on the splendid effort which had already raised by voluntary enlistment over five million men, warmly congratulated the Prime Minister on the patience and skill with which he had surmounted a dangerous situation. Some soldiers and many sciolists, who did not know enough of the essential demands of other services, or of the state of feeling in the country, to appreciate, as the King did, the political difficulties involved, and who saw only too clearly the urgent need of fighting men, were inclined to attribute to lethargy or misdirection the Government's guarded action in this matter. But Sir William Robertson has frankly admitted that it was owing to the action taken during Mr. Asquith's tenure of office that the strength of the British Army in France was greater in the summer of 1917 than at any period of the War.[1] And Lord

[1] See *Soldiers and Statesmen*, Vol. I, p. 285.

Kitchener's last public words are worth recalling here:

" In my opinion compulsion came at the right time and in the right way as a military necessity, and for no other reason."

Some of Mr. Lloyd George's new friends were active in contrasting his enthusiasm for compulsory service with the reluctance felt by some of his colleagues. But when Mr. Lloyd George came into power as Prime Minister he was faced with just the same demands as his predecessor, and was forced, like him, to acknowledge the difficulties involved. Labour, he then told the Chief of the Staff, would not stand any more compulsion. With one eye always on popular feeling, he hesitated to apply the compulsory principle too strictly. Mr. Asquith's Military Service Act brought our fighting strength in France to its highest point in June 1917. But from that date, under Mr. Lloyd George's Administration, it declined. And in the judgment of Mr. Lloyd George's military advisers, the defective arrangements in regard to man-power were allowed to drift on, until they resulted in the disasters of the early spring of 1918.[1] The truth is that the difficulties of the statesmen in this matter were greater than the soldiers knew. But there is little doubt that in 1916 Mr. Lloyd George's readiness to identify himself with every intensification of military effort was widely extolled at the expense of his colleagues by the public which followed the Northcliffe Press. It supplied a reason for suggesting

[1] See *Soldiers and Statesmen*, Vol. I, p. 302 *seq.*

that he, and he only, was the Minister to win the War. Did Mr. Lloyd George always resist the temptation to make political capital out of this idea?

VI

At last, in December 1916, the crisis came. The disappointing record of the year's campaigning, the demand for more successful leadership, the feeling, almost inevitable in a time of stress and partial failure, that the Allied Governments were unequal to coping with their difficulties, the cruel losses—some thought the unnecessary losses—in the Somme offensive, the complaints of lack of vigour at the Admiralty then in Mr. Balfour's charge, and finally the dramatic collapse of the Roumanian Army, had produced a general depression, a vague but natural desire for change.

" Few, if any, people," one busy Diarist noted, " see the end of the war except by stalemate."

Fewer still realised that Ludendorff was even then noting that the Germans were " completely exhausted on the Western Front," and was indulging in the gloomiest auguries of what would happen if the Allied attacks were renewed and continued without pause. The depression in London seemed to find an echo in the secret Memorandum which Lord Lansdowne presented to the Cabinet in November,[1] urging that the time had come to consider whether

[1] This remarkable State paper is printed in Lord Oxford's *Memories and Reflections*, Vol. II, pp. 138–147.

the Allies were in a position to refuse all idea of negotiation and to insist on nothing but a dictated peace. And the gravity of feeling in the Cabinet was deepened by the ever-increasing anxiety caused by the submarine war. But the Government's resolution remained unshaken, and responsible soldiers refused to consider the possibility of anything but a decisive victory, at a time when our superiority was quietly increasing and when England's effort had still only in part been made. It may be, however, that Lord Lansdowne's Memorandum made it easier for Mr. Lloyd George to persuade himself that the winning of the War depended on his taking control of it into his own hands. He remained in the Government, but laboured hard to dissociate himself from the unpopularity which it incurred. He held constant meetings with its principal opponents.

" Groups were at work inside the House of Commons," writes one of his admirers frankly, " backing him up and carrying on a guerilla warfare against the Government. Newspapers of the Northcliffe type assailed one Minister after another with more or less malignity and more or less injustice."

And at last, while protesting his desire " to avoid all appearance of adding to the Prime Minister's difficulties," he grasped the occasion to put himself in the Prime Minister's place. " It is L. G.'s opportunity to become P.M., and he is seizing it," wrote one observer. Other observers, both inside and outside the Government, were persuaded that Mr. Lloyd George had been watching for the opportunity for some time past.

The facts of an episode which no excuses can make creditable were set out at the time with careful fairness by Lord Crewe.[1] On December 1, 1916, while Ministers were working at plans for speeding up procedure, Mr. Lloyd George, acting in concert with Mr. Bonar Law and Sir Edward Carson—rather strange confidants for a Liberal leader—suddenly presented to Mr. Asquith a demand for the formation of a new Committee or Council to control the conduct of the War. This Committee was to consist of three or four persons,[2] excluding the Prime Minister, but including Mr. Bonar Law, the Conservative leader, Sir Edward Carson, then an active opponent of the Government, and Mr. Lloyd George himself. View the circumstances as we may, it must be doubted whether any member of a Cabinet ever presented to his chief a more wounding or intolerable demand. Mr. Asquith received it with extraordinary patience. He was ready to consider, without regard to his own claims, any proposal that seemed likely to help in winning the War. He did indeed feel that, if he was to remain Prime Minister, he must effectively control the War Committee. But he was prepared to delegate his functions as chairman to a large extent to Mr. Lloyd George. Only he was not persuaded that the triumvirate proposed to him, even with Mr. Arthur Henderson added as a

[1] See *Memories and Reflections*, Vol. II, Chap. XIV.
[2] The original suggestion, apparently, was a triumvirate, but the proposal for a fourth member, a Labour leader, soon followed.

representative of Labour, would be specially efficient or successful in carrying on the War. So public-spirited and conciliatory was Mr. Asquith's attitude, so unwilling were several Ministers, Unionists as well as Liberals, to substitute Mr. Lloyd George for Mr. Asquith as their chief, that many suggestions were made for a reconstruction of the Government on lines which both Mr. Asquith and Mr. Lloyd George could accept. Mr. Asquith would even have agreed to take a secondary place. But most of his Liberal colleagues, who deeply resented the attack made on him, felt that, if he surrendered to such pressure, his influence would disappear. While negotiations were still in progress, *The Times* published on December 4 an article which sufficiently indicated the views of the triumvirate at work. It was announced that Mr. Lloyd George, Mr. Bonar Law and Sir Edward Carson—described four days later as " in some respects the backbone of the new movement "—were to take out of the hands of Mr. Asquith and his " old digressive colleagues " the supreme direction of the War. Mr. Asquith's closest supporters, it was added, must have convinced him that his qualities were better fitted to preserve national unity than " to force the pace of a War Council." Lord Grey and others were obviously included in the attack.

It is impossible to doubt the intention of this article, whatever may have been its source of inspiration. After such an avowal the negotiations with Mr. Asquith necessarily failed. They were probably never intended to succeed. Mr. Lloyd George resigned. He might have been allowed to go, had he not threatened, in the very crisis of the War, to conduct a campaign in the country against his old colleagues, which would have made it difficult for any Government to carry on.[1] Mr. Asquith's resignation followed. In opposition, as in office, he at least could be counted on never to allow his own personal interests to endanger the interests of the State. In the afternoon of December 6 Mr. Lloyd George declared that he was not a candidate for the Premiership. Before the day was over he had accepted the post. Mr. Balfour threw his great influence into the same scale, and helped powerfully to persuade Conservative Ministers to join Mr. Lloyd George's Administration. They joined it in some cases reluctantly enough. Mr. Balfour's rapid adhesion to the new Prime Minister caused surprise to those who knew that Mr. Lloyd George had been urging his removal, a demand which Mr. Asquith had refused to allow. The Labour Party's adhesion—another surprising feature of the bargain—was secured by lavish promises, among which schemes of nationalisation played their part, by the offer of no less than eight places in the new Administration, and by the creation of two new Ministries, of Labour and of Pensions, to be filled by Labour politicians.

[1] Lord Crewe's Memorandum may be compared with an account of the Ministerial crisis, less well-informed but not widely dissimilar, given in *The Atlantic Monthly* for February 1919 and entitled "Unwritten History."

6

" His offers to Labour," says one sympathetic writer, " were such that the Party could not resist his appeal."

And it seems difficult to doubt that Mr. Lloyd George's arrangements for displacing his old colleagues had already been elaborately thought out. Even so, the adhesion of the Labour Executive was only secured by a small majority. And before long Mr. Lloyd George's Labour colleagues found, as his Liberal and Conservative colleagues have found also, that the confidence which they gave him he was unable to retain.

To secure the support of the Press has generally been with Mr. Lloyd George a supreme consideration, and of that support, at least of the support of those newspapers which had most vociferously attacked Mr. Asquith's Government, the new Prime Minister had already made sure. Before many months were over Lord Northcliffe was induced to accept a mission to America, which removed from the scene for a time at least one confidential and highly embarrassing supporter. Mr. Balfour's Mission was then in America, doing very useful work, and at an early date Lord Reading and other distinguished emissaries followed. It is a little difficult to understand the need for so many special envoys in a country where we were already admirably represented. But Colonel House, a singularly well-informed observer, has borne witness to the value of their labours. And a good deal of " co-ordination " must have been needed if there were presently, as Lord Northcliffe stated, five hundred officials of the

British War Mission with ten thousand assistants in the United States.[1] In connection with Lord North-cliffe a curious incident had occurred at Mr. Lloyd George's meeting with the Labour Party. He had been asked whether the policy of prosecuting small newspapers for expressing their opinions was to be continued, whilesome large newspapers were allowed to say what they liked; and he had replied with emphasis that if Lord Northcliffe were guilty of offence, he would be treated like a labourer or anybody else.[2] The labourer in question was destined before long to return from America to the scene of his labours, and to prove once again a powerful but precarious ally. Lord Northcliffe was a man of great energy and force, and of genuine, at moments almost truculent, patriotism. He used all his efforts to make Mr. Lloyd George Prime Minister and to support him— for a time—in office. He is said to have been invited more than once to join his Cabinet. He shared perhaps the Prime Minister's conviction that it was given to one man only to see clearly how to win the War. Yet within three years they had wholly ceased to trust each other. Lord Northcliffe was describing Mr. Lloyd George as a " chameleon," and the Prime Minister, in the same strain of fancy, was replying that he would " as soon rely on a grass-hopper " as on his recent friend :

" When a man has deluded himself, and all the people whom he ever permits to go near to him help him into the belief that

---

[1] See *The Intimate Papers of Colonel House*, Vol. III, p. 246.
[2] See *Lloyd George and the War*, pp. 107-8.

he is the only man who can win the War, and he is waiting
for the clamour of the multitude that is going to demand his
presence there to direct the destinies of the world, and there
is not a whisper, not a sound, it is rather disappointing; it is
unnerving; it is upsetting. Then the War is won without him.
There must be something wrong." [1]

Lord Northcliffe might perhaps have retorted in
much the same vein on Mr. Lloyd George. But we
need not dwell upon these strenuous dialectics. In
1916 and 1917 at any rate Lord Northcliffe rendered
Mr. Lloyd George great service. He may have been
at times a difficult colleague. He was often unsure
in judgment and unguarded in expression. But can
it be wholly the fault of others that so many eminent
men of all parties, who have tried to work closely
with Mr. Lloyd George, have sooner or later lost
faith in their ally?

When Mr. Lloyd George formed his Government,
however, the Harmsworth Press had for the moment
been captured. Tory Ministers were induced to
replace the old Liberal associates, with whom Mr.
Lloyd George was so ready to dispense.[2] Lord Curzon and Lord Milner, Mr. Bonar Law, Mr. Balfour
and Sir Edward Carson accepted important posts
under the new Liberal leader.[3] Mr. Arthur Henderson proved to be one of the four Englishmen selected

---

[1] For Mr. Lloyd George's singular outburst in the House of
Commons see *Parliamentary Debates*, April 16, 1919.

[2] It is understood that Mr. Lloyd George made an offer to
one of them only, Mr. Herbert Samuel, who declined. Later
he secured the services of Mr. Churchill and Mr. Montagu.

[3] Mr. Lloyd George did not, after all, find it possible to put
Sir E. Carson in the War Cabinet at once.

to control the operations of the War, in a War
Cabinet from which the Head of the War Office, the
Head of the Admiralty and the Head of the Foreign
Office were eccentrically excluded; and the singular
discourtesy which Mr. Henderson soon afterwards
experienced at the hands of the Prime Minister
shows how little value, except for what may be
called purposes of "window-dressing," Mr. Lloyd
George attached to some choices which he made.[1]
A certain number of Liberal members of Parliament, who had been prominent in Lobby efforts to
win support for Mr. Lloyd George, received places
in the new Coalition. It was necessary that it should
contain some representatives of Liberalism. But of
these Liberals the most conspicuous have since transferred themselves to other parties. A few men who
had won reputation or made large fortunes in business were introduced into the Government. The
Daily Mail demanded business men and hustlers, and
to the demands of the *Daily Mail* and kindred papers
the new Prime Minister never failed to lend attentive
ears. His Administration could only live by meeting
the requirements of the man in the street. One or
two interesting appointments were made, others
neither specially interesting nor successful. When all
was done, few Liberals were persuaded that in intellect, resolution or executive ability the new Govern-

[1] The strange incident on August 1, 1917, when Mr. Henderson was kept waiting for over an hour outside the doors of the
Cabinet of which he was a member, has been related by more
than one writer.

ment was equal to the old. The truth is that the new appointments were largely a matter of camouflage, intended to meet the newspaper demand and to give the impression of some new and popular departure. Political allies and party support the Prime Minister must have, to keep him in office. For the rest, the *personnel* of his Government did not greatly matter, for he meant to keep essential things in his own hands.

Many excuses may be made for statesmen who are led to differ from their colleagues. In December 1916 the outlook on all sides was alarming, public opinion was disquieted, and its self-constituted leaders were often excitable and ill-informed. Demands as vague as they were natural were heard on all sides for something different, for some change of leadership, of method and of fortune, to quicken and reanimate the counsels of the Allies. In such a situation any man will be listened to who has the force and cleverness to convince the public for the moment that he might find a remedy for their perplexities if he were given the chance. Intense self-confidence may be an asset. Party loyalties count, and ought to count, for nothing in comparison with national necessities. The supreme consideration is the safety of the State. But admitting all that, it is yet difficult for those who value what is scrupulous and loyal to justify Mr. Lloyd George's methods of making himself supreme. It is not hard for a popular politician in an hour of public misfortune to gather round him a group of discontented critics—soldiers, journalists,

politicians, quidnuncs—to feed them with more or
less confidential information, to allow them to suggest how different things might be were he in power.
Only this is not often done by an English statesman
while in office, to discredit the colleagues whose responsibility he shares. Few fair-minded men will
deny the justice of Mr. Asquith's conclusion that " a
well-organised, carefully engineered conspiracy "
had been formed to turn him out of power. For myself, if I may be allowed to add a personal reminis-
cence, I was in December 1916 very unwilling to
condemn Mr. Lloyd George. I shared the general
feeling that things were not going well. I wished,
like everyone else, for more effective and successful
action. Standing then outside Parliament, I had no
special knowledge of the Government's grave difficulties or of the embarrassments caused them by
their Allies. I had no special ties to Mr. Asquith
beyond those of a loyal Liberal, who had for a brief
time held office under him. In earlier days, when
the Boer War had divided Liberal opinion, I had
been strongly on Mr. Lloyd George's side. In my
difficulty I went for advice to Mr. Harcourt, still a
member of the House of Commons, who of old had
shared my admiration for Mr. Lloyd George's
courage, and who knew the Cabinet situation from
inside; and I asked him if no explanation or excuse
could be found for the new Prime Minister's conduct. He shook his head. I reminded him of our
sympathy with Mr. Lloyd George in the past, of his
intrepidity and resourcefulness in politics, all of

which Mr. Harcourt readily admitted. " But for the last few years," he added, " it has been nothing but intrigue, intrigue, intrigue." The more the records come to light, the more the real history of those months is examined, the more remorselessly this judgment is confirmed.

CHAPTER III

MR. LLOYD GEORGE AS A WAR MINISTER

Mr. Lloyd George was now in power. He had attained to political supremacy. He could count on the support of the Conservative Party, of the Labour Party, of a certain number of independent or unstable Liberals, and of a carefully censored and manipulated Press. He alone, with his great political adroitness, could hold together the combination which he had created; and a threat at critical moments to resign—a weapon which the Prime Minister did not hesitate to use—was generally sufficient to induce his colleagues to submit to his decisions. " L.G. was the War Cabinet," said one of his colleagues, " and nobody else really counted." [1] Lord Curzon, it may be added, was an important member of the small body created " to devote itself unremittingly to the conduct of the War." But it is significant that his biography contains no indication that he was allowed to exercise any special influence on military affairs in all the critical months between June 1917 and the Armistice. And in October 1918

[1] See Colonel Repington's report of a conversation with Mr. Arthur Henderson (*The First World War*, Vol. II, p. 278).

we find him complaining to Mr. Austen Chamberlain that the War Cabinet were not consulted as they should be, that meetings to discuss vital questions were constantly postponed :

" Things are being or may be done, for which we shall bear the responsibility but of which we are not aware." [1]

Mr. Lloyd George was sufficient to himself. His strength lay in the fact that none of his colleagues were prepared to replace him, to take over the responsibilities which he had fearlessly assumed. And he had this advantage over his predecessor, that he had gathered in everybody likely to attack him. He felt sure that Mr. Asquith would not encourage any action calculated to weaken national unity in time of war. He could, in fact, count with confidence on a magnanimity which he had not shown.

I

It is needless here to speak at length of some curious features of the new Administration. An impression of intense activity, or at least of intense restlessness, was given. It was necessary to convince the man in the street that something drastic and original was going forward. But the impression of activity was largely true. Mr. Lloyd George's energy was unceasing. The War Cabinet met repeatedly, sometimes two or three times a day. One great Admiralty official is reported to have told them

[1] See Lord Ronaldshay's *Life of Lord Curzon*, Vol. III, pp. 259–60.

that he could not attend all their meetings and conduct a war at sea at the same time. All sorts of administrative experiments were started, at no small cost to the Exchequer, and sometimes with insufficient gain to the public service. The partial breakdown of contractors in the early days of the War had led to the establishment of the Ministry of Munitions. The railways had passed automatically under Government control. And the ever-increasing pressure of circumstances seemed to render almost inevitable the control of shipping, of food, of coal and raw materials, the limitation of imports in order to save tonnage, the attempt to control production and distribution upon every side. A vast scheme of State Socialism was improvised under very difficult conditions, and this system was in some cases administered by inefficient amateurs. It is easy to point out the blunders which accompanied it, the troubles which, when the War ended, were certain to ensue. But it is only fair to make full allowances for a situation which was at all times seriously perplexing, and which in the spring of 1917, when the submarine peril was at its height, threatened the gravest danger to the State. And it is perhaps too early yet to decide how far these hurried and ambitious experiments in Socialism could have been avoided, and in what proportions they did harm and good.

Of the business men whom Mr. Lloyd George imported into Government Departments some undoubtedly had large views and large capacity, and did vigorous and useful work. Others knew certain sections and aspects of the business world as Civil Servants could not know them. Others again exhibited at least the best intentions and a genuine readiness to sacrifice their pecuniary advantage to the public interest. But a breezy manner and an ebullient patriotism are not always an adequate equipment for administrative work. Mr. Lloyd George has never shown in a high degree the gift of choosing men. And it is not always safe to assume that because a man has made a large fortune in business, where considerations of profit are paramount, he is necessarily the best man to work an administrative machine where the element of profit does not enter in. The one common failing of most of these administrators was their astonishing readiness to pour out public money when the element of profit and loss was removed. And this spirit spread from the new Departments to the old. The figures of expenditure, it was observed, under Mr. Lloyd George's Administration were like the figures of astronomy, measureless by the minds of ordinary men. The public accounts are full of examples of the almost universal waste. But it is interesting to notice that the success of the business men in some measure depended on the extent to which they allowed themselves to be guided by expert Civil Servants in their administrative careers. Most of them, let it be added, were both shrewd and generous in acknowledging the assistance which the trained civilians gave and the high standards of conduct on which the civilians insisted. And on their side the ablest Civil Servants came to realise not the weak points only, but the ability and vigour of many of the new colleagues by whose side they served.

Less easy to defend were some of Mr. Lloyd George's experiments in administrative reform. One observer, who had been very ready to criticise the late Prime Minister, now found his successor strangely inaccessible, and complained that he kept an extraordinary apparatus of secretaries and clerks about him. In his genial conversation a new note of dogmatism appeared. Mr. Lloyd George had been " the head and front of the demand for men under the Asquith leadership "; but he now seemed unwilling to face a question which had done its part in placing him in power.

" He said that he was ' not prepared to accept the position of a butcher's boy driving cattle to the slaughter, and that he would not do it.' " [1]

The observer noted a new assumption of fierceness in listening to criticism, which had not shown itself when Mr. Lloyd George was listening to criticism of his colleagues. But if men could not be spared for the Army, there was no lack of them apparently in the offices of State. No Socialist ever had a more pathetic belief than Mr. Lloyd George in the virtue of multiplying public officials. New Departments sprang up like mushrooms. The roll of Government

[1] See Repington, *First World War*, Vol. I, p. 455.

servants grew as rapidly as the bungalows in St. James' Park. Downing Street became a Garden Suburb. A brand-new Prime Minister's Department arose, called by some a Secretariat, by others a kindergarten, and by patriots who repudiated German terms a crèche—" intelligence officers," one sympathetic biographer explains, appointed to " feed the Prime Minister with facts." This Secretariat included presently a hundred and fourteen persons,[1] tumbling over each other, no doubt, in their desire to diet the Prime Minister, reporting to the Head of this strange Administration what was going on in the Departments of his colleagues, disseminating with the best intentions facts, theories, gossip, rumours, and at times also confidential information which ought not to have been allowed to pass through many hands. Mr. Lloyd George insisted, the Chief of the Imperial General Staff has told us, on receiving, contrary to precedent, copies of all communications which passed between the General Staff and Commanders-in-Chief:

" It unavoidably led to secret plans being seen by far too many people, some of whom, such as the numerous Secretaries, paid and unpaid, who thronged the precincts of No. 10 Downing Street, had no concern with them beyond sheer curiosity." [2]

Mr. Lloyd George was never able to explain clearly what his over-crowded Secretariat was for. " They

[1] See the details taken from the Civil Service Estimates and reprinted with comments in the *Liberal Magazine* for July 1922.
[2] See *Soldiers and Statesmen*, Vol. I, p. 178.

are a recording Department, they are a communi-
cating Department," he suggested later. "The
Cabinet Secretariat simply transmit," he told the
House of Commons. "They copy. They have no
other function." The activities of these agents must
not be confused with the official record of Cabinet
proceedings, placed under a distinguished public
servant whom Mr. Asquith had appointed as Secretary of the Committee of Imperial Defence.[1] In fact
the whole proposal, like so many of its author's proposals, had never been properly thought out. The
one conclusion which emerged was that the new
Department was intended to enhance the Prime
Minister's personal authority and personal prestige.
Mr. Lloyd George, as one admirer tells us, "was
not going to allow himself to be misinformed " about
what was going on around him " through lack of
sufficient assistants." But the public had to be dieted
also, and the feeding of opinion was probably an
important part of the Secretariat's work.

Even inside the Cabinet, it seems, the same
curious multiplicity of helpers and the same lack of
regularity reigned. Ministerial meetings became
reunions in which a surprising number of outsiders
took part. Mr. Lloyd George's Cabinet, it was
proudly claimed, did " not carry on its proceedings
behind closed doors " [2]—except presumably when

[1] Lt.-Col. Sir M. Hankey, who rendered conspicuous service
in more capacities than one during the War.

[2] For these explanations and admissions see *Lloyd George and
the War*, by " An Independent Liberal," written in praise of
Mr. Lloyd George's War service, Pt. II, Chap. II.

Mr. Henderson or other Ministers happened to be shut out. It did not trouble about old-fashioned conventions, privacy, collective responsibility or the like.

" Ministers, heads of departments, officials, officers, experts and visitors come and go according to the programme of the proceedings."

There must have been an immense amount of discursive talk. But a War Cabinet which did not include the Heads of the fighting Departments probably needed to consult experts and officials; and the Prime Minister's quickness in apprehending the views of these advisers often roused admiration. On the other hand, his " fruitfulness in ideas," it was admitted, made him " a bit of a trial to his colleagues." He launched proposals and then dropped them, hurried on to a new scheme before he had finished with the first—" left his babies," one colleague remarked, " lying about " for someone else to nurture. But that did not matter, we are assured, because the Prime Minister never forgot what he wanted to remember! Other critics, perhaps more impartial, noted that Mr. Lloyd George had also the faculty of never remembering what he wanted to forget.

II

To an impressionist Prime Minister, however, the supreme consideration was always to convey the right impression of the Government's activities to the public mind. Popularity first was Mr. Lloyd

George's watchword. If Mr. Asquith had erred on the side of neglecting, even disdaining, some managers of Press opinion, Mr. Lloyd George was determined not to make the same mistake. Certain newspapers had been invaluable in helping him to power; and it is probably no exaggeration to say that to secure newspaper support in shepherding opinion was, even in days of great national anxiety, the most absorbing task to which those close to him devoted their time. He rarely overlooked a journalistic friend or neglected a journal that could serve him. If the *Daily Mail* was a little uncertain, the *Daily Express* might be counted on for support; its proprietor was understood to have played a large part in cementing the alliance between Mr. Lloyd George and Mr. Bonar Law. If the *Times* should prove capricious, the Prime Minister had the *News of the World* [1] at his command. *John Bull* was prepared to patronise him, and did so. The *Daily Telegraph*, the *Morning Post*, the *Observer* and other prominent journals were only anxious to help the national cause. The Conservative Press, carefully tuned, would, it was thought, follow the Conservative leaders; and most of the Conservative leaders likely to give trouble, Sir Edward Carson, Lord Milner, Mr. Bonar Law, Sir F. E. Smith, had been safely brought into the new Administration. But as Mr. Lloyd George's distaste for military advice developed, murmurings developed also, even in the

[1] Its representative became one of Mr. Lloyd George's chief Press agents.

7

closely censored Conservative Press.[1] Of the Liberal Press the *Daily Chronicle* was in due course bought in Mr. Lloyd George's interest. The *Daily News* and *Nation*, long critical and independent, were brought into line later on; and the *Daily News* ultimately absorbed the *Westminster Gazette*.[2] The *Manchester Guardian*, if at times bewildered and uneasy, was held in check for the most part by the unremitting courtesies which Mr. Lloyd George paid to the old Liberal friend and colleague at its head.

" In the ' breakfast diplomacy ' of Mr. Lloyd George," one admirer has told us, " intelligence and will-power move on a fulcrum of sympathy and confidence."

This " fulcrum " few guests at his table could resist; and his breakfast diplomacy had undoubted value in retaining recalcitrant colleagues and in comforting uncomfortable friends. In matters of publicity the Prime Minister added to the powers given him by a rigid censorship the influence of a personality which could at times be very frank and winning, the authority which his great position and his unrivalled command of information bestowed. No British politician ever showed such skill or assiduity in using for his own benefit the resources of the Press. The result was that for two critical years most people in this country knew very little of their rulers' doings

[1] The vindictive attack made on Colonel Repington and the *Morning Post* later showed how deeply Mr. Lloyd George resented independent criticism.

[2] But this was not till the War and the Coalition were over, and an energetic campaign for " reunion " had won wavering minds in the Liberal Party.

except what the Prime Minister wished them to know. And Mr. Lloyd George found his reward in the silencing of criticism, in the legend which grew up to dignify his efforts, and which, transmuted into common belief by the alchemy of victory, gave him the unexampled prestige that he enjoyed at the end of the War.

Nor was that legend quite devoid of substance, mingled with dross as to some extent it was. The two years of war which saw Mr. Lloyd George almost a dictator, though a dictator at times strangely uncertain as to what he should dictate, were years of grave peril, of long-delayed and long-uncertain triumphs, but of the growing and at last irresistible ascendency of the nations which possessed the greater resources and the greater staying-power. In that story it is not the individuals who principally count. The War was won, in spite of innumerable, perhaps inevitable, blunders, by the spirit and devotion of the masses of our people. We produced no Chatham, no Wellington, no Nelson. But the heroes of the days of Frederick and Napoleon had a far less complicated task. We committed many mistakes, encountered many disappointments, both on our own part and on the part of our Allies. And those mistakes and disappointments continued almost to the end. But from first to last they were accompanied by acts of incomparable service, by the unexampled efforts of a great number of able men. If there are ample opportunities for criticism, there are still more ample opportunities for paying tribute to every class of public servant, statesmen, soldiers, sailors, factory-workers, even politicians, journalists, contractors, who contributed at any stage to the result. The " Old Contemptibles " [1] of the Army and the picked men of the Navy would be the last to grudge the special honours which the Territorials, the New Armies and the Merchant Service won. So far as Mr. Lloyd George kept alive and represented the unconquerable spirit of the nation, he has a place in history which no one will dispute. The mistake of some of his partisans has been that they have claimed for him an immunity from error to which he has no title, and almost a monopoly of qualities which so many of his contemporaries shared.

It was a piece of peculiar good fortune which gave Mr. Lloyd George, to control the Coalition, a colleague as loyal and as supple as Mr. Bonar Law. No more adroit politician and no more accomplished debater had emerged for years in the Conservative Party. Mr. Bonar Law won beyond question esteem and confidence from those who knew him well. And even those who knew him little had grounds for believing that behind his political armour was a man not only of high gifts, but of high character, and of a nature singularly free from self-seeking. But many Liberals, watching him in Parliament in days of acute political conflict, men of moderation who did

---

[1] This phrase has passed into tradition. But it is more than doubtful if the Emperor William ever used it. (See Ponsonby's *Falsehood in War-Time*, pp. 84–7.)

not fail to appreciate the finer qualities of those with whom they disagreed, could not help wondering sometimes at his apparent bitterness of partisanship, and asking themselves if he were really a victim of the angry suspicions which he seemed to show. I know that my own feeling on this point was shared by others who did not often lack respect for their opponents. Men who could listen with composure to Mr. Balfour or to Mr. Austen Chamberlain, even to Mr. F. E. Smith or to Sir Edward Carson, could not listen with patience to Mr. Bonar Law. It was not only that his shafts went home: so did the shafts of other speakers. It was that they dealt wounds which rankled. There was something a little rasping in his methods of debate, something which gave opponents an impression of unfairness. But as party animosities diminished, that impression died away, and of Mr. Bonar Law's public spirit there never was a doubt. Under the second Coalition he had to do most of the unpleasant work for the Prime Minister in Parliament. And yet the House grew to like him more and more. He was not altogether a strong man. By nature perhaps, like Mr. Lloyd George, he was something of a political schemer. But he would not scheme for personal or private ends. He had a good deal of Mr. Lloyd George's pliancy, of Mr. Lloyd George's dexterity in dealing with Parliament and managing men. Able, adaptable, kindly and resourceful, he made an ideal lieutenant; and he had no wish to usurp the leader's place. It is probable that he felt neither the power nor the confidence to take that grave responsibility upon him. For he had little of the deep-rooted self-assurance which was the secret of Mr. Lloyd George's strength.

III

There are materials now available, which ten years ago had no existence, for forming a judgment on the events of 1917 and 1918. We have had an outpouring of histories, memoirs and biographies, to illuminate almost every aspect of the War. We have had some candid revelations from German soldiers and German statesmen. We have had from France a number of acute, instructive studies. And we have had commentaries of great value made by British writers who were in a position to know the facts. In asking ourselves what part Mr. Lloyd George played, and what influence he really exercised, in the critical decisions of those two difficult years, there are four English writers in particular whose evidence on military questions it seems impossible to set aside,[1] because they had close and confidential access to most of the leading actors in the drama, and, with all allowances for prejudice, exceptional opportunities of arriving at the truth. Colonel Repington's diaries, discounted as some of his gossipy material may be, reveal an observer whose familiarity with military problems and intimate relations with British and French soldiers lent

[1] And many others might easily be added, *e.g.* the biographers of Lord Kitchener, Lord Haig, Lord Rawlinson, etc.

weight to his comments on the management of the War, while his connection with the *Times* and his personal sympathies predisposed him to give Mr. Lloyd George a cordial welcome on the formation of his Government in December 1916. But from that time onwards Colonel Repington's story is little but a story of growing disillusionment, ending in deep distrust of Mr. Lloyd George's methods and in amazement at his headstrong disregard of military advice. Mr. Winston Churchill, from the standpoint of an intimate colleague, is naturally less inclined to criticise Mr. Lloyd George. He has no undue respect for military opinion. He is quick to detect its failings. And he has a much wider understanding of the political difficulties which surrounded the Prime Minister on every side. Mr. Churchill's presentment of the facts and his deductions from them have therefore, in judging of Mr. Lloyd George's decisions, apart from their vivacity, an importance of their own. Sir William Robertson is first and foremost a professional soldier, who saw the conditions of the military problem as most able soldiers saw them, and who proved to be entirely right in his conviction that the fate of Europe must be settled on the Western Front in France. He had the power of stating his opinions to the Cabinet with a knowledge, steadiness and candour which impressed almost all the statesmen who heard him except Mr. Lloyd George. Whatever one may think of the professional soldier's limitations—and their existence will be admitted by many who yet doubt whether a gifted politician's intuitions are always the best guides in conducting a campaign—no one who wishes to judge fairly can refuse to listen to Sir William Robertson's sincere and disinterested comments on the military operations which it was his duty to control. And if it be thought that he, like other soldiers, learned to distrust Mr. Lloyd George too quickly, lacked the *finesse* and the imagination to appreciate the Prime Minister's flights of fancy in the art of war, we may turn to the diaries of Sir Henry Wilson, who was Mr. Lloyd George's own special selection, and probably his most intimate military adviser in the critical months of 1917 and 1918.

Sir Henry Wilson at any rate was no obstinate and hide-bound Englishman—like so many, it seems, of the distinguished Generals whose warnings Mr. Lloyd George swept aside. It is difficult to believe that his astonishing diaries were all intended for the public eye. But it is impossible to doubt that, allowing for prejudice, exaggeration, indiscretion, eccentricity, they contain a genuine and candid picture of the events in which he took a leading part. Of Sir Henry Wilson himself opinions have varied. Mr. Asquith, with whom he had little sympathy, found him voluble and impetuous, " an indefatigable intriguer," with a loose tongue and a loose pen, and deficient on the professional side in prescience and judgment. Lord Kitchener shared some of Mr. Asquith's opinions. Mr. Winston Churchill was more appreciative. He found in General Wilson not only " an expert adviser of superior intellect," whose lucidity in setting forth his views was a delight, but " the most comprehending military mind of our day in Britain." And there is no doubt that Mr. Lloyd George was attracted by Sir Henry's freshness and unconventionality, by his humour, resourcefulness, audacity and cheeriness, by his readiness in speech, his readiness in scheming, and his great power of explaining the military position in an interesting and vivid way. Above all, Sir Henry Wilson was prepared at first to listen to the Prime Minister's ideas of strategy as sympathetically as the Prime Minister listened to his, and Mr. Lloyd George found this inclination on the part of a British General as irresistible as it was perhaps unique. The Prime Minister's uncomfortable habit of consulting Sir Henry Wilson without regard to the feelings of his responsible advisers, and his determination to force Wilson, as soon as he felt strong enough to do so, into Sir William Robertson's place, made Sir Henry's position one of exceptional difficulty, and he met the situation with exceptional skill. He never lost touch with the distinguished British Generals whom the Prime Minister so obviously distrusted. He won and kept the cordial friendship of distinguished Frenchmen like M. Clemenceau and Marshal Foch.[1] And if his views of Mr. Lloyd George as a ruler deteriorated woefully as his familiarity with the Prime Minister's methods increased, that experience alone is no sign of eccentricity, for it was only too common

[1] Foch had been a friend of Wilson for years before the War.

with those who enjoyed the same opportunities as he.

But it may be said, and with truth, that it was not in military matters that Mr. Lloyd George's aptitude in leadership was shown. It was rather in the general sense of effort and activity, in the buoyancy of mind and doggedness of spirit, for which in the popular opinion of the time he stood. The Prime Minister, like the nation, was beset by anxieties. If at the moment he made his countrymen believe that all was being done that could be done to secure victory, did he not render valuable service in at least stimulating confidence and effort? The answer is that undoubtedly he did. There is a curious little passage in Colonel Repington's diaries, purporting to record Mr. Edwin Montagu's opinion in May 1917, when he had not yet been invited to join Mr. Lloyd George's Administration:

" M. said that L.G.'s whole attitude before he took office was one of pessimistic criticism. He had done nothing since he came in, and yet his attitude was now one of the utmost optimism." [1]

But optimism alone has an invigorating effect, even if it has been cynically suggested that optimism was the prevailing attitude of everybody in the War who was doing something, and pessimism the prevailing attitude of everybody who watched what was being done. Mr. Lloyd George, Mr. Churchill tells us, lived in the present. He was always ready to face

[1] See *The First World War*, Vol. I, p. 566.

emergencies, to grapple with any problem that arose. He roused enthusiasm. He set people to work at something, many people to work at many things—if not invariably at things that needed to be done. He was rarely without an expedient. And if the improvised nature and the indifferent management of some of these expedients resulted in confusion and unnecessary cost, still they had value in keeping up the general impression of activity, and a more substantial value if they helped in any degree to keep up the nation's heart. The greatest danger which this country had to face in the early months of 1917 was the alarming success of the German U-boat campaign. It reached its climax in April; and—apart from the inexhaustible resource, the unbreakable tenacity, of British seamen—it was chiefly overcome by the adoption of the convoy system in May. The credit of instituting the convoy system, which authoritative naval opinion with some notable exceptions long resisted, but which is now recognised as one of the boldest and wisest decisions ever made in naval war, has been claimed mistakenly for several men. The Admiralty at last adopted and applied it with remarkable vigour and success. But in spite of all the resource and ingenuity brought to bear by the Admiralty on the submarine problem, it remains very doubtful if the true solution would have been recognised and accepted in official quarters, had there not been strong insistence from outside. For that insistence Mr. Lloyd George and his War Cabinet, and those who advised them, deserve high praise.[1] Mr. Churchill conceives that Mr. Lloyd George's greatest service to the nation lay in facing the submarine peril " with unquailing eye." But to the unquailing eye there was in this case happily added the power to discriminate between conflicting opinions, and the skill and courage to make the right view prevail.

IV

It is certainly far from the wish of Liberals who look back with unforgotten sympathy on many episodes in Mr. Lloyd George's early career, to grudge him any honours which he may legitimately claim. But the more closely we examine his actions as head of the Executive which directed our campaigns abroad—and in the War Cabinet, it must be remembered, he was, even when his colleagues distrusted his decisions, to all intents and purposes supreme—the more difficult it is to answer the criticisms which that direction has aroused. Mr. Lloyd George's weaknesses as a military adviser were illustrated only too quickly by the ardour with which he threw himself into the Salonica scheme. We had, of course, great interests to care for in the East, in Egypt, in Asia, even in the Balkans. We had a command of sea-power such as no nation had ever had before, and in the Mediterranean at any rate a vast

[1] Sir Henry Newbolt's *Naval Operations* (Vol. IV, pp. 325–83) should be studied on this subject. But it is understood that Sir M. Hankey was chiefly responsible for the advice on which the War Cabinet acted.

extent of apparently vulnerable enemy sea-coast. There were strong reasons in political feeling and in natural sentiment for a determined effort to save Serbia, for action which might help to warn Bulgaria, to win over Roumania and Greece. The French Government, from mingled motives, committed themselves to the Salonica adventure, without perhaps realising how large a share of the strain and effort which it called for must fall on the British Navy and the British Exchequer. And before the end of 1914 Mr. Lloyd George had adopted the idea, and was pressing it in season and out of season on his colleagues. But from the first the whole enterprise was a grave mistake. It was undertaken too late. Even if undertaken earlier, it would probably have failed to save the Serbians from destruction or the Bulgarians from declaring against us. For some three years it struggled on, achieving no useful object, a woeful example of misplaced enthusiasm, of wavering and mismanagement in war. And the fact that, when our enemies at last collapsed, it was convenient to have an army on the spot to occupy the Balkans, was no adequate compensation for the waste and loss incurred. We are all familiar now with the melancholy story:—the inevitable divisions of opinion on the subject; the reluctant decision in 1915 to send troops, which were to be withdrawn immediately if communications with the Serbian army could not be opened and maintained; the urgent demand for additional troops which followed; the dissatisfaction with the operations undertaken and, it must be added, with the French General in command;[1] the efforts of our General Staff to remind the Cabinet that it was not so easy as Mr. Lloyd George perhaps imagined to move troops from France to Salonica for the winter and back again to France from Salonica for the spring, and that the enemy could always move troops across Europe much faster than we; the doubts and conferences in 1916 as to whether we should persevere or draw back; the Government's fluctuations between the two alternatives, more marked than ever after Mr. Lloyd George's accession to power; the unending drain on our resources in men and ships and money and supplies—some 150 ships, some 400,000 tons of shipping, were required in 1917; the folly of maintaining a great inactive army in the Balkans when the danger from the submarines was at its greatest, and our very existence depended on our saving all the tonnage that we could.[2] The tale of men whose services were wasted there and often so badly needed in the West—414,000 is the figure given for British troops,[3] and they were only a part

[1] It is significant to note the dread expressed by some French officers in General Foch's *entourage* lest General Sarrail should be recalled to France and given military preferment there. (See Repington's *First World War*, Vol. II, p. 59.)

[2] Sir Henry Newbolt puts the sinkings of Allied tonnage in the Mediterranean at 101,000 tons in February 1917, at 72,000 tons in March, and at a very much higher figure in April (*Naval Operations*, Vol. IV, pp. 277–80). One division is said to have taken two months to get from France to Salonica (*First World War*, Vol. I, p. 407).

[3] See *Soldiers and Statesmen*, Vol. II, p. 145.

of the vast forces diverted to the East—and the tale of the unremitting effort needed to keep these men fed, reinforced, sustained, rendered the Salonica episode, in the words of no mean judge, " the most persistent, exasperating and unfruitful " of all the military adventures to which Mr. Lloyd George committed this country.

But the episode of Salonica does not stand alone. A word should be added about the campaign in Mesopotamia, for which Mr. Lloyd George afterwards claimed special credit in a speech neither ingenuous nor fair. At first a failure, Sir Stanley Maude made it in the end a great success. It may be worth while to quote together Mr. Lloyd George's statement and Mr. Asquith's reply.[1] Here are Mr. Lloyd George's assertions:

" What about Mesopotamia—that blessed word? It was not I that went to Mesopotamia. It was Mr. Asquith who supported the Mesopotamian campaign. It was perfectly true that he did not make a success of it, but when we took it up we did. We found it with a great army defeated and captured. We reorganised it when it was in a very bad condition. We captured Baghdad and Mosul. We found the army at Jaffa or the Canal. But the only difference between us was that they began it badly and we did it well. But Mesopotamia was not my policy. I found the British Army there, and only did my best to make it a success, once we were there."

Few people reading this statement would gather that Mr. Lloyd George, as a leading member of Mr Asquith's Cabinet, was responsible from the begin-

[1] I take them from the *Liberal Magazine* of March 1921, where they are given, with references, side by side. The dates were February 10 and February 19, 1921. Mr. Asquith's facts can be verified.

ning for the whole Mesopotamian campaign. Mr.
Asquith made no such attempt to shirk responsibility, though he admitted frankly that the operations in Mesopotamia had been mismanaged by the
Indian Government at first.

" We reorganised the General Staff here, and I put that
great and gallant soldier, Sir William Robertson—to whom
this country is under an immeasurable and not sufficiently
acknowledged debt of gratitude for the winning of the War—
I put him at the head of the General Staff. He reorganised
the whole thing. He developed, with the assistance of the
Quartermaster-General—another very distinguished soldier,
Sir John Cowans—a totally new system of communications, of
transport, of supply, of all the necessities of an Army, and I
myself appointed that great soldier, Sir Stanley Maude, to the
command of the expedition. From the time when I left office
in the second week of December 1916 to the end of that
campaign not a thing was done, nor was any step taken by
the Government which succeeded us, which contributed in
any way to its success."

Yet Mr. Lloyd George's description is " they began
it badly and we did it well." Even if it could be
shown that some of Mr. Lloyd George's administrators contributed in matters of transport or otherwise to the success of the campain, lack of generosity
could hardly go further than Mr. Lloyd George's
statement goes.

v

Apart from Eastern controversies, it seems that
Mr. Lloyd George's extreme facility in absorbing
new ideas prevented him from arriving at any settled
convictions as to what the main objects of British
strategy ought to be. Nor could he always bring

himself to listen with patience to the experienced men who did. The result was a number of restless suggestions, which redoubled the uncertainties and anxieties of war. The desire, natural enough, to secure a victory somewhere, in order to encourage public opinion, was the Prime Minister's strongest wish on taking office. Within six weeks the plan of campaign for 1917, already agreed on by Sir Douglas Haig and General Joffre, was dropped.[1] An ambitious scheme for a great transference of men and guns to Italy for an attack on Austria was propounded—without previous consultation with our General Staff. And directly afterwards a third project was put forward for a new offensive in France—the very policy to which Mr. Lloyd George had recently expressed himself as resolutely opposed. But in this last scheme the Prime Minister was singularly unfortunate in the arrangements which he made. If there be any obligation binding on Ministers who undertake to conduct a war, it is the obligation to trust and support their Generals so long as they employ them, and to cease to employ them when their trust has gone. Mr. Lloyd George's method, unfortunately, both with the Chief of the Imperial General Staff and with our Commander in France, was to distrust and even at times to thwart the Generals he retained. He was dissatisfied already with Sir Douglas Haig, and he had con-

[1] But the French Government was largely if not chiefly responsible for this. General Foch at the same time was left without any effective command. (See M. Painlevé, *La Vérité sur l'offensive du 16 Avril, 1917.*)

demned in no measured terms the costly offensives on the Western Front. Yet in February 1917 he flung himself suddenly into a scheme for a new offensive on the largest scale. Conferences were held in Calais and in London. General Nivelle, General Joffre's successor in the Chief Command in France, appeared at the War Cabinet in London, where his eloquence, his charm and his command of English captivated Mr. Lloyd George, who could not understand inarticulate people, and who was never at his best in judging men. The British Prime Minister agreed to put the British troops under General Nivelle's orders, without consulting either the British Commander or the British General Staff.[1] His sudden confidence in the new French General surprised even French observers. One has gone so far as to suggest that the British Government " sought an occasion to drag the French Government into an intrigue against Marshal Haig." [2]

" To the historians of all time," says one of Lord Haig's biographers,[3] " the Calais Conference will always be the high-water mark of ineptitude of civilian interference with the conduct of military operations. It has no parallel in history. All British military advice was deliberately discarded. The British Government through its responsible head decided to commit the fortunes of the armies in the forthcoming campaign, and the fate of the nation, to the plan of an allied

---

[1] See Churchill's *World Crisis, 1916–1918*, pp. 267–9, and Repington's *First World War*, Vol. I, p. 555.

[2] See Abel Ferry, *La Guerre, vue d'en bas et d'en haut*, p. 197; Robertson, *Soldiers and Statesmen*, Vol. II, pp. 203–34, and Dewar, *Sir Douglas Haig's Command*, Chaps. X and XI.

[3] See General J. Charteris' *Life of Field-Marshal Earl Haig*, p. 243. This criticism has been disputed, but it seems to have force.

Commander-in-Chief which had received no support from our military advisers, and which was already the object of sharp criticism from many leading French soldiers."

The whole of General Nivelle's plan, ill-judged, ill-timed and delayed in execution, was ruined by the Germans' adroit retirement. Sir Douglas Haig did his part gallantly at Arras and at Vimy. But General Nivelle led his troops to disaster in Champagne. Deep murmurs broke out in France, where the new Government had little sympathy with General Nivelle. And General Pétain was called in at a most anxious moment to re-establish confidence and to suppress mutiny among the French troops.

The episode reflected little credit on the military judgment of Mr. Lloyd George. Yet even after General Nivelle's unhappy failure, the British Prime Minister took the extraordinary course of trying to back his claims against those of General Pétain, to the not unnatural indignation of the French Minister of War.[1] And early in May, at a conference in Paris, the politician who had inveighed so bitterly against the military Moloch in the previous year, was active in demanding the continuance of the offensive without allowing the enemy a single moment of rest:

" After full consideration, the British War Cabinet asks of its French colleagues to push the offensive during the course of this year with all the force of which our two armies are capable." [2]

---

[1] See Repington, Vol. I, p. 541 and Vol. II, pp. 68 and 72.
[2] See Churchill, *World Crisis, 1916–1918*, p. 284. On the whole episode M. Painlevé's *Comment j'ai nommé Foch et Pétain* is worth study.

Events soon proved that the French were not in a condition to push their offensive, and the British armies had to undertake by far the heaviest task. In July the War Cabinet telegraphed their whole-hearted support to Sir Douglas Haig. But the losses which followed appalled the Prime Minister, the losses and the lack of visible results. Passchendaele, Mr. Churchill assures us, was " the end of illusions." Mr. Lloyd George viewed with horror the cost of the offensive which he had so energetically urged. His distrust of the British Commanders deepened. He made little allowance for their difficulties. His ever-veering views swung back again. He seems to have determined to prevent, for a time at any rate, any further active operations by Sir Douglas Haig on the Western Front in France. And the results of this disastrous change of purpose were seen in March 1918.

We cannot wonder if Mr. Lloyd George's direction of the campaign in France in 1917 was sharply criticised by military opinion. But even sharper criticism was roused by the apparent light-heartedness with which at different moments in the same year he proposed to throw our forces hither and thither in campaigns elsewhere. " Always starting new hares," was the Chief of the Staff's comment on these embarrassing enthusiasms. And even Sir Henry Wilson has noted the terror which the Prime Minister's " mad schemes " inspired. One day Mr. Lloyd George was urging a grand attack upon Trieste. On another the objective was to be Alexan-

dretta, on another Jerusalem, on another Aleppo.
" Firework strategy," commented the soldiers, " a
victory somewhere quickly, a victory while you
wait." There was much to be said, no doubt, for
fresh ideas and unceasing activity. But the constant
changes of plan tended to bewilder and unsettle
those who had to carry them out. It has been estimated that at least twenty per cent. of the time of
the General Staff at the War Office was occupied
in explaining that the projects put forward by the
Prime Minister were from a military point of view
impracticable or unsound. The campaign in Pales-
tine, when at last adequately organised, proved to
be a very great success. But the strain which it
imposed on our man-power was very serious; and
its brilliant Commander never lost sight of the fact
that no successes in Jerusalem could settle the issue
of the War.

" I recognise," he wrote to Colonel Repington, " that the
West is the essential battle-ground, where victory will be
decisive. Make sure of victory there." [1]

If only Mr. Lloyd George could have been persuaded to listen to wiser men's advice! But so far
from listening to people of military experience, we
find that in March 1918 he was dissatisfied even with
General Allenby's successes, and was accusing both
him and Sir William Robertson of having exagger-
ated the difficulties of the campaign.[2] The work of
the War Cabinet inevitably suffered from its leader's

[1] See General Allenby's letter of February 4, 1918 (*First
World War*, Vol. II, p. 237). [2] *Ibid.*, p. 247.

multiplicity of schemes. In July 1917 General Smuts found it overwhelmed with its labours, and the Prime Minister struggling, of course unsuccessfully, to do the work of six men. The General that month attended a Conference at Paris, remarkable chiefly for the number of people present, and pronounced it " the most futile exhibition of incompetence that he had ever witnessed." [1] In August there was another Conference, in London, and General Foch's description of it, as given by General Wilson, represents Mr. Lloyd George as tired, peevish, " *maladroit*," as complaining that we were always late, but as unwilling to accept Foch's proposal to get ready for the 1918 campaign. That Conference appeared to the great Frenchman " an absolute fiasco," without direction and without result. [2] In September Sir Henry Wilson, already much in Mr. Lloyd George's confidence, noted that there was not only no common plan for the whole front, but no common plan even for our section of it. In October Wilson found the Prime Minister profoundly dissatisfied, but not knowing what to do. In the same month Mr. Lloyd George appointed Wilson and Lord French as " technical advisers," hoping apparently that this would drive Sir William Robertson to resign. In the same month newspapers known to respond to the Prime Minister's suggestions began a Press attack upon the General Staff. [3] Why, one asks,

[1] See Sir H. Wilson's *Life and Diaries*, Vol. II, p. 7.
[2] *Ibid.* p. 9.
[3] See especially the *Manchester Guardian* of October 29 and November 1, 1917.

if Mr. Lloyd George thought Sir William Robertson and Sir Douglas Haig unfitted for their great responsibilities, did he not remove them, and face with courage any criticism which his action roused? From America our representative wrote:

" The President repeats most earnestly that he will risk any adverse criticism in order to win the War." [1]

In England the one thing which Mr. Lloyd George would not do, even when he believed the fortunes of the War to be at stake, was to face the possibility of a newspaper attack.

Meanwhile the want of war direction obviously increased. The losses in Flanders had been very serious. The news from Russia grew steadily worse: when Lenin secured control, Russia practically ceased to be an Ally. At the end of October 1917 the Italian Army was overwhelmed at Caporetto; and in face of that disaster Mr. Lloyd George, whose high spirit in danger rarely failed him, showed the energy and concentration which his schemes so often lacked. " You are our Kellermann," he told Sir Henry Wilson, " and you must save us in our desperate situation." But the Italian failure necessitated, as Sir Douglas Haig reminded us, " the transfer of five British divisions from France to Italy, at a time when their presence in France might have had far-reaching effects." At Rapallo in November a Supreme Council for the Allies was set up. To secure unity between the politicians this Council had

[1] In February 1918. See the *Intimate Papers of Colonel House*, Vol. III, p. 444.

its uses, and Mr. Lloyd George's outburst at Paris on the need for unity among the Allies was listened to with such respect as it deserved.[1] But as a machine for military action it had little use or none. The opinion of the British Chief of the Staff was not even asked upon the subject. The new Kellermann had little doubt that Mr. Lloyd George's real object was to get rid of Sir William Robertson and Sir Douglas Haig, while Sir William Robertson, on his part, only too well aware of the Prime Minister's perplexities, was "genuinely anxious to help him if no more tricks were played." M. Clemenceau wanted one Commander-in-Chief. Mr. Lloyd George would not hear of it. It was impracticable; Sir Henry Wilson thought it impossible.[2] Failing that, M. Clemenceau would have had the leading Generals, Foch and Pétain, on the new Council. Again Mr. Lloyd George would not hear of it: that would compel him to appoint Robertson and Haig. Neither Clemenceau nor Pétain concealed his belief that the Supreme War Council as constituted by Mr. Lloyd George was for military purposes valueless. The American Generals shared this opinion. Colonel House, an exceptionally shrewd and detached observer, who fully appreciated the value of the Inter-allied Conference for co-ordinating economic resources, was driven to the conclusion that the

[1] See *Times* of November 13, 1917. Its tone was sharply criticised.

[2] See Wilson's *Diaries*, Vol. II, p. 30. Carson, Sir Henry notes, is "angry with Lloyd George for his constant abuse of Robertson." (*Ibid.* p. 47.)

Supreme War Council as at present constituted was
" almost a farce." He attended its meeting at Versailles on December 1, 1917. He found it was " all
talk and no concerted action." He dined with Mr.
Lloyd George afterwards, and found him happy and
in good form.

"Just why he was happy, excepting that the Conference
had adjourned and he was returning to England, is more than
I can fathom, for certainly we have not done one half of what
should have been done. The Supreme War Council has taken
up but few of the matters which properly should have come
before it, and instead of sitting for one morning it should have
sat for a week." [1]

Wherever one looks in Mr. Lloyd George's record
the same qualities appear : the large plans, the abun-
dant energy, the variable judgment, depending so
often upon public opinion, the love of talk, the love
of scheming and the noticeable lack of thoroughness
and grip. The year 1917 closed in gloom. It could
not be said that Mr. Lloyd George's Government
had as yet solved the problem of how to win the
War. The Prime Minister kept a bold front. But his
optimism was shaken. He set to work with vigour
to explore the possibilities of peace.

VI

But if we are to judge of Mr. Lloyd George as a
War Minister, there is a gloomier episode still to
record. At the beginning of 1918 the situation was
obviously threatening, and especially threatening for

[1] Colonel House's *Papers*, Vol. III, p. 279. But see the whole
of Chapter IX of this volume.

our armies on the Western Front in France. They had suffered very severely in the fighting of the previous year. Mr. Lloyd George is said to have consulted M. Clemenceau as to the possibility of avoiding such losses, and Sir Henry Wilson has set out, not too tenderly, M. Clemenceau's reply:

> " He told me that Lloyd George had written to him a couple of days ago saying he understood Pétain had a plan of attacking without losing life, and would he tell Lloyd George the secret and send it over by an officer! Clemenceau said Lloyd George was a fool, and the way to save life was not to attack." [1]

Obsessed with the idea that the British Generals in France could do little but lose life and exhaust their resources, the Prime Minister was now, it seems, determined not to supply them with more troops than he could help. Such action would seem to be incredible were not the evidence beyond dispute. There could be no question as to the German forces gathering for attack. From November to March the German infantry divisions in France were increased from 146 to 192.[2] The Government were well aware of this alarming concentration. Mr. Lloyd George afterwards claimed that the German offensive had been foretold with extraordinary accuracy by the military Staff at Versailles.[3] Yet for week after week in the winter of 1917–18 the War Cabinet could come to no decision in regard to the campaign immediately ahead, while the Prime Minister han-

[1] See *Wilson's Diaries*, Vol. II, p. 41.
[2] See Dewar, *Sir Douglas Haig's Command*, Vol. II, p. 14.
[3] See *Parliamentary Debates*, April 9, 1918.

kered still for schemes of Eastern conquest and was largely occupied in fighting against the advice of his own General Staff. It was only, Sir William Robertson tells us, after ten weeks of delay that this all-important question was referred to the Supreme War Council. Then, on February 1, the Council recommended that, " subject to the Western Front being made secure," a decisive offensive should be undertaken against Turkey. And when M. Clemenceau criticised this question-begging compromise, and pointed out the dangerous concentration of German troops on the Western Front, the Prime Minister was indignant with Sir William Robertson for endorsing M. Clemenceau's views.[1] When General Foch asked for more men for our armies in France, Mr. Lloyd George replied that that meant revolution in this country. When Sir Douglas Haig, only too well aware of the gaps in his battalions, pressed for reinforcements, Mr. Lloyd George turned a deaf ear. He distrusted the British Commander, but he feared it might be unpopular to replace him. He expected him to hold the Western Front, now a widely extended front, against a very serious danger. He knew how heavy Haig's losses had been. He had compelled him to send divisions to Italy. But he was reluctant to give him the men that he needed to make his deficiencies good. History may agree with Mr. Lloyd George in thinking that there had been grave errors of generalship and needless waste of life in some of our offensives in

[1] See *Soldiers and Statesmen*, Vol. II, pp. 285-7.

France. But, though Mr. Lloyd George had mourned over these offensives, he had not stopped them: he had even insisted, in May 1917, that they should go on. He had retained in command, though he had sometimes disregarded, the Generals responsible for them. And then, at the critical moment, when it was not a question of a British offensive, but of defending the British Army against an overwhelming attack, he failed to give our Generals the force which they required. To the last, in fact, Mr. Lloyd George was confident that he could judge the needs of the military situation better than his military advisers, and, though large numbers of troops were available to draw on in England and elsewhere, he refused to entrust them to Sir Douglas Haig.[1]

This in plain terms is the conclusion forced upon us by the narratives we now possess. Is it possible to dismiss it as merely the result of prejudice or partisanship? Or is it the bare truth, which, in spite of many an effort to slur it over, can no longer be denied? Sir William Robertson's evidence, generally restrained in statement, cannot be swept aside as unsupported. Sir Douglas Haig's language entirely bears it out, though some significant passages in his despatch of July 20, 1918, which dwelt upon his shortage of men and his need of reinforcements, were omitted—it cannot be by accident—when the Government allowed the despatch to be issued, after

[1] Towards the end of 1917 we had not less than 1,200,000 men in distant places. Many could have been brought from the East. (See Robertson, *From Private to Field-Marshal*, p. 324.)

withholding it from publication for three months.[1]
Colonel Repington, no ill-informed critic, could not
in January 1918 control his indignation at the
Cabinet's refusal to listen to military warnings in
regard to the deficiencies in men, and at the orders
issued by the War Office to reduce the number of
battalions in each division:

"This is terrible, and will mean the reduction of our
infantry in France by one-fourth, and confusion in all our
infantry at the moment of coming crisis."

A week later he estimated that the Boche divisions
in the West already outnumbered the Allies, and
were coming in at the average rate of nine a month. In
February he was prosecuted by the Government for
publishing his views and was for the moment silenced.

"They have starved the Army for men, have dispersed our
military resources about the world, and now have to face the
consequences of their folly. Upon the Army and the country
will fall the retribution which Lloyd George and his War
Cabinet alone deserve." [2]

Sir Frederick Maurice's testimony, clear, detailed,
authentic, is to the same effect.[3] He was then
Director of Military Operations, and had been
lately ordered not to talk with Colonel Repington
about the War! Our armies in France were not
given the reinforcements wanted. "They should
never and need never" have been called upon for
the cruel sacrifices which they had to face. Sir

[1] See *Sir Douglas Haig's Command*, Vol. II, pp. 17–21.
[2] See *The First World War*, Vol. II, pp. 180, 191, 234, 238.
[3] See the careful, documented statement called *Intrigues of
the War*.

Henry Wilson, Mr. Lloyd George's chosen adviser, is little less emphatic in condemning the Minister's action. In December 1917 he warned Haig's Chief of the Staff that Sir Douglas was " going to have three attacks—by the Boches, by London, by Paris " —and he added, " We shall want D. H. badly when bad times come." In January 1918 he noted a new Press campaign against Sir William Robertson and in a lesser degree against Sir Douglas Haig, and asked himself, " Is this Lloyd George? " In the same month he recorded that General Foch could not understand why Mr. Lloyd George could not or would not take any decisive action, and begged the Prime Minister " to make Versailles into a real Council, and not a mass meeting." In February he complained of " six days of chaos," directly attribut-able to lack of purpose on the part of the Prime Minister, and reported some startling expressions of Lord Milner about the " vacillations and uncer-tainties " which went on all day. On March 11 he estimated that there were 186 German divisions already in France, of which ninety-two faced our armies. Haig, forced to disband twenty-five per cent. of his infantry battalions in order to find men for the rest, was afraid of the penetration of his line. There was great talk at Versailles of a General Reserve; but on March 14 the Supreme Council decided that for the present our General Reserve in France should consist of divisions in Italy alone.[1]

[1] " Of course, in a sense, this is nonsense," comments Wilson. See Wilson's *Diaries*, Vol. II, pp. 42, 52, 53, 55-6, 58, 61, 66, 68, 70.

On March 21, when the Germans were attacking our armies in overwhelming force, the War Cabinet seemed to Sir Henry Wilson to be occupied in " long discursive and useless discussions " about Russia, Japan and the United States.

It is a melancholy story, and Mr. Winston Churchill has summed it up. He had rejoined the Cabinet as Minister of Munitions in July 1917, and had of course the closest access to his chief. He recalls the situation in the early days of 1918, the French desire to reserve their strength, the slowness of arrivals from America, the demand from Allenby for more troops, the need of additional forces in Mesopotamia, the " constant drain " of the Salonica front.

" It was in these grave circumstances that we had to anticipate a German onslaught far exceeding in power and fury anything that had yet been experienced."

The Russian collapse had relieved masses of German and Austrian troops. The Intelligence reports " revealed week after week an unending flow of men and material to the West." The British infantry were " woefully depleted." The battalions " were far below their proper strength." Sir Douglas Haig " vehemently and naturally " called for all the officers and men he needed. The Chief of the Imperial General Staff supported him. Mr. Churchill himself, knowing the facts and seeing the Prime Minister constantly, " never ceased to press for the immediate reinforcement of Sir Douglas Haig." But Mr. Lloyd George was sure that he knew best. He viewed with horror, we are told, the task of driving men to the shambles. He dreaded lest our resources should be expended in another Passchendaele. He feared that, if the troops were once in France, he would not be able to resist the military pressure for a fresh offensive. So he gathered reserves in England and deliberately refused to send Sir Douglas Haig the reinforcements he desired.

"But I held, and hold still, that the War Cabinet should have been resolute, as I believe it would have been found strong enough, at once to support and to restrain the High Command in France."

In Mr. Churchill's view, Mr. Lloyd George and his Cabinet failed not only " to make their Commander conform to their convictions ": they failed also " to do full justice to the Army because of their disagreement with the Commander-in-Chief." [1] And some fifty-five or fifty-six weakened divisions of British infantry were left to face the onslaught of overwhelming numbers of Germans,[2] an onslaught in power, equipment and intensity never yet equalled in the history of war.

What were the consequences of Mr. Lloyd George's refusal to listen to military advice? On March 7 his deputy, Mr. Bonar Law, assured the

[1] See *The World Crisis, 1916–1918*, pp. 375–8 and 422. Mr. Churchill is convinced that the front could have been held on March 21, had the War Cabinet reinforced Sir D. Haig, as they could and should have done.

[2] The figures given by different writers, and sometimes by the same writer, differ slightly; but the Germans were often two or three to one.

House of Commons that he was still a little sceptical about the threatened offensive, and that in any case the Germans would have no dangerous superiority in men or guns! Mr. Churchill, his colleague, reports that the Germans set in motion rather more than three-quarters of a million men against our 300,000, and that their guns on a front of forty miles numbered nearly 6,000 as against 2,500 on our side.[1] The failure to give Sir Douglas Haig the reinforcements which he needed had been aggravated by the demand that he should take over more line, a demand strongly pressed by the French and very difficult for us to refuse altogether. The attack came as and when the military authorities expected. The only surprise was in its weight and scale and power. The Fifth Army, " shamefully undermanned," and left to face an irresistible enemy, was driven back in unavoidable confusion and lost some sixty per cent. of its strength. By the evening of the second day the British tale of deaths and wounds and captures exceeded 100,000. By April 4 the worst was over. The stubborn and heroic resistance had stemmed the German advance. But the battle went on, and the cost paid was terribly high. During the forty days which began on March 21 our tale of killed and wounded, prisoners and missing, exceeded 300,000.[2] No such cruel and disastrous losses had ever been suffered by the British Army. No episode in the history of the War reflects so gravely on the

[1] *The World Crisis, 1916–1918*, p. 412.
[2] *Ibid.*, p. 446.

9

mismanagement of the Minister in charge. None illustrates so fatally the headstrong self-assurance which had come near to ruining the cause of the Allies.

VII

These considerations ought not to be forgotten, however humiliating and painful they may be. But let it be remembered also that, if Mr. Lloyd George brought disaster upon us, he faced it with the courage and resourcefulness which are among his greatest gifts. He was quick enough to realise—one wishes he had been franker to acknowledge—his terrible mistake. " Opportunist methods " were for the moment abandoned and instant measures taken to avert defeat. Reinforcements were summoned from the East. Urgent appeals for help were sent to America. The men whom Sir Douglas Haig had asked for vainly, and whose presence might have saved so many lives, were hurried across the Channel with astonishing speed.[1] Steps were at last taken, as the military authorities had for long entreated, to draw additional men from the munition works, the coal-mines and civil life. A new Man-Power Bill raised the military age to fifty or even fifty-five. And the country accepted without a murmur demands which would never have been refused had

[1] The decision was to send over 170,000 men in seventeen days, if ships could be provided (Wilson, *Diaries*, Vol. II, p. 74). Sir W. Robertson speaks of 140,000 men being sent (*Soldiers and Statesmen*, Vol. I, p. 332). From all quarters in April some 400,000 men, it seems, were found.

the truth been told and the need explained before. On April 9 the Prime Minister moved for leave to introduce the Bill. When he declared that the attack of overwhelming German forces had been accurately foretold by the Army authorities, one Member broke in with an awkward question:

" Were preparations made to meet it? "
" My hon. Friend," the Prime Minister answered, " must really allow me to speak in my own way."

With that observation Mr. Lloyd George left the subject, and never returned to this vital but embarrassing question during the whole of his speech. He pointed out, indeed, the critical nature of the battle, praised the almost incredible courage and coolness of our troops, explained the vigorous measures taken afterwards to meet the emergency, dwelt on the new appointment of General Foch. Incidentally he spoke of General Gough's retirement in terms which it is now admitted were neither generous nor just. But the most misleading part of the speech was contained in one sentence which conveyed the impression that, in face of the German concentration, the strength of the British forces had been fully and satisfactorily maintained:

" What was the position at the beginning of the battle? Notwithstanding the heavy casualties in 1917, the Army in France was considerably stronger on the 1st January, 1918 than on the 1st January, 1917."

The comparison of figures for January was only true if in the latter case, January 1918, some 300,000 non-combatants, unarmed labourers and coolies,

were included. But the figures for January 1 were
in any case misleading, because the attack began on
March 21, and between January 1 and March 21
1918, as Mr. Lloyd George was well aware, the
Germans had been pouring reinforcements—" an
unending flow of men and material "—into France.
The War Cabinet, on the other hand, while pressing
for an extension of our line, had refused our Commander the troops he needed, and had compelled
him to break up one battalion out of four in every
British infantry brigade. It is no wonder that the
Prime Minister avoided the question of what had
been done to meet the attack foretold.

Mr. Lloyd George's speech of April 9 caused grave
dissatisfaction among men who knew the facts.
General Sir Frederick Maurice, moved by a strong
sense of public duty, and deliberately disregarding
considerations of discipline and of his own personal
interest, published on Tuesday May 7 a letter
impugning the accuracy of the Ministerial statements. On the same day Mr. Bonar Law, speaking
as Deputy-Leader of the House of Commons, declared that General Maurice's allegations affected
the honour of Ministers, and that the Government
proposed to invite two Judges to inquire into the
misstatements alleged. He added that the inquiry
must be held in private, as it would involve " the
examination of the most secret documents." The
proposal for an inquiry by two judges was not very
popular. It was evident that several Members, not
on one side only, would have preferred a Select

Committee of the House. On Thursday May 9 Mr. Asquith moved for an inquiry by a Select Committee, a proposal which he had some reasons for thinking the Government would accept. And then Mr. Lloyd George, throwing over both the Government's offer and Mr. Bonar Law's statement that publicity could not be allowed, announced that he would deal with the whole subject then and there, and would give the House " the whole of the sources of information " on which his statements had been based. Considerations of the honour of Ministers were dropped. Mr. Asquith's motion, advocated with great restraint and moderation, was treated as a vote of censure. And Mr. Lloyd George's speech, though again unfair and evasive, won for the moment a substantial Parliamentary success. He began in his worst vein, declaring that Mr. Asquith, in suggesting a Select Committee, had been egged on and prodded by a Party press:

" Why, for the last two or three years, since I have thrown myself into the vigorous prosecution of the War, according to my view, I have been drenched with cocoa-slop."

He directed much of his speech to an attack on General Maurice, who could not be there to reply and who was refused the inquiry promised. He tried to defend his comparison of the figures for January 1917 and January 1918:

" As a matter of fact there was an increase as between the 1st of January and March 1918, but it just happened that I thought I would take the first month of the year."

He declared that his figures came from General Maurice's own Department, and he made great play with some figures supplied by that Department at short notice for an answer given by the Under-Secretary for War on April 18, nine days *after* his own incorrect statement had been made. Fortune favours the brave. These particular figures, sent in without General Maurice's knowledge on the very day when he handed over his Department to his successor, had hurriedly included the strength of our army in Italy in the strength of our armies in France. This curious accident gave Mr. Lloyd George just the backing which his careless statement needed, and he persisted in taking advantage of it long after the error had been pointed out. But no Departmental error made on April 18 could justify a misstatement made on April 9, though it might, in default of reply or explanation, be used a little later to confute an absent adversary in the House of Commons.[1] No one knew better than Mr. Lloyd George how steadily he had refused to listen to the warnings which the War Office had supplied.

From this triumphant misuse of statistics the Prime Minister passed on in his speech to discuss at length the reasons for extending our front in France. But he again ignored the real charge, that he had refused to give Sir Douglas Haig the reinforcements

[1] Those interested will do well to read Sir F. Maurice's explanation and comments (*Intrigues of the War*, Appendix). When Mr. Lloyd George quoted in debate the figures supplied on April 18, there was at his disposal a return showing those figures to be incorrect.

he required. Very few Members present had the knowledge necessary to check his statements, though one or two insisted on the main point, the unpardonable failure to maintain our Army's strength in France.[1] Sir Edward Carson—" the backbone " of Mr. Lloyd George's combination had very soon dropped out—warned the Prime Minister not to try " to bluff the House of Commons." Lord Hugh Cecil did not think the attack on General Maurice fair:

" It does not seem to me a very desirable thing to make an attack upon a man who is necessarily not present, while at the same time you are refusing an inquiry."

And he was not impressed by Mr. Lloyd George's method of meeting the charge:

" Of all forms of inquiry, the least desirable seems to me that of the Prime Minister, sitting alone in judgment upon himself, selecting the evidence, reviewing it, and ultimately pronouncing himself clear and acquitted from all blame."

But the Unionists as a party would not support Mr. Asquith.[2] Many Members, little moved by Party considerations, felt that nothing would be gained by recriminations at a time of national danger. For the time being the Prime Minister's dexterity prevailed, and all inquiry into the most disastrous episode of the War was stifled and suppressed.

But the matter did not end there. The vote on Mr. Asquith's motion became a dividing-line be-

[1] See, for instance, Sir H. P. Croft's speech in the debate (May 9, 1918).
[2] See Repington, *First World War*, Vol. II, p. 298.

tween Liberal politicians, between those who were prepared to support Mr. Lloyd George blindly and those who, even at the risk of political proscription, were determined to retain their liberty of judgment. In his election speeches six months later Mr. Lloyd George revived this episode, and tried deliberately to shift the issue and to confuse it with the question of unity of command. One example of his argument will suffice:

" So they began to attack us, and a section of the Liberal Party took up opposition to unity of command, and I say without hesitation it was because the Government were in difficulties in trying to put it through. It was challenged once or twice in Parliament. The Government were in a precarious position over it. Ultimately it culminated in the Maurice debate with a decision on a point of confidence. What was the occasion? At the time the German Army was in the ascendency. One terrible blow—a reeling blow—had been delivered at the British forces. They had staggered back twenty miles under this terrible blow, and were awaiting another. The Germans had accumulated a gigantic Army opposite the British forces, intending to attack them. We were engaged with all our power and strength in pouring men, munitions and guns into France." [1]

What are the natural inferences from this speech? That the issue at stake was the unity of command, and that on this issue a base Opposition attacked the Government in the Maurice debate, at a moment when they were pouring men into France to face the gigantic army assembled to attack us. What are the facts? That the question of unity of

[1] See Mr. Lloyd George's speech at Newcastle-on-Tyne reported in the *Times* of November 30, 1918. His speech at Wolverhampton on November 23 was another example of the same methods.

command had been settled by General Foch's appointment some weeks before the Maurice debate began; that it had nothing whatever to do with that episode, and was not mentioned either in General Maurice's letter or in Mr. Asquith's speech; and that the whole charge was that, not in May 1918, but in January, February, March and before that, when the Germans were in fact accumulating a gigantic army to attack us, Mr. Lloyd George had refused to pour into France the men needed to reinforce Haig's shrunken battalions, though the military authorities had repeatedly warned him of the " terrible reeling blow " foreseen. In the heat of the Khaki Election Mr. Lloyd George's dexterous confusion of facts and dates was crowned with success. Some politicians still seem to think that dexterity of this kind is characteristic of a " born leader." Others will find it hard to persuade themselves that it is characteristic of a scrupulous or candid mind.

VIII

There are only two or three other points to mention in considering Mr. Lloyd George's record as a War Minister here. Great play—especially for electioneering purposes—has been made with the phrase "unity of command," a point which, in spite of Mr. Lloyd George's assertions, was never an issue between the Government and the Opposition. The need of co-ordinating and unifying as far as possible the military efforts of the Allies was forced in turn on every Government, and was obvious alike to soldiers and to statesmen. It was not a belated discovery by any particular politician's partisans. The principle was easy enough to acknowledge. The whole problem was how to apply it. And that practical difficulty Mr. Lloyd George found as perplexing as every one else. As early as October 1915 Lord Selborne had proposed to the first Coalition Cabinet the creation of an Allied Council to control the War, to which each Great Power concerned might nominate one Minister, one soldier and one sailor.[1] About the same time Sir Henry Wilson had suggested to Mr. Bonar Law a Franco-British Council, to consist of the two Foreign Ministers, the two War Ministers and the two Commanders-in-Chief.[2] Other leading soldiers like Foch and Robertson advocated an Allied Council in July 1917. The fact is that unity of command was always an ideal, that few people saw how to secure it,[3] and that it came in the end through the teachings of adversity, and not by the consistent efforts of any single man. But Mr. Lloyd George's movements in that direction— his colleague Mr. Churchill calls them his " extremely laborious and mystifying manœuvres "—are worth a moment's study. Early in 1917 he endeavoured in a rather surreptitious manner to give General Nivelle control of the British forces in France. And though that experiment ended in dis-

[1] See Robertson, *Soldiers and Statesmen*, Vol. I, p. 192.
[2] See Wilson's *Diaries*, Vol. I, p. 258.
[3] See Repington, *First World War*, Vol. II, pp. 131–3, and Wilson's *Diaries*, Vol. II, p. 31, etc.

aster, he returned to the idea in January 1918, with the eccentric suggestion that General Joffre, who had by that time lost the confidence of the French Government, might be made Generalissimo, with Sir Henry Wilson as his Chief of Staff.[1] But that suggestion may have been only one of the transient inspirations with which the Prime Minister so often embarrassed his colleagues. With French Generals, as with English Generals, Mr. Lloyd George's judgment was frequently at fault. In General Nivelle he proved to be mistaken. With General Joffre he would probably have been disappointed again. General Pétain's merit he was very slow to realise, and almost to the last he showed little appreciation of the great qualities of General Foch.

"Not once did Mr. Lloyd George, during my time as C.I.G.S., express any admiration for General Foch's qualifications either as a commander or a counsellor, while there were occasions when he seemed to hold quite a contrary opinion about them." [2]

Sir Henry Wilson seems to corroborate this view. And, strangely enough, it was from Sir Douglas Haig and others, not from the British Prime Minister, that at the critical moment the demand for General Foch's appointment to the first place came.[3]

In the interval, however, there was more than one experiment. In August 1917 we hear that Mr. Lloyd

[1] See Wilson's *Diaries*, Vol. II, p. 51. In public Mr. Lloyd George was wholly opposed to one Generalissimo still.
[2] See Robertson, *Soldiers and Statesmen*, Vol. I, pp. 221-2.
[3] See *Sir Douglas Haig's Command*, Vol. II, p. 133.

George was " distinctly taken " with a plan of Sir Henry Wilson's to create an International Allied Staff, which might at least enable the Prime Ministers to overrule their military advisers.[1] In November the Supreme War Council was set up at Rapallo, but it did little to secure unity of command, though it gave Mr. Lloyd George more choice of military opinions. For effective co-ordination either joint action by the Allied Chiefs of Staff or the appointment of a Generalissimo was needed. But Mr. Lloyd George would not agree to the first so long as Sir William Robertson was C.I.G.S. in England. And on November 19 he told the House of Commons that to the appointment of a Generalissimo he was "utterly opposed." [2] He afterwards declared that a proposal to place the British armies under a foreign General, if made before March 21, 1918, would have overthrown his Government.[3] And the preservation of that Government was unhappily too often the first consideration in his mind. The experiments and embarrassments at Versailles went on. Sir Henry Wilson and others have described them. A General Reserve was decided on, to be placed under an Executive Committee. The idea of a Reserve was admirable—more admirable perhaps than the idea of a Committee. But the idea of a Reserve on paper only did not much help our armies in France.

[1] See Wilson's *Diaries*, Vol. II, p. 10.
[2] See *Parliamentary Debates*, November 19, 1917.
[3] See W. H. Page's *Life*, p. 366.

" The decision, like many others of the Supreme War Council, remained a dead letter; and events moved forward without the British Army receiving either the reinforcements for which Haig had pleaded or the reserves which Lloyd George had laboured to supply." [1]

The proposal, however, enabled the Prime Minister to change the Chief of the British Imperial General Staff. In February 1918 Sir William Robertson " imprudently quitted " London for a few days, and Mr. Lloyd George seized the opportunity to create a vacancy in his office by methods which Mr. Churchill has described with singular candour, and which painfully recall Lord Harcourt's phrase, " intrigue, intrigue, intrigue." [2] Sir Henry Wilson ultimately became Chief of the Imperial General Staff, and worked with vigour and ability to secure some sort of control and unity through the Supreme Council at Versailles. But Mr. Lloyd George's Executive Committee in command of a paper Reserve broke down,[3] and in the battles of March our troops paid the penalty for the mistake. When the disaster came Sir Douglas Haig was one of the first to suggest General Foch's appointment—" I can deal with a man, not with a Committee "; and he made the suggestion not only because he knew General Foch as a comrade, but also because, while

[1] See Churchill's *World Crisis, 1916–1918*, p. 387.

[2] Sir W. Robertson's account of this transaction is substantially the same as Mr. Churchill's. (*Soldiers and Statesmen*, Vol. I, pp. 232–5.)

[3] General Pétain seems to have promised some divisions for this Reserve, but Sir Douglas Haig could not (Wilson's *Diaries*, Vol. II, pp. 66–70).

General Pétain threatened to withdraw on Paris, General Foch was, like Haig himself, determined to cover Amiens and to prevent the separation of the British Army from the French.[1] M. Clemenceau, it has been said, had for some time had Foch's appointment in view.[2] Lord Milner and Sir Henry Wilson arrived almost simultaneously at the same decision, to ask for the appointment of General Foch. But Lord Milner had no authority to do so from the War Cabinet or from Mr. Lloyd George. The memorable conference at Doullens on March 26 gave General Foch the power to co-ordinate and in effect to control the Allied forces on the Western Front. " Douglas Haig," commented Wilson when the conference ended, " is ten years younger to-night than he was yesterday afternoon."

The worst was almost over, but the " mystifying manœuvres " went on. To the last Mr. Lloyd George would not trust our Generals in France, though Sir Douglas Haig had readily and generously accepted the authority of the French Commander. At the end of March 1918 Lord Milner was finding the Prime Minister almost impossible to work with.[3] In April Sir Henry Wilson was fighting in the War Cabinet against proposals for removing Sir Douglas Haig.[4] There were difficulties with the

[1] See *Sir Douglas Haig's Command*, Vol. II, pp. 133–5.
[2] This is a difficult point. But the French evidence does not all of it bear out Mr. Lloyd George's statement (in the *Daily Express* of November 26, 1929) that M. Clemenceau " always disliked and distrusted Marshal Foch."
[3] See Wilson's *Diaries*, Vol. II, pp. 81 and 154.
[4] *Ibid.*, p. 87.

French when things went wrong: unity of command did not solve every problem. A meeting of the Supreme Council on July 7 is reported as the angriest yet known. Wilson had constantly to struggle for consideration for the British point of view. But above the clash of personalities and jar of interests there rose ever more clearly the figure of the great French General, not yet completely trusted either in England or in France, but cool, tenacious, confident, persistent, and already foreseeing almost alone the victory ahead. On July 1 Wilson notes Foch's astonishing statement that all great anxiety would be over in ten days. A fortnight later he reports that Mr. Lloyd George is difficult and fractious, complaining again of our commanders, and protesting that " nothing was being done." Mr. Lloyd George was dissatisfied now because Sir Douglas Haig was supporting General Foch in all his demands; and when Haig supplied Foch with British divisions to help the famous counter-attack which turned the tide of war, Mr. Lloyd George's Government threw upon Haig the responsibility for weakening the British front. Lord Milner, it seems, was still convinced that we should " never thrash the Boches." The Dominion Prime Ministers at a meeting in London on July 31 were still dominated, all except Mr. Hughes, by Mr. Lloyd George's theory that it was impossible to beat the Germans on the Western Front.[1] Yet even before that Foch's genius had seen that the turning-point had come. On August 8,

[1] Wilson's *Diaries*, Vol. II, pp. 112–120.

" the black day of the German Army," Sir Douglas Haig struck a blow which resulted in one of the most significant victories of the War. But neither Mr. Lloyd George nor his War Cabinet seem in the least to have realised its importance. They were even then contemplating the reduction of Haig's divisions,[1] and showed little consideration towards the British General whose troops were making such astonishing progress. On September 1, on the eve of another great attack, a warning came from London: " The War Cabinet would become anxious if we received heavy punishment in attacking the Hindenburg line without success." It is not unfair to quote Lord Haig's biographer upon this point:

" Although the telegram came from the Chief of the Imperial General Staff, it could only have been sent with the cognisance of the War Cabinet. Haig never had a moment's doubt what it was intended to convey. The Cabinet were ready to meddle and interfere in his plans, but would not accept the responsibility for their own views." [2]

Haig for once allowed himself to comment on the " weaklings in London " who knew nothing of war. There are moments when one is glad to remember that the War Cabinet was often for practical purposes Mr. Lloyd George alone. As late as September 23 Haig was thought in London to be " ridiculously optimistic "; it was feared he was embarking on another Passchendaele.[3] A week later the Chief

---

[1] See Repington, *First World War*, Vol. II, p. 358.

[2] See Charteris' life of *Field-Marshal Earl Haig*, p. 356.

[3] Lord Milner shares the responsibility for this opinion. (Wilson's *Diaries*, Vol. II, p. 126.)

of the Imperial General Staff, visiting our Front in France, reported the general indignation at the Prime Minister's unwillingness to spare thanks or praises for the Field-Marshal and his splendid troops. And returning, he told Mr. Bonar Law his opinion that the Government were " tumbling " into victory just haphazard, with " no concerted action and no far-seeing plans." [1] These views may not be complete. But they do not lack corroboration; and they show at least the impression made on a keen-minded man who had exceptional opportunities of judgment, and who was in close and confidential intercourse with the War Cabinet of Mr. Lloyd George.

[1] See Wilson's *Diaries*, Vol. II, p. 128. It was not till October 9, Sir H. Wilson tells us, that he could induce Mr. Lloyd George to telegraph praise to Sir Douglas Haig (*Ibid.*, pp. 128, 135).

CHAPTER IV

MR. LLOYD GEORGE AS PEACE-MAKER

History, unfolding her resources slowly, may, as the years go by, have more to tell us as to the methods by which our long-delayed victory was won. Some laurels may yet need to be distributed afresh. But in the intense relief which followed the unexpected collapse of our enemies, criticism was naturally silenced and only a deep feeling of thankfulness remained. The nation knew only what it had been told. The Prime Minister, with the Press at his disposal, had in the eyes of the public borne the heat and burden of the day; and he secured in overwhelming measure the credit for the triumph which the nation's tenacity had won. No man within living memory had attained such ascendency in British politics. How did he use the powers and opportunities which he had acquired?

I

The most urgent tasks, once the Armistice was agreed to, were to guide the country through the difficult transition from war to normal life, and to induce our Allies to co-operate in laying the foundations of a lasting peace. These great tasks were urgent. They required the closest study, the most determined patience and the noblest temper which statesmanship could bring to bear. But from both Mr. Lloyd George turned aside to precipitate a General Election at the moment most favourable to his own interests. Within twenty-four hours of the Armistice his Whips were summoning the first Election meeting by telegrams curiously headed " O.H.M.S." [1] In this enterprise Mr. Bonar Law again proved a useful and adaptable ally. Few politicians will blame Mr. Bonar Law, a strong party man with Conservative attachments, for seizing the opportunity to extinguish the Liberal Party. Liberals might have looked for a different attitude in Mr. Lloyd George. But Mr. Bonar Law was able to assure his friends that " in essence " the aims of Mr. Lloyd George had become " much the same as those of our Party." And the electioneering which followed tended to confirm this view. The Labour Party left the Coalition, but the Conservatives and Mr. Lloyd George's adherents remained. And their leaders, acting together, proceeded, in the spirit of Signor Mussolini, to prescribe the gentlemen whom the electors should elect. Mr. Lloyd George added to the gaiety of Conservative circles by proscribing at the same time nearly all the old official colleagues in whose company he had spent his public life. Pursuing his attack upon Liberal Members who had voted for an inquiry into

[1] Captain Guest afterwards undertook to bear the expense.

his fatal military blunder of March 1918, the Prime Minister exerted himself to secure the defeat of Liberal candidates up and down the country, and administered a blow to the Liberal Party from which it has not yet recovered. The simplicity of the new electioneering was happily illustrated in a speech made at Warrington by Sir F. E. Smith:

" I am authorised by the Prime Minister to say to you that if there be any Liberal in Warrington who recognises his leadership, if there be any Liberal in Warrington who recognises him as, perhaps, the greatest Welshman in the whole history of Wales "—could the speaker for the moment have confused the boundaries of Warrington and Wales ?—" if there be such men, they will listen to his message and his wishes. It is his desire that my brother, and no one else, should be returned from this borough to represent it in his Parliament." [1]

Mr. Lloyd George's speeches in the Election campaign were almost equally naïve and outspoken. They cannot by any process of illusion be regarded as the speeches of a statesman driven to abandon his party connections in a moment of national peril, and anxious, as soon as that peril was over, to return to his old principles and his old friends. He began by demanding that criticism of the Coalition should stop. Only two years before he had declared free speech to be " vital " even in war-time, and had denounced Members of Parliament who were content to be " mere penny-in-the-slot machines." Now, when the War was over, an Opposition was unnecessary. It was merely " organised fault-finding."

[1] Quoted in the Liberal Magazine of January, 1919, from the *Warrington Guardian* of December 7, 1918.

He wanted a Parliament that would " take no heed of criticism " ; and his former colleagues were singled out for attack. Later on Mr. Lloyd George mentioned the pain which it gave him to " sever his relations with his old comrades in arms," and to damage a party with which he had been associated " from the moment he was able to lisp the accents of his wild tongue." [1] But the pain was endured. In 1918 Mr. Lloyd George's triumph over his old comrades was complete. Not a single Liberal of Cabinet rank was returned to the House of Commons.

Apart, however, from personal or party issues, Mr. Lloyd George's electioneering speeches in 1918 were interesting to watch. They illustrated afresh the orator's keen susceptibility to the temper of the audience he addressed. To his Liberal followers, summoned to Downing Street on the day after the Armistice, he spoke of a peace based on the " fundamental principles of righteousness," and scouted " base, sordid, squalid ideas of vengeance and of avarice." Even his first Election Manifesto, on November 21, was moderate and guarded. There was nothing about hanging the Kaiser or impossible indemnities there. A week later, however, the tone was changing. Indemnities now bulked more largely. Germany must pay to the limit—though there was still a good deal of caution as to what the

[1] See Mr. Lloyd George's speech to the Manchester Reform Club, made later, on December 8, 1919, at a moment when he was doing all he could to prevent Sir J. Simon's election in Spen Valley.

limit might be. But, as the polling-day approached, Professor Keynes reminds us, " the debauchery of thought and speech progressed." [1] Mr. Barnes, a Labour Member who had stayed in the Government, had incautiously demanded the hanging of the Kaiser. Sir Eric Geddes, another prominent Minister, proposed to squeeze Germany like a lemon —to squeeze her " until you can hear the pips squeak." The leader of a patriotic Coalition could not afford to be outdone by his subordinates; and on December 11 the trial of the Kaiser and a promise to demand from Germany the uttermost farthing, the whole cost of the War so far as that was practicable, appeared to be within the scope of the Prime Minister's programme. The whole cost of the War was lightly estimated at twenty-four thousand millions sterling. It might be a little difficult to get all that. The Prime Minister, an impressionist, did not go much into details. But three years later the Secretary to the Treasury announced that the total sum received by Great Britain was insufficient to cover the expenses of our Army of Occupation on the Rhine. These golden expectations, linked with other promises of equal value—Britain for the British, social and industrial regeneration, and a happier country for us all—won an excited nation's heart. Soldiers like Sir Henry Wilson might find Mr. Lloyd George's bribery " simply disgusting." Candid economists like Professor Keynes might deplore such concoctions of prejudice, deception, sentiment and

[1] *The Economic Consequences of the Peace*, p. 130.

greed.[1] Mere politicians might have their own opinions, and express them unavailingly with more or less reserve. Criticism at that moment had no effect upon the public mind. The confederates, with the assistance of the " coupon," secured an overwhelming majority in Parliament. And early in 1919 they were able again to turn their attention to the national interests which had been too long set aside.

II

Of the Coalition Government which followed it is not possible to speak with much respect. Few Liberals have desired to dwell upon its record. They are content to remember gratefully the rare courage and sincerity of purpose with which, until Mr. Asquith's return to Parliament, Sir Donald Maclean led the small group of Liberals who had secured re-election, and, in face of Mr. Lloyd George's undisguised hostility, kept genuine Liberalism alive. And few perhaps of the Ministers who shared the Coalition's counsels now look back on its performances with pride. No Government of recent times has so quickly disappointed the hopes of its supporters. No recent House of Commons has proved itself so void of interest, independence or initiative, or so successful in bringing Parliamentary Government into disrepute. The Prime Minister made no pretence of respecting the House which he had created. He left its leadership to others, and rarely

---

[1] *The Economic Consequences of the Peace*, p. 131.

appeared on the Government Bench. His appearances were not always popular, for in moments of difficulty he was apt to give his colleagues away. Somewhere behind the scenes, men knew, that busy and dominant personality was asserting itself as vigorously as ever, and in its absence Mr. Bonar Law was equal to any explanations or excuses required. The truth is—be it respectfully spoken—Mr. Lloyd George was to some extent swept off his balance by his phenomenal success, and he showed for a time serious symptoms of a malady which in lesser men is termed swelled head. " Office is very heady wine," he once warned Mr. Ramsay Mac-Donald; and a Dictatorship, one may imagine, goes to the head more quickly still. The " booming " of the Prime Minister by his publicity department became one of the absurdities of public life. A new magnificence marked his movements. His progresses abroad from Conference to Conference—Circuses irreverent critics called them—were rendered comical by the immense attendance of Ministers, officials, experts, tyros, journalists, busy-bodies, secretaries, typists, body-servants, housemaids, all upon the noblest scale. No such paraphernalia, paid for by a patient Exchequer, had ever waited on democracy before. But the calls upon the Prime Minister's energies were endless; and to these endless calls, it must be readily admitted, whether in the battles over peace-making in Paris, or in the strange incursions into diplomacy which followed them, or in the manipulation of public opinion, or in the multiplication of schemes of reconstruction at home, the new Dictator was rarely backward to respond.

It would not be fair to hold Mr. Lloyd George responsible for all the disappointing and impracticable clauses of the Peace Treaty to which he agreed. The story of those Conferences is familiar, and M. Clemenceau's description of his two most powerful colleagues—" one of whom thought he was Napoleon," while the other believed himself something auguster still—has been recently recalled.[1] The circumstances were exceptionally difficult, and in meeting them Mr. Lloyd George often showed a certain largeness and liberality of temper, a notable resourcefulness and versatility, an untiring readiness to bargain, argue and persuade. But on essential points he failed. He often saw the right course. He often deviously followed it. He realised how short-sighted was the policy of rancour, of grasping bitterness, recommended in some quarters. He could appreciate, though he might not attain to, President Wilson's nobility of tone and aim. But all through he was handicapped by his own electioneering statements and by his perpetual anxiety to have popular opinion at his back. There was more than one indication of his nervousness lest, while manœuvring in favour of moderate courses at Paris, he should be suspected of any such weakness by the Khaki majority in Parliament or the more vindictive organs of the London Press. Early in January 1919 Sir

[1] See Sir L. Guillemard's statement in the *Times* of November 28, 1929.

Henry Wilson, visiting Downing Street, found the Prime Minister in conference with Mr. Horatio Bottomley and others,[1] and discussing, no doubt, " the fundamental principles of righteousness " in the making of a peace. *Flectere si nequeo Superos*— Lord Northcliffe's support had become precarious, and the Prime Minister was determined to have at least the popularity of *John Bull* at his back. But for such support Prime Ministers must pay. A little later three hundred and seventy Members of Parliament, perturbed by an authentic rumour from Paris that Mr. Lloyd George was inclining to moderation on the question of indemnities, instead of exacting the uttermost farthing or squeezing the lemon till it squeaked, telegraphed to warn him that his Election pledges must be kept. Mr. Lloyd George, answering to the spur, came home and assured the House of Commons that he was bound by every pledge that he had given. His Government had put forward their terms from the beginning. They had " never swerved one iota from them." [2] The terms themselves were left conveniently hazy. But for a Khaki House of Commons full-throated generalities sufficed.

III

Mr. Lloyd George's efforts to direct the foreign policy of this country, after the terms of peace with Germany had been agreed, are equally character-

[1] See Wilson's *Diaries*, Vol. II, p. 161.

[2] This speech, of April 16, 1919, contained the violent and undignified attack upon Lord Northcliffe, which has been already mentioned.

istic. They offer perhaps the strongest example of the difficulties which attend a political system based largely upon manœuvre and intrigue. Here again there is often evidence of quick intelligence and generous intentions. But in the result few Ministers could have been more unfortunate in alienating allies, in exasperating opponents, and in weakening our national reputation for good faith. Mr. Disraeli once, for purposes of epigram, declared that his political leader had a stable mind. But not even Mr. Lloyd George's most devoted followers would choose that epithet to describe their chief's. In diplomacy, as in campaigning, he was always full of expedients, expedients which might alter every month; and each fresh expedient required some fresh Conference, generally at a European watering-place, to work it out. Some of the expedients were, no doubt, useful and suggestive. But their variety was such that neither English Ministers nor Foreign Ministers, neither allies nor enemies, could at any given moment be certain for what policy Mr. Lloyd George stood. And yet, as has been pointed out, side by side with these ever-varying expedients, the Prime Minister sometimes showed a curious persistency in clinging—secretly, if publicity seemed undesirable—to opinions he had formed. We see it in his obstinate conviction that the Germans could never be beaten on the Western Front in France. We see it, in a better form, in his broadminded endeavours, concealed when necessary from a Khaki House of Commons, to reduce indemnities to reasonable terms. We see it in his desire to come

to an understanding with the Soviet Government—
varied by disguises, denials, even measures of
hostility, as that was. We see it in his headstrong
backing of Greece, which led the Greeks to disaster.
We see it in his frequent disregard of economic
laws. Unvarying self-assurance tempered by an
ever-varying opportunism is perhaps the most
dangerous equipment that statesmanship can have.

In Mr. Lloyd George's diplomatic dealings the
atmosphere of perplexity was not diminished by the
fact that the Coalition Government had one Foreign
Office, the official establishment, on one side of Downing Street, and another Foreign Office on the other
side, in the Garden Suburb, looking for inspiration to
Mr. Lloyd George alone. Cabinet responsibility is
not a doctrine by which Dictators can be lightly
bound; and the hapless position of Mr. Lloyd
George's colleagues, whose decisions were liable at
any moment to be overruled or thwarted, found its
most pathetic expression when Lord Curzon became
Foreign Secretary in Mr. Balfour's place.

" There are in reality two Foreign Offices," Lord Curzon
was finally moved to protest, " the one for which I am
responsible and the other at Number 10. . . . I could, if
required, draw up a list of important cases in which agents
have been employed, instructions given, policies initiated at
Number 10 Downing Street, all in the Department of Foreign
Affairs—of which the Foreign Office has either known
nothing or has been informed only when the action had
already been taken." [1]

---

[1] See the *Life of Lord Curzon*, Vol. III, pp. 316–17. But this
letter, drafted in October 1922, was never sent, because the
Government broke up.

For some months Lord Curzon was a *locum tenens* only. Mr. Balfour was acting in Paris and Lord Curzon was acting at home. " A. J. B. is in Paris pursuing one policy," he writes frankly. " I am here pursuing another." [1] And, to add to the picturesque confusion, the Prime Minister, with a cloud of subordinates round him, was probably all the time pursuing a third. A little later Lord Curzon and Mr. Montagu were developing Eastern policies in flat contradiction of each other; and again the Prime Minister, for aught either of them knew, might be developing a separate Eastern policy of his own. It was inevitable that inconveniences should arise. Such a happy-go-lucky collection of counsels perhaps never proceeded from a Cabinet before.

Conferences became a great resource. But as time passed they grew in ineffectiveness. Mr. Lloyd George apparently delighted in them; yet it has been cruelly pointed out by an observant critic that the only success won in four years by British foreign policy was achieved at Washington, the one Conference which Mr. Lloyd George did not attend. [2] We hear of the Prime Minister at one Conference " in tearing spirits." But the meeting seems to have had a less exhilarating effect on our Allies. San Remo in April 1920, with its six hundred gendarmes, its numberless photographers, its journalists and visitors and quidnuncs as plentiful as the

[1] See the *Life of Lord Curzon*, Vol. III, p. 203.
[2] See Sir V. Chirol's article on " Four Years of Lloyd-Georgian Foreign Policy " in the *Edinburgh Review* for January 1923.

sands on the seashore, was followed by Spa in July,
by Lympne in the next year—to which our Foreign
Minister, singularly enough, was not invited—by
Cannes, and finally by Genoa, in 1922.[1] The picnic
element attached to the Conferences, and the
unceasing efforts of Mr. Lloyd George's publicity
department to exploit them in his interests, became
more and more surprising. The journalists in the
Riviera wrote of " a wonderful vision of mundanity,"
rivalling a London crush in June. A Coalition candidate told his constituents that Mr. Lloyd George
had gone to Italy to look for their lost markets. But
the Prime Minister rose to loftier heights. He preferred these Conferences, he said, to the old diplomacy, because reason prevailed when he got together
his " fellow-men made in the image of God." And
the fellow-men at any rate entertained each other
with assiduity, and incidentally discussed a multitude of problems on the largest scale—French and
German differences, Bolshevik overtures, Polish
ambitions, doubtful doings in the Ruhr Valley, in
Silesia and in Asia Minor, finance and self-deter-
mination, war-criminals, reparations, coal. It may
be hoped that they contributed something to solve
the troubles of a Europe which had drawn perilously
near meanwhile to famine and disintegration. But
they clearly contributed to mutual irritation also,
and round the activities of Mr. Lloyd George in
particular an uncomfortable atmosphere of suspi-
cion grew up.

[1] This, of course, is not a complete list.

The last of these Conferences, Genoa, was perhaps the worst fiasco, because it had been the most widely advertised and most had been expected of it. Designed as a background for a duel between Mr. Lloyd George and Lenin, it turned into a duel between Mr. Lloyd George and M. Poincaré.[1] The French Government had long been growing more and more dissatisfied. The Russians made no pretence of trusting anyone. The Germans were suspicious and afraid. Lord Grey had noted with alarm in January 1922 that there appeared to be less confidence, less good understanding between the French and British Governments than at any period since 1904. Another not unkindly critic added that the " five feverish weeks " at Genoa accomplished extraordinarily little.[2] A third assured us that Mr. Lloyd George assumed the Prime Ministership of Europe, and tried to treat the assembled statesmen as he treated his own Cabinet.[3] The result was not a success. Mr. Lloyd George's scheme for bringing about an understanding with the Russian Government—his " expert " adviser on this occasion was a leader of the Student Christian Movement—may have been admirable in design. But his way of working for it, his " laborious and mystifying manœuvres," created as usual a wide-

[1] Mr. J. D. Gregory's comments are interesting (*On the Edge of Diplomacy*, p. 194 *seq.*). He was one of three Foreign Office representatives in a total delegation of 120.

[2] See Lord D'Abernon's *An Ambassador of Peace*, Vol. I, p. 314.

[3] See Mr. J. M. Keynes in the *Manchester Guardian* of April 20, 1922.

spread distrust. And the Bolsheviks were not likely to forget that it was only after vehement denunciations of Bolshevik policy, and vain and costly efforts to put down the Russian Revolution by war, that Mr. Lloyd George's Government had swung round to the opposite policy of negotiating with them. The Conference at Genoa resolved itself largely into bickerings and farce. M. Poincaré, it seems, had been promised by Mr. Lloyd George that there should be no politics at Genoa. So the discussions began with finance. Russia was invited, not exactly to pay her debts, but to admit that she owed them. The Allies presented a little bill for £2,600 millions. M. Litvinoff, quite equal to the occasion, replied with a counter-claim for £5,000 millions. From this, M. Krassin was afraid, one item, compensation for the ice-breakers seized by the Allies in Northern waters, might have been left out. But M. Litvinoff was good enough to hint that, if the Allies proved reasonable, a detail of that kind would not be pressed too closely; the Bolsheviks might even grant them a rebate.[1] Two days later this atmosphere of comedy was darkened. The nerves of the Conference were shaken by the news that the Russians and Germans, treated as suppliants and outsiders, had quietly made a Treaty together behind the backs of the Allies—the one thing which Allied diplomacy had been most anxious to avoid. The Allies protested " with astonishment " and in " the frankest terms." Newspapers broke into reproaches. It was even

[1] See the *Times* for April 17, 1922.

suggested that Mr. Lloyd George had been "fooled."
But this Treaty remained the only positive achievement of the Genoa Conference, and at last one sorely
tried member of Mr. Lloyd George's Cabinet lifted
up his voice and vented feelings long and bitterly
repressed.

" Genoa," wrote Lord Curzon, " has now finally collapsed
and the Prime Minister is coming back with nothing—entirely
his own fault. I hope it will be the last of these fantastic gather-
ings which are really only designed as a stage on which he is
to perform." [1]

Even Mr. Lloyd George's high spirits were damped.
He felt bound to warn an Anglo-American Press
dinner of the storms which he saw " gathering on the
horizon, rising higher and higher in the firmament
of Europe." But before he left Genoa he had at least
the crowning satisfaction of addressing the assembled
representatives of the newspapers of the world.

IV

The two outstanding examples of Mr. Lloyd
George's diplomatic methods between the signing of
the great Peace Treaty and the break-up of the
Coalition, were his attitude towards the revolutionary Government of Russia and his handling of the
issues between Turkey and Greece. In both cases he
seems to have forfeited equally the confidence of
his colleagues and of our Allies. No incidents perhaps illustrate more clearly his open-mindedness,
his large and ranging views, his incurable love of

[1] See the *Life of Lord Curzon*, Vol. III, pp. 297–8.

manœuvring, and his want of steady purpose, judgment, grasp. From the first he saw the desirability of bringing the Bolsheviks into the settlement of Europe. He was alert to open communications with them. But he would not frankly admit it. He kept assuring the public that there could be no question of recognising the Russian Government. When an American mission was sent to Russia, its leader had a discussion with Mr. Lloyd George's Private Secretary on his way out, and a breakfast with Mr. Lloyd George in Paris on his way back.[1] But all that Mr. Lloyd George could remember of the incident, when questioned in the House of Commons, was this:

" No; we have had no approaches at all. Of course there are constantly men of all nationalities coming from and going to Russia, always coming back with their own tales from Russia. But we have had nothing authentic. We have had no approaches of any sort or kind. . . .
" There was a suggestion that there was some young American who had come back. All I can say about that is that it is not for me to judge the value of these communications." [2]

What did he gain except mistrust by mystifications of this kind? What had become of that " allegiance to Truth " which his first political leader regarded as " the supreme duty and the supreme joy of life " ? Mr. Lloyd George more than once laid stress on the folly of invading, the impossibility of conquering, so

[1] See the *Times* of November 10, 1919. Mr. Bullitt stated that he showed Mr. Lloyd George the proposals handed to him by the Soviet Government in Moscow on March 14, 1919.
[2] See Mr. Lloyd George's speech in the House of Commons on April 16, 1919.

vast a country. It was his " earnest conviction," he assured the House of Commons in April 1919, " that to attempt military intervention would be the greatest act of stupidity that any Government could possibly commit." Yet this earnest conviction did not prevent him from sending British troops to Russian ports, British ships to Russian seas, and British assistance to Admiral Koltchak and General Denikin.[1]

" We have sent a hundred millions' worth of material and of support in every form," he told the Guildhall banquet in November 1919, " and not a penny of it do I regret."

It was the tax-payer who had reason to regret the Prime Minister's habit of running two opposite policies at once. But if one failed, he could always fall back upon the other. His publicity department would supply excuses for both.

" What we have been doing in Russia," said one powerful critic in October 1919, " whom we have been attacking, whom we have been opposing, what object or aim of any consistent or coherent kind inspired or dictated our policy, I have never been able, notwithstanding constant interrogations, to find out."

By the end of 1919 Mr. Lloyd George had probably decided that a war with the Soviet Government was not likely to succeed. " We have failed," he said in February 1920, " to restore Russia to sanity by force. I believe we can save her by trade."[2] And the next feelers were put out to obtain a sort of under-

[1] The help sent to Admiral Koltchak had been promised by the Supreme War Council in 1918 and again in 1919.

[2] See *Parliamentary Debates* for February 10, 1920.

standing, which might begin with commercial intercourse and gradually lead the way to peace. The
policy was reasonable enough, if only Mr. Lloyd
George could have been persuaded to be frank about
it. But other questions complicated the issue—the
sharp conflict between Russia and Poland, the adventures of General Wrangel, the uncertainty about
Russian debts. The " zigzag of improvisations and
insincerities " continued. And when the Bolsheviks
at last were brought to Genoa to negotiate, they
proved to be quite as dexterous in the artifices of
diplomacy as the Allies. Mr. Lloyd George has
recently spoken of one part of his Russian policy as a
" mad adventure " for which Mr. Winston Churchill
was to blame. But he seems to have overlooked the
fact that Mr. Churchill had neither power nor
opportunity to take action except as a member of
the " ramshackle Government " of which Mr. Lloyd
George was the responsible head.

The story of Turkey and Greece, however, is a
still more unfortunate example of diplomacy ending
in disaster for our friends and very nearly for ourselves. It might have seemed impossible to alienate
Russia, Turkey and Greece together. But even that
result Mr. Lloyd George's impressionist methods
achieved. Our victory over the Turks had been
brilliant and decisive. But almost all the fruits of
victory were thrown away. Mr. Lloyd George and
his colleagues were apparently too busy at first to
give their attention to Turkish problems; and while
the Allied Councils and Conferences drifted, the

Turks were slowly recovering their strength. In
1917 the War aims of the Allies included " the
setting free of the populations subject to the bloody
tyranny of the Turks, and the turning out of Europe
of the Ottoman Empire." But instead of taking steps
to enforce that policy, the Great Powers failed to
check the Turkish Nationalist revival or to develop
any definite policy at all.   Italy, on the other hand,
began to develop separate ambitions, without much
regard for the feelings of her Allies.   And in May 1919
the three chief members of the Supreme Council
suddenly invited the Greeks to occupy Smyrna.

" Not a moment to be lost," comments Sir Henry Wilson
characteristically, " as the three think Italy is up to tricks.
I asked Lloyd George if he realised that this was starting
another war, but he brushed that aside. . . . Of course the
whole thing is *mad*." [1]

A massacre of Turks accompanied the Greek
success. But there for the moment the policy of
breaking up the Turkish Empire lagged; and as the
vigour of the Turks revived it became almost certain
that retaliatory massacres would follow. There were
grave reasons for anxiety about Armenia. We all
knew Turkish methods there. In November 1918
the Allies had promised " undoubted security of
life " to subject nationalities under Turkish rule.
But in October 1919 Mr. Lloyd George thought it
necessary to tell the House of Commons that " we
left Armenia because we wanted to economise." We

[1] See Wilson's *Diaries*, Vol. II, pp. 189–90.

really could not police the world.[1] In February 1920 the Government decided, without consulting Parliament, to leave the Turks in Constantinople. But the Turks were to be warned that, if they continued to massacre Armenians, this decision might be reversed.[2] In April the Allies were in conference at San Remo, and Sir Henry Wilson, who was present, could not conceal his indignation at the decisions taken:

" I think this was the most incompetent, impotent, cynical meeting of all the hundreds I have been present at. Subject —Turkey. Nitti opened, and then Lloyd George said it had been decided that morning that none of the three Powers would send a single battalion to Armenia; that they had decided to arm the Armenians and to let them fight it out with the Turks; if their cause was just, and if they were strong enough, they would win, and if not then they were not worth saving." [3]

Mr. Lloyd George, no doubt, stated his case at the Conference less crudely. But Sir Henry's summary was not remote from the facts. There were fresh and shameful massacres of Armenians by the Turks that spring.

In June 1920 the Greek forces were again advancing, " with a Mandate from the Allied Conferences of Hythe and Boulogne."[4] In July Mr. Lloyd George told the House of Commons that Turkey was " broken beyond repair." [5] He was convinced that the Greeks were splendid soldiers and that the

[1] See *Parliamentary Debates*, October 30, 1919.
[2] *Ibid.*, February 26, 1920.
[3] See Wilson's *Diaries*, Vol. II, p. 233.
[4] See the *Observer*, June 27, 1920.
[5] See *Parliamentary Debates*, July 21, 1920.

Turks were perfectly useless—" a most dangerous obsession " in Sir Henry Wilson's view. In August the Treaty of Sèvres, which proved a wholly futile document, was signed. It was ignored by Mustapha Kemel and his National Assembly. In November Mr. Balfour assured the League of Nations that Mustapha Kemel was merely the head of a band of brigands. But the brigands proved able to destroy the Armenians and before long to get the better of the French.[1] In December Mr. Lloyd George announced that the Greeks had scattered Kemel's forces " without the slightest difficulty," and were prepared, if asked, to march " right through " to Angora or the Dardanelles:

> " I have not the slightest doubt about that." [2]

In March 1921 the Allies were trying to revise the Treaty of Sèvres on terms highly favourable to the Turkish " brigands," who had by that time disposed of the Armenians, and had come to terms with the Government of Russia. But Greek ambitions were by no means satisfied. They could count on the sympathy of Mr. Lloyd George. And while the Allies proclaimed their neutrality, they at least permitted the Greeks to attack the Turks again. Mr. Lloyd George was quite sure that the Greeks were only acting in self-defence. But Sir Henry Wilson, the Government's chief military adviser, summed up the position differently after attending a Cabinet Council on March 22 :

[1] *E.g.* in Cilicia, in March and April, 1921.
[2] See *Parliamentary Debates*, December 22, 1920.

"This coming attack is entirely uncalled for and wholly provocative. And Lloyd George knows this. The whole thing is a ramp, and a disgusting ramp. Because the Turks are at this moment considering the terms offered to them a fortnight ago here in London, the Greeks with the full knowledge of Lloyd George attack the Turks."

Sir Henry added with curious foresight:

"In my opinion the end of this will be the total ruin of the Greeks—the friends of Lloyd George." [1]

In July there were Greek successes, and Greek atrocities too. In the autumn the Greeks were trying hard to raise money in London, not, it was suspected, without the active sympathy of the British Government, while French agents were busily engaged in securing friendly and profitable relations with the Turks. In the spring of 1922 both Greeks and Turks accepted an Armistice, and peace proposals came into view. Peace of course was the single object which Mr. Lloyd George ought steadily to have pursued. The Angora Government, having now made friends with Italy, pressed for the evacuation of Asia Minor. But the Greeks had their own views about evacuation, and in July they threatened to occupy Constantinople instead. On August 4, 1922, while the Allied Ministers were supposed to be doing their utmost to secure a peaceful settlement, Mr. Lloyd George made a speech in the House of Commons which both Greeks and Turks regarded as a direct incitement to renew the war. He enlarged on the heroic sacrifices of the Greek

[1] See Wilson's *Diaries*, Vol. II, pp. 281-2.

soldiers and on the atrocities committed by the Turks:

> " Millions of Armenians have been exterminated, and the same policy is being applied to the Greeks."

He had " absolutely no doubt " that, if we were not in Constantinople, the Greeks " would occupy that capital in a very few hours." He declared that we had overthrown the Turks, and that the responsibility for the establishment of peace was ours:

> " We cannot abrogate the predominance which has been won by the sacrifice of our own people." [1]

Passages from this speech were issued as an Order of the Day to the Greek forces. In the Council Chamber at Angora it was immediately decided to risk an offensive. Before August was over the Turks struck their blow. And within a few weeks the Greeks were driven in panic and disorder out of Asia Minor by the Turkish Army of whose uselessness Mr. Lloyd George had been so perfectly assured.

It is a depressing story of bad judgment and bad faith, and it moved quickly to an astonishing climax. The British Prime Minister, who had left the Armenians to their fate and had led on the Greeks to their ruin, now found himself on the verge of a new war with the Turks. His courage, as usual, was equal to the occasion; but all traces of discretion disappeared. On September 16, 1922, Mr. Churchill

---

[1] See *Parliamentary Debates*, August 4, 1922, and the *Life of Lord Curzon*, Vol. II, pp. 298-9. The " millions " of Armenians exterminated must be taken as an example of Mr. Lloyd George's impressionist style.

gave to the Press an alarmist statement, which the Cabinet as a whole had not sanctioned and the Foreign Secretary had not seen,[1] which caused consternation in Government circles and gave serious offence in Italy and France. " No more bellicose manifesto," said a great French newspaper, " has been circulated in Europe since 1918." Lord Curzon rushed off to Paris to undo its effects. But Mr. Lloyd George proceeded to telegraph for aid to the Dominions, and intimated that, whatever our Allies decided, the British Empire must be prepared to go ahead.[2] A reference to the League of Nations was suggested. But the *Daily Chronicle*, Mr. Lloyd George's organ, retorted that the League which the Labour Party used " like an incantation to cure every boil in Foreign Policy, would have played its wheezy harmonium in vain to soothe the savage breasts." [3] To be rebuked as a filibuster by Mr. Hughes was, no doubt, unexpected. But the statement in the *Daily Chronicle* is significant, as showing how little value Mr. Lloyd George's friends attached to the idea of arbitration by the League of Nations, to which he has often paid lip-service. The Angora Turks, it seems, were not unfriendly to Great Britain. But their leader said frankly that he could place no confidence in the words of Mr. Lloyd George. By the end of September the " fire-eaters and war-mongers " in the Cabinet, as the Foreign

[1] See the *Evening Standard*, September 18, 1922.
[2] See the *Daily Telegraph*, September 19, 1922.
[3] See the *Daily Chronicle*, October 3, 1922.

Secretary described some of his colleagues, had so far succeeded that an ultimatum was sent out for General Harington to use. Mr. Lloyd George's methods seemed only too likely to plunge us back into hostilities. Yet only a few weeks before he had been imploring his friends at a Nonconformist luncheon to " put the explosives under lock and key," and assuring them that he would consecrate all that remained of his energies " to make it impossible that humanity should in future have to pass through the fire, the torment, the sacrilege, the horror and the squalor of war."

Happily, to General Harington on the spot the torment and horror and squalor of war were realities, not merely rhetorical recollections. The General showed in dealing with the Turks a restraint and moderation which had been deplorably lacking in some Ministers at home. Lord Curzon laboured with energy and judgment to secure the French Government's help for a peaceful solution of the crisis. The ultimatum sent from Downing Street was not delivered. And as soon as bluff and threats were eliminated a reasonable settlement was found. But the Prime Minister's headstrong action had now thoroughly alarmed his colleagues. The Conservative Party and the Conservative Press were in revolt. On October 17 Lord Curzon, driven at last to the point of resignation, visited Mr. Lloyd George, and found himself subjected, as Mr. Asquith had been in 1915, to a strange emotional appeal. Mr. Lloyd George implored him, " in a voice charged with emotion," to remember their common comradeship to the last.[1] And two days later the historic meeting at the Carlton Club put an end to a Government whose divisions could no longer be disguised. Is this, one asks, as one reads the almost incredible story, the record of a " born leader " or of an irresponsible adventurer in public life? Will any Liberal trained in the school of Mr. Gladstone, or accustomed to the steady sincerity of Lord Grey, again entrust the interests or obligations of this country to a politician who can play with them as light-heartedly as this?

[1] See the *Life of Lord Curzon*, Vol. III, p. 319.

CHAPTER V

MR. LLOYD GEORGE AS A CONSTRUCTIVE STATESMAN

It is not possible to follow Mr. Lloyd George here through more of his foreign adventures as Head of the Government from 1918 to 1922. The story of Coalitionist policy in Egypt is another story of drifting and divided counsels, ending at last in a surrender to Egyptian sentiment, liberal and large-minded in intention, but so ill-timed and ill-managed as almost entirely to fail of its effect.[1] Mr. Lloyd George's domestic adventures as Prime Minister are even fuller of significance, if we are to form any balanced judgment of the man. But of these it must suffice to take a few examples, and to deal with them as briefly as may be. Was his direction of home affairs after the War marked by greater wisdom or discretion than his direction of policy abroad? Does it encourage Liberals to believe that any tradition or principle they care for would be safe in his hands if he were again returned to power? There were many issues of the greatest difficulty to be faced

[1] The story may be read in J. A. Spender's *Life, Journalism and Politics*, Chap. XXVI, in the *Life of Lord Curzon*, Vol. III, pp. 245–51, and elsewhere.

in those four years, enough to test the powers of any statesman. But Mr. Lloyd George had many advantages—a personal position of extraordinary strength, a well-tended Press, a House of Lords controlled by his Conservative colleagues, and an unusually subservient House of Commons. What was his attitude, what were his achievements, in dealing with the greater problems which came up—with the Government of Ireland, with Housing, Labour, Unemployment, with Agriculture and Railways, with imperative questions of Taxation and Economy, of Reconstruction and Free Trade? It is, after all, by their actions, and not by their professions, that public men in this country must be judged.

I

Take Ireland first. Mr. Lloyd George's alliance with Mr. Bonar Law had at least the result of putting an end to the Unionist Party, by inducing Mr. Bonar Law and most of his followers to admit the necessity of some form of Home Rule. Sir Edward Carson, indeed, whose faith in Mr. Lloyd George had not long survived his becoming his colleague, spoke angrily of broken pledges, and occasionally repeated his threat to call out the Ulster Volunteers. But Mr. Balfour, Mr. Walter Long, Mr. Austen Chamberlain and Lord Birkenhead, once Mr. Galloper Smith of the Ulster Army, appeared ready to acquiesce in self-government for Ireland, which had rather suddenly ceased to be a party question.

In spite of the troubles of 1916 and the indications of revolutionary and anti-English feeling in that country, the Unionists as a whole accepted the new policy with surprising ease. Amid all the War perils of 1917 the Government set up a Convention of representative Irishmen who were to endeavour to draft a constitution for themselves. And in a letter to the Chairman of this Convention, written in February 1918, Mr. Lloyd George laid it down that a single Parliament for an united Ireland was an essential part of the settlement to be secured.

The Convention worked hard. But after nearly a year of close deliberation the members of the Convention proved unable to agree. The efforts of the conciliators were unhappily thwarted, in part by the inherent difficulties of the problem, in part by the Government's ill-judged and belated attempt to enforce conscription in Ireland, and in part by the growth of disaffection and the dangerous influence of the Sinn Fein leaders.

" The question of Irish conscription," Mr. Winston Churchill has recently admitted, " was handled in such a fashion during 1918 that we had the worst of both worlds, all the resentment against compulsion and in the end no law and no men."

Never perhaps had Mr. Lloyd George's opportunism shown itself more maladroit. At the General Election of 1918 the Prime Minister laid down in a letter to Mr. Bonar Law the basis of the Coalition policy, and claimed the right to bring Home Rule into operation, while vouchsafing few details to show what Home Rule meant. But he recognised that the attempt must be postponed until the condition of Ireland made it possible; and the replacement of the old Nationalist Party by Sinn Fein Members, who refused to attend the British Parliament, did not bring the possibility nearer. Nor was Lord French's administration of the Irish Government of a character to improve the situation. Before another year had passed we were back in the worst days of coercion, with a singularly unfortunate or incompetent Executive aggravating the disorder which had been allowed to grow up. Still the Prime Minister persisted with his plans of Home Rule: he could never appreciate the difficulty of running two incompatible policies at the same time. In December 1919 Mr. Bonar Law, whose self-effacement on this subject seemed astonishing to those who remembered his utterances in days gone by, announced that the Government were bringing in a new Home Rule Bill:

" We are ready to give anything in the nature of self-government—these are the principles—which does not imply the coercion of Ulster, and which does not imply the breaking away from the bond of union of the United Kingdom." [1]

Mr. Gladstone could not have asked for more, nor have veiled details in a more generous vagueness. Before Christmas, however, Mr. Lloyd George added that the new Bill would create two Irish Parliaments: the " essential " single Parliament of 1918 had now become " an outrage on the principle

[1] See the *Glasgow Herald*, December 5, 1919.

of self-government." So quickly do some politicians move. But Liberals would have readily pardoned such minor aberrations had the Prime Minister persisted in the conciliatory policy announced.

What followed? In March 1920, while Mr. Asquith was pleading for Dominion Home Rule and for the end of military government in Ireland, the new Home Rule Bill passed its second reading in the House of Commons. It roused no enthusiasm. Captain Redmond on behalf of the Nationalists protested bitterly against " the permanent dismemberment " of his country. Sir Edward Carson protested not less bitterly. " Make the world safe for hypocrisy," he cried. Lord Robert Cecil pronounced it " a very bad Bill," with no weight of Irish opinion behind it. Mr. Asquith declared that it satisfied no need, and renewed his plea for the grant of Dominion status to Ireland. But Mr. Lloyd George and Mr. Bonar Law both refused to entertain the idea of Dominion Home Rule. The Bill went forward, but in Ireland crime increased to an alarming extent. In July Sir Edward Carson threatened that, if the Government could not protect the persons and property of loyal subjects, he would organise his friends to do so. And hand in hand with the reports of outrages went ugly rumours of the methods adopted by the authorities to avenge them. In August the Chief Secretary, Sir Hamar Greenwood, introduced a new and sweeping Coercion Bill, designed to remedy the paralysis of justice in Ireland. The Bill practically put the whole population at the mercy of military tribunals.

12

Mr. Lloyd George took the opportunity to denounce afresh the idea of Dominion Home Rule, and to declare—a curious admission on which to found a Home Rule measure—that there was no proposal which the British Government could put forward which was acceptable to any party that had authority to speak on behalf of Ireland. Nevertheless the Government persisted with their two-fold plan—a Home Rule Bill, which they agreed that nobody wanted, and a Coercion Bill abolishing every safeguard for constitutional freedom in a country which they proposed to hand over to the men whom they were trying to proscribe. And, to add to the confusion of counsels, the agents of the Irish Executive apparently allowed themselves to organise a sinister scheme of reprisals, designed to punish outrage by outrage, murder by murder, crime by crime.

The facts about these Irish reprisals are no longer seriously disputed, though the Government did all they could at the time to prevent their being known. A number of recruits, enlisted in England for a wage of ten shillings a day and perquisites, were added to the Royal Irish Constabulary—ex-soldiers many of them, inured perhaps to " frightfulness " abroad and permitted to practise it on the Irish population. Their black caps and khaki uniforms soon became a symbol of terror. But the strangest feature of the scheme was that it was terrorism undertaken by the agents of the law. The *Manchester Guardian* will not be suspected of any desire to be unjust to Mr. Lloyd George.

" There is one aspect of Irish crime," it wrote, " that is not fully realised in this country because it is utterly alien to our ordinary conception of law and government, that is the systematic destruction committed by the soldiers and constabulary. . . .

" The reprisals almost necessarily fall upon perfectly innocent people . . . and convert an armed force into a body of freebooters. Yet day after day this goes on in Ireland. Town after town is ' shot up,' shops are looted, liquor stores are rifled, houses burnt, the inhabitants of the whole town or village driven by indiscriminate fusillade into the cellars for safety. Even the creameries of the admirable Agricultural Co-operative Society, a score or more of them to date, have been wantonly destroyed. Yet the authorities make no move, and no one is punished or called to account." [1]

On September 21, 1920, the sack of Balbriggan, by no means a solitary example, concentrated public attention on the methods of the Black-and-Tans.

" In its brutality, wantonness and destructiveness last night's work of the uniformed forces of the Crown is comparable only to the story of some Belgian village in the early days of the War. Two men were dragged from their homes to the police barracks, bayoneted and beaten to compel them to reveal secrets, and then taken out into the street and shot in cold blood, their bodies left to be picked up by any passer-by.

" To kill men without trial and on mere hearsay and gossip is no law at all, but it does coincide more or less with the rough methods of justice to which Ireland is given over. One states this merely because it represents the spirit animating a large section of the R.I.C. and of the military forces in Ireland : ' Murder must be met by murder.' . . .

" It is only free-booting callousness that could have made the ' Black-and-Tans ' I saw yesterday in Balbriggan yell and cheer when they passed the smouldering ruins of poor cottage homes." [2]

---

[1] See the *Manchester Guardian News Bulletin* of September 6, 1920, quoted in the *Liberal Magazine* for October 1920, p. 518.
[2] See the *Manchester Guardian*, September 22, 1920.

At Balbriggan rows of cottages and shops were burned, and the people driven panic-stricken into the fields and ditches. A big hosiery factory employing 300 workers was destroyed. The largest mill was saved from destruction at the hands of Government agents only by the intercession of the local police. In place after place the creameries were burned. There were promiscuous burnings and shootings in Tuam, Galway, Limerick, Carrick-on-Shannon and elsewhere. At Cork, which had a military Governor—into whose action " no Government could tolerate an inquiry by civilians "—300 buildings were fired in December 1920, including the City Hall, the Carnegie Library and the Corn Exchange, in revenge for an attack on twelve cadets. These official outrages were in no sense acts of self-defence in hot blood. They were organised and deliberate acts of vengeance taken indiscriminately, with apparently no effort to discover whether the victims were guilty or not. Again and again quiet, law-abiding people, farmers and shopkeepers, unconnected with Sinn Fein, had their premises burned over their heads and were fortunate if they escaped with their lives. And the attempt to ruin local industries was the most unpardonable incident of all.

Of the British Government's connivance there was no doubt. No Irish Executive could have taken such action without it. No Commander could have allowed his troops to burn and shoot at random unless he knew that he had the Government at his back. Lord French was Viceroy. General Macready

was Commander-in-Chief. Sir Hamar Greenwood
was Chief Secretary. These men were all Mr. Lloyd
George's selections: in Ireland as in England Mr.
Lloyd George was supreme. General Macready,
when challenged, thought the conduct of the police
was " only human." They must act on their own
initiative if they could not get redress from the law.
Punishment for such acts was " a delicate matter."
The Chief Secretary, while trying to deny the
Government's complicity, alleged that reprisals were
few, and talked in the same breath of the discipline
and the intolerable provocation of the police. The
Daily Chronicle, Mr. Lloyd George's chief organ,
explained that the Government, while intending to
check reprisals, refused to apply " the strict letter of
civil law." Mr. Lloyd George himself, in one of his
worst speeches, recited the attacks made, shameful
enough, on the constabulary, and justified the policy
of hitting back.[1] He did not appear to see any difference between hitting people who were guilty and
people who were not:

" If it is war, give the soldier and the policeman a fair
chance, and they will give a good account of themselves."

He had no patience with people who talked pomp-
ously about outrages and discipline when gallant
men were defending themselves. In Ireland evidence
was difficult to get. Men suspected of murder had
sometimes in the past escaped:

[1] For this speech at Carnarvon see the *Times* of October 11,
1920.

" Now, when men attempt to escape and they refuse to stop, then undoubtedly the police now fire on them. Can you complain of it ? Why should that be characterised as murder ? It is the only way in which they can defend themselves."

To such arguments—it was not the *Times* only which thought them " the sheer negation of Liberalism "—Sir John Simon found the reply; and let it be added that no Liberal did finer service in exposing the folly and wickedness of the action which the Government allowed :

" The soldiers and constabulary are not responsible for the policy of the country. It is the meanest of subterfuges to exploit the losses and trials of these men when what is really designed is to throw a cloak over a method deliberately approved by their superiors."

Sir Henry Wilson was a soldier and an Irishman, who, whatever his foibles, had no sympathy with Sinn Fein. He saw with amazement Mr. Lloyd George " hugging to his heart " the idea that for every loyalist murdered two Sinn Feiners were now being done to death. To Wilson it seemed inconceivable that a British Prime Minister should be satisfied to accept " a counter-murder association " as the remedy for the disgraceful condition of Ireland. On September 29, 1920, he had an opportunity of expressing his opinion to Mr. Lloyd George and Mr. Bonar Law :

" I pointed out that these reprisals were carried out without anyone being responsible; men were murdered, houses burnt, villages wrecked, etc. . . . I said that this was due to want of discipline, and this *must* be stopped. It was the business of the Government to govern. If these men ought to be murdered, then the Government ought to murder them. Lloyd George danced at all this, said no Government could possibly take the responsibility."

But Sir Henry's conclusion was that neither of the two Heads of the Government " had the faintest idea of what to do." [1] If Sir Henry Wilson be thought too censorious, one grave, impartial witness may be quoted. " You do not cast out Beelzebub by Beelzebub," the Archbishop of Canterbury was driven to say.

II

For months together this cruel and reckless policy went on. Facts accumulated. Even the Chief Secretary could not deny them, though he took refuge in evasions and in self-congratulations equally deplorable in tone. " We are succeeding," he told the House of Commons in November. He had smashed the boycott. He had smashed the hunger-strike. Every Irish creamery which had a manager suspected of Republican sympathies—suspected only, because no trial took place—was, the Chief Secretary boasted, " in peril ": that is, liable at any moment to be destroyed by the agents of the law. The only question in Sir Hamar Greenwood's mind was who was on the side of the assassins; and he indicated not obscurely his old Liberal friends. Mr. Lloyd George, in the same vein, asserted at the Mansion House that the Government had got " murder by the throat." But the outrages of Black-and-Tans only

[1] See Wilson's *Diaries*, Vol. II, pp. 247–8, 251, 263–4.

stimulated the Republicans to worse offences, and Mr. Lloyd George's vaults were immediately followed by fresh massacres of officers in Dublin and of auxiliary policemen near Macroom.

" No Cabinet," Sir Henry Wilson commented on the Dublin murders, " as the Cabinet do not seem to think that anything out of the way has happened."

Mr. Lloyd George's satisfaction in his policy found vivacious expression in a banquet at the Constitutional Club. The " accents of his wild tongue " were now quite different from those heard at the Manchester Reform Club. He kept a Conservative audience in a roar of laughter with gibes about the " Bolshevists and Sinn Feiners and faddists and cranks of all sorts "—in other words, the great Liberal gathering at the Albert Hall which had protested against the outrages of the Black-and-Tans.[1]

All through the winter these methods of argument and statesmanship continued, while the volume of public indignation rose. On February 15, 1921, Mr. J. H. Thomas laid before the House of Commons some carefully verified facts in regard to reprisals at Mallow, where railway men, with no evidence whatever against them, had been savagely maltreated and shot by the police. It was clear that organised Labour in this country could no longer be hoodwinked, and Mr. Lloyd George began to take alarm. A week later the Archbishop of Canter-

[1] See the *Times* for December 4, 1920.

bury spoke out with fine vehemence in the House of Lords, and denounced the attempt to " punish wrong-doing by lawlessly doing the like." In the same month a judicial report on reprisals in County Clare was made public; the report on the burning of Cork the Government had so far suppressed. The County Court Judge found that in one county alone 139 cases of criminal injuries in a few months had been proved against the agents of the Crown, and that in none of these cases " was there any evidence to suggest that the victims had been guilty of any offence." It was pointed out in the House of Commons that the Government's methods were in fact increasing crime. Sinn Fein outrages had risen from 599 in 1919 to over 9,000 in 1920— singular evidence of the Government's success. Still Mr. Lloyd George insisted that reprisals must continue. But Mr. Bonar Law took occasion to say that the Government did not like what was going on. They would be thankful to see it ended.[1] Only how to end it they had no idea. In March Mr. Lloyd George began to speak more doubtfully of failure. Leaders of religion, Bishops, a Cardinal, Free Churchmen, joined openly in denouncing the policy of reprisals. In April the Prime Minister brought himself to admit that " a certain number of undesirables," guilty of " deplorable excesses," must, without any fault on the part of the Government, have found their way into the forces which the Government employed. But so long as Sinn Fein

[1] See *Parliamentary Debates*, February 21 and March 1, 1921.

Ireland demanded a Republic, so long " the present evils " must go on.[1] It was vain for Mr. Asquith to plead for a truce, for at least a cessation of outrage, for " a breathing space in which reason and argument could make their way."

Then suddenly there came an extraordinary change. On the Government's feelings at this date, April 1921, Mr. Winston Churchill has made an interesting statement.

" The Prime Minister," he tells us, was still " markedly disposed to fight the matter out at all costs, and to rely for this purpose upon ' the age-long loyalties of the Conservative Party.' "

The phrase " age-long loyalties " is a little puzzling; presumably the Tories' inveterate loyalty to the idea of Irish coercion is meant. But from Mr. Churchill's account it is evident that Mr. Lloyd George was startled to find that even his Conservative colleagues were revolted by his policy of " unmitigated repression." Mr. Churchill, indeed, with his Napoleonic outlook, saw little difficulty in providing a hundred thousand new special troops and police, thousands of armoured motor-cars, cordons of blockhouses and barbed wire, and " a systematic rummaging and questioning " of the Irish population, if the most unlimited exercise of " rough-handed force " were to continue to be the Government's policy in Ireland.[2] But in May Sir Nevil Macready, who commanded the rough-handed forces, made it clear

---

[1] See the *Times* of April 20, 1921.
[2] See *The World Crisis, The Aftermath*, pp. 291-2.

that he had no expectation that even these magnificent measures would succeed. He told the Government plainly that the morale of his men was yielding to the strain:

" Unless I am entirely mistaken, the present state of affairs in Ireland, so far as regards the troops serving here, must be brought to a conclusion by October, or steps must be taken to relieve practically the whole of the troops together with the great majority of the commanders and their staff." [1]

Sir Henry Wilson endorsed General Macready's report. And then at last Mr. Lloyd George, faced by a Cabinet revolt and by the soldiers' warnings, was compelled unwillingly to realise that the game of reprisals was up. In June the King opened the new Parliament in Northern Ireland, and the Prime Minister seized the opportunity to swing away from the policy of violent coercion and back to ideas of conciliation once again. As usual, there was no indication that he realised how surprising his gyrations seemed. And there is something irresistibly comical in the air of innocent benignity which the obstinate advocate of Government by outrage now assumed. " Can you tell me why Liberals attack me ? " he asked plaintively at a banquet in July, six months after the famous dinner at the Constitutional Club. What was there for Liberalism to quarrel about ? What did it matter what had been done or said, now that " the heights of the Beatitudes " were actually in sight ?

[1] See *The World Crisis, The Aftermath*, pp. 293–4. In June 1921 Sir N. Macready declared himself " thoroughly fed up with this business." (See Macready, *Annals of an Active Life*, Vol. II, p. 563.)

" I feel that all men of all parties, whatever their personal feelings may be, whatever their partisan feelings may be, should, like men, drop everything, remember that the destiny of mankind is in the making; drop everything, all trivialities, personal or otherwise, and help the Prince of Peace." [1]

When the Government were making war on Ireland, one very able critic commented, nobody must speak, or they were encouraging the rebels. When the Government were making peace with Ireland, nobody must speak, or they were traitors to the Prince of Peace. Why, in studying Mr. Lloyd George's versatile eloquence, does that old description " gammon " so irresistibly recur? Why, whenever Mr. Lloyd George turned with tears in his voice to the Liberal Party, did his friends feel sure that he was becoming uneasy about Conservative support?

But once a complete *volte-face* had been determined on, the new policy was carried through with vigour and adroitness. In July a truce with the " assassins " was proclaimed. Reprisals stopped. It was announced that the Prime Minister would be " happy to see " Mr. de Valera in Downing Street, and to propose to him " that Ireland shall assume forthwith the status of a Dominion "! Dominion Home Rule had been contemptuously derided when urged by Mr. Asquith a few months before. In August all members of Dail Eireann, interned, imprisoned or undergoing penal servitude—even, when Mr. de Valera insisted, one member convicted of murder—were set free without conditions. In

---

[1] See *Daily Chronicle* of July 15, 1921.

September an active and ingenious correspondence ended in discovering a formula on which the Irish Rebel leaders could be got to treat. And after weeks of anxious and arduous deliberation a second Parliament was established in a divided land, on terms which made the greater part of Ireland in most respects an independent State. Few now may wish to quarrel with the terms adopted. Few will deny the force and ability which pushed them through. But the Treaty signed in December 1921 was largely an act of obliteration, designed to wipe out not only the past of the Unionist party, but one of the ugliest chapters in Irish history and in Mr. Lloyd George's political career. Lord Birkenhead, a prominent figure in the negotiations, spoke of some heart-searchings. The *Manchester Guardian* asked itself how Mr. Lloyd George could ever have consented to " the abominations of lawless violence " which he had let loose, to his own and the country's " indelible disgrace." But the significant thing is the demoralisation within Mr. Lloyd George's Cabinet, which the whole episode of Black-and-Tan reprisals showed. There were men of character and honour in the Government. One of them at least was deeply disquieted by proceedings which he could neither deny or defend. Others must have shared his views. Some, for aught we know, may have protested. But not one of them resigned. Under Mr. Lloyd George's leadership all sense of collective Cabinet responsibility had vanished. No man was his brother's keeper. If Ministers did not like their leader's methods, they shut their eyes or looked the other way.

III

There were elements of tragedy too often in Mr. Lloyd George's conduct of affairs. But in his Home Administration, it may be thankfully admitted, we are more conscious of the comedy at work. No Minister, when electioneering, ever entered into larger obligations. Even Lord Curzon was driven into poetry to describe the Coalition's prospects:

> " The World's great age begins anew,
>   The Golden years return."

We are entitled to ask how far this radiant forecast was accomplished, what proofs of practical capacity or leadership the Head of the Coalition Government displayed. Of Mr. Lloyd George's energy and fecundity in propounding plans there can be no question. As a producer of schemes he is unequalled. His weakness lies in carrying them out. And this weakness is largely due to the fact that, for all the " experts " called into council, his schemes are by no means invariably founded on the knowledge and study required. They are apt to be too obviously got up for the occasion. And the occasion is generally some electioneering need. Housing was one of the most urgent problems which Mr. Lloyd George undertook to solve. " We must have habitations fit for the heroes who have won the war." Some half-a-million houses needed to be supplied without delay. In a speech at Manchester in September

1918 the Prime Minister's enthusiasm overflowed its borders. The project of housing had been played with for half a century. He would show the world how it should be done:

> " You cannot plough the waste land with writing paper "
> —a metaphor astonishingly true—" you cannot sweep away slums with paint-brushes, and you cannot bind the gaping wounds of the people with red tape."

In January 1919 we were informed that the Local Government Board were devoting much attention to the subject. The Government were to become builders on the greatest scale. A Chief Commissioner and eight District Commissioners of Housing, of course with adequate staffs, were to get to work immediately. A manual with all sorts of plans was to be issued. Doors and windows, baths and kitchen-ranges were being standardised already. All the new living-rooms were to have as much sunshine as possible, and all the new larders as little as might be. In February Dr. Addison announced that the Government had ordered 300,000,000 bricks and had surveyed every brickyard in the country. In April a Housing and Town-Planning Bill passed its second reading in the House of Commons. The Local Authorities were to be associated with the Central Government in various ambitious schemes. In June, however, it appeared that, though some 28,000 acres of land had been surveyed and valued, very few houses had so far been built. In December another Housing Bill conferred additional powers upon the Government. Dr. Addison had a new plan for subsidising private effort. Everybody who could build a decent house must be brought in. No money needed would be spared by the State. But only 149 houses had been built by that time: the rest of the half-million were still to come.

Dr. Addison, now Minister of Health—the Local Government Board had been merged in a new Department—took the unusual course of suggesting that the slow progress made was really due to his predecessor's neglect at the old Board; and that predecessor—an old colleague—retorted that Dr. Addison was too easily satisfied with setting up Committees and with appointing highly paid officials at " enormous and useless expense." In commenting on the work of one another Mr. Lloyd George's Coalitionist colleagues were the most candid Cabinet of modern times. In February 1920 the Minister was still battling with his difficulties. Tenders were still being accepted. Grandiose plans were still being approved. There was " a ghastly shortage " both of bricklayers and of houses; but the Minister was certain that no blame could be attributed either to the Government or to the Ministry of Health. Another year passed. The ghastly shortage still continued. Instead of half-a-million houses, some 38,000 had been built. By July 1921 Dr. Addison had become a Minister without portfolio, and the complete failure of the Government's methods could no longer be concealed. By entering the building industry the Government had run up prices against itself. It had drawn the

Local Authorities into all sorts of expensive and inefficient schemes. It had, as usual, multiplied officials: that is always the first step, and too often proves to be the chief step, in Mr. Lloyd George's schemes of social reform. Another Minister, Sir Alfred Mond, was appointed to get things on to a business footing; in other words, to get out of the muddle as best he might.

A new phase in the proceedings opened, with less " vision," perhaps—there could hardly be less progress—but with a larger admixture of common-sense. The number of houses to be built by Local Authorities and Public Utility Societies was now to be limited to 176,000, at a cost to the State of about £10,000,000 a year for many years. The number built or building under the scheme of subsidy to private builders was estimated at about 23,000, and the cost of the subsidy at a few millions more. It is a curious and significant fact that, as the cost of housing subsidies rose, the cost of house-building rose with them, and that when the subsidies were reduced the cost of building also went down.[1] The Government now considered that the time for " a policy of judicious retrenchment " had arrived. But Mr. Lloyd George was still as positive and confident as ever. The Government were only " crying a halt." There would not be " a single house the less built." Somehow or other there would be more houses and cheaper; though how this result would be obtained

[1] See the interesting official figures given in the *Times* of April 15, 1929.

13

by cutting down both numbers and expenditure was neither lucidly nor satisfactorily explained.[1] Critics even permitted themselves to doubt if the new promise had any meaning. It certainly found no fulfilment while Mr. Lloyd George remained in power. Under this system of " judicious retrenchment " the great building programmes lagged: one wonders if they might not have moved faster had Mr. Lloyd George and his Ministers never intervened at all. Projects for slum clearance had to stand over, to be revived when Mr. Lloyd George was out of office. In July 1922 some 120,000 houses had been finished, and 35,000 more were being built.[2] Sir Alfred Mond did his best; but with these meagre figures of achievement the Coalition Government had to be content. In November of that year Mr. Bonar Law, who had countersigned his colleague's promises, admitted that the situation was as bad as even Labour candidates alleged. Seven years later, Mr. Lloyd George, on the eve of a General Election, recurred to the subject, and dilated picturesquely on the Conservative Government's shortcomings and on the prevalence and iniquity of slums. A Government's efficiency, he told his audience, depended on two things: first on the soundness of their plans, and next on the capacity of the men who put those plans through. The shades of Dr. Addison and of Sir Alfred Mond, now gathered

[1] See *Parliamentary Debates*, July 21, 1921.
[2] 120,800 built, 35,971 building, and 17,000 not yet begun *Times*, July 26, 1922).

to other parties, must be left to ask each other what these ironical generalities could mean.

IV

Mr. Lloyd George's record on Housing is a significant story. But not less significant is the story of his dealings with the land. Here, again, as an impressionist speaker, Mr. Lloyd George has won and deserved many a success. His deep distrust of the landed interest is one of his earliest and strongest passions. He has stimulated useful and fruitful inquiries on land taxation and land reform. And though on this point, as on many others, his political faith has undergone some curious permutations, a real wish to revolutionise our land system is probably a permanent part of his political creed. His Election Manifesto of 1918 was liberal in its agricultural pledges. Scientific farming and increased production, the development of rural industries, the improvement of village life, extensive schemes of afforestation and reclamation, were essential parts of the Coalition policy, and were to be entered on, all of them, without delay. But if "you cannot plough the waste land with writing-paper," it is equally ineffective to cultivate it with promises alone. And similar schemes, it will be noticed, still for the most part awaiting their fulfilment, were to be found in his election promises of 1929.

Here, again, in practical administration Mr. Lloyd George proved to be lamentably weak. The Corn Production Act of 1917, announced as " simply and solely a temporary war expedient," guaranteed a minimum level of prices; and in October 1919 Mr. Lloyd George made the sweeping claim that the Act had benefited everyone concerned, had increased production, raised wages, reduced hours and kept down the price of bread, without the loss of " a single penny " to the State.[1] It did not seem to occur to him that for all these combined and contradictory blessings somebody, possibly the over-charged consumer at the mercy of Government con-trols, had had to pay. And he omitted for the moment to remember that the bread subsidy was costing fifty millions sterling, while the prices of mutton, beef, butter, bacon, milk, sugar and eggs had risen respectively by 110, 114, 154, 156, 197, 200 and 229 per cent. as compared with the prices of 1914.[2] Filled with enthusiasm, Mr. Lloyd George went on to offer guarantees of good prices to the farmer, guarantees of good wages and shorter hours to the labourer, and a guarantee to the public that both farmers and labourers would do their best to increase production for the State. He failed in one point only—in explaining how it could be done. But to Mr. Lloyd George, in his impressionist pictures, economics present no difficulty at all.

" You have your market here at your own doors," he told the farmers gathered at the Caxton Hall. " It is computed by men who understand this business much better than I do "—

---

[1] See the *Times* of October 22, 1919—the speech at Caxton Hall.

[2] See the Food Controller's estimate up to March 1920, quoted in the *Liberal Magazine* for October 1920, p. 549.

those anonymous experts again—" that you could raise in this country of food commodities 150 millions worth which is now being brought from abroad. Just think what that means. If you could take away £150,000,000 of what we have to pay across the water the sovereign would look up. There would be a new shine on its face."

To tune in with these economic theories, Lord Lee, a strong Protectionist, had been appointed Minister of Agriculture, and he was prompt to show himself a convinced advocate of the old Protectionist ideas. The Government, he announced, " would stop at nothing " to extend the area of arable land. The " temporary war expedient " of 1917 became the foundation for an Agriculture Act in 1920, which continued the system of Government interference and guaranteed prices as " an urgent provision for national safety." The Bill represented, we were told, the " definite reconstruction policy " of the Government. It was now to be the " permanent policy of the country." It was to make certain of the nation's daily bread. Mr. Lloyd George too would stop at nothing in maintaining agricultural production, on which " the security of this land depends."

It is sad to confess how quickly these bright hopes broke down. From the first the Agriculture Act was gravely distrusted not by Liberals only, but by Conservatives familiar with the management of land.[1] And in a very short time it became evident that the Government had entirely omitted to calculate its cost. They had indeed assured their

[1] Its opponents included Colonel Courthorpe, Lord Bledisloe, Lord Chaplin and the Duke of Buccleuch.

supporters that it might prove, in a world where all economics were imaginary, to cost nothing at all. But they quickly discovered that the financial liability was so serious as to involve the dropping of most of its provisions.[1] Another comical *volte-face* occurred. Every argument used to defend the Act was now, with astonishing promptitude, thrown over. The Minister was instantaneously persuaded that guaranteed prices, State control, the Wages Board, the safety of the nation and its daily bread, must go. A " happy and contented peasantry," it was discovered, was not dependent upon guarantees of this kind, but could best be secured " without the interference of the State "! And actually within a few months of its adoption the whole egregious scheme had disappeared. Many amusing lessons in politics may be learned from the Coalition Government's efforts to reconstruct their long-suffering country. But this strange attempt to impose agricultural protection, to mingle with it democratic safeguards for the protection of the labourer, and to ruin it all by hasty breaches of faith in regard to the financial pledges given,[2] will rank among the most unfortunate and ridiculous of all. In 1929 Mr. Lloyd George was still perorating as picturesquely as ever on agricultural revival and the necessity of reanimating country life. But when we come to ask what, as a Minister, he contributed to that difficult

[1] " The whole of the Corn Production Act," said the Minister soon after, " and of Part I of the Agriculture Act must go." Sir A. Griffith-Boscawen had now succeeded Lord Lee.

[2] The debates of June and July 1921 are worth study.

problem in four years of unexampled power, the answer is the Agriculture Act of 1920, consigned to the scrap-heap in 1921.

v

On a par with Mr. Lloyd George's schemes of agricultural revival were his schemes for dealing with Reparations and Free Trade. Dependent on the support of a large Conservative contingent, led by Tariff Reformers as devoted as Mr. Bonar Law, Mr. Chamberlain and Lord Birkenhead, Mr. Lloyd George realised that all his adroitness would be needed to introduce Protection while paying lip-service to Free Trade. " It would be premature," he announced in 1918, " to prescribe a fiscal policy intended for permanence." But meanwhile Colonial Preference was to be established, dumping and unfair competition prevented, vital key industries fostered and sustained :

" Beyond this I should say that we should face all these questions with new eyes."

And with new eyes the members of his mixed Administration set to work to discover that Free Trade and Protection were really indistinguishable things. In this optical adventure Mr. Lloyd George, who loves nothing better than to fuse contradictory policies together, was well qualified to give a lead. The War had been fruitful in Socialistic experiments, and Socialism and Protection are fruits of the same tree. A " transitional " system was invented for restricting our imports and our exports—to old eyes an odd way of stimulating trade. Preference began. Tea, tobacco, clocks and motor spirit were among the articles selected as the soil from which Imperial loyalties should spring. It was, as Mr. Austen Chamberlain said, a small beginning, so small that old eyes found its value to the Dominions difficult to detect. One almost recalled a phrase of Mr. Joseph Chamberlain about the uselessness of " fiddling with those little things." The loss to the revenue was certainly more visible. And presently the small beginnings grew. Import duties, imposed as purely war measures, were continued—duties which " absolutely reek and stink of the old-fashioned Protection," cried a Coalition Liberal whose eyes were out of focus and whose party discipline had gone astray. And licences controlling trade, arbitrary restrictions dictated by interested committees, clogged with uncertainty for traders and dangerously liable to political abuse, roused some resentment among commercial men.

A further step followed. In August 1919 Mr. Lloyd George announced that these import restrictions would be abandoned, but that dumping would still have to be prevented, key industries protected, and floods of foreign goods curtailed. In the November following Mr. Lloyd George took occasion again to dilate on unfair competition, and an Anti-Dumping Bill was introduced, directed against foreign goods sold here, not below their cost of production, but—a different thing—below their

selling price abroad. The Bill had a short shrift.
It was badly conceived and badly managed. Like
so many of Mr. Lloyd George's legislative experiments, it was founded on temporary convenience
rather than on any clear conception of economic
laws. It aimed confusedly at all sorts of objects—at
injuring Germany, at keeping up prices in Great
Britain, at checking imports and supplies which
were often needed in this country, at giving fresh
opportunities for departmental interference in business men's concerns. In December the Coalition
Liberals found it necessary to intimate that, new
eyes or old eyes, they could not see their way to vote
for such a worthless Bill. It was postponed and
dropped. The Head of the Government discovered
that he could not bind himself " either to the words
or to the machinery " of his own Government's
measure. But he found an opportunity to explain to
the Manchester Reform Club, on whose devoted
simplicity he seems to have thought that he could
always count, that the Anti-Dumping Bill had been
intended " to strengthen the whole line of Free
Trade." [1]

So far Mr. Lloyd George's efforts to see Protection
with new eyes had failed. But his pledges to the
Conservatives had—for obvious reasons—to be
honoured, though those to the electors were sometimes overlooked. Before the end of 1919 an interesting judgment in the Courts revealed the illegality of
the proclamations under which the Government had

[1] See the *Times* of December 8, 1919.

for months past been imposing embargoes upon imports. That expedient received a rude shock; fresh methods of introducing Protection unostentatiously had to be sought. The Dyestuffs (Import Regulation) Bill of 1920, largely protective in its character and objects, was excused on the ground that it was a necessity for national defence. But it was followed by a proposal for the recovery of reparations from Germany, which has a special interest, because it was supposed to be largely due to Mr. Lloyd George's own fertile invention, and was supported by economic arguments which only Mr. Lloyd George appeared to understand. The proposal passed the House of Commons in March 1921. It was intended to make the German Government co-operate in collecting reparations. They were to pay to German exporters fifty per cent. of the price of German goods sold to us. The British buyer would only pay half the price to the German seller; the other half he would pay to the British Treasury instead. Mr. Lloyd George's followers could not quite conceal their apprehension that British purchasers might ultimately suffer, and that the contribution of the German Government might prove very difficult to get. But Mr. Lloyd George was quite confident as to what would happen:

" The man who buys a thousand pounds' worth of German goods would pay £500 into the British Exchequer . . . who will give the purchaser a receipt. He will then send over to Germany either by bill of exchange or whatever other method by which he pays, the balance, and he will pin on to that the Treasury receipt. . . The German seller will then go to his

Government, and he will say, ' Here I have got a bill of exchange for £500. I have got a British Treasury receipt, or a French Treasury receipt, for another £500. I ask you to cash this £500.' He cashes it in currency which is quite useful to him, but no good to us, because he can pay his wages, he can pay for his goods, and he can pay his costs in the currency of his country. So we get our currency and they get theirs, and we are both satisfied." [1]

Thought " is the citadel," as Mr. Gladstone once said. But Mr. Lloyd George's thought proved strangely baffling to business men.

" I was under the impression," said Sir John Simon gently, speaking from some experience of commercial law, " that, when Germans sold goods to Englishmen, it was probable that it was the German who sent the bill of exchange to the Englishman in order that it might be accepted by his customer, and that in many cases this bill was discounted, negotiated or held by a bank, and passed into the possession of third parties long before the goods were delivered."

Other practical men of hardly less authority pointed out the fantastic nature of this attempt to solve the reparations problem by putting duties upon German exports. And the plan was no sooner attempted than it broke down.

" Merchants almost without exception state that the German exporter refuses to deliver goods until he or his agent is paid in full. The general result is that either business is suspended altogether, or that the British importer pays the German exporter in full, and himself pays the duty to the British Customs authorities." [2]

---

[1] See the debates on the Reparations Recovery Bill in the House of Commons on March 7, 10 and 14, 1921.
[2] See the statement issued by the Chemical and Dyestuffs Traders Association in April 1921.

It was found that the " fifty-fifty " cry had no foundation. For every £100 which the British buyer paid to the German seller he had to pay £100 to the Customs here. The effect of the Act was either to stop importation or to make the Englishman, and not the German, pay. The French Chamber accepted the Act without illusions, simply " to consecrate the agreement between the Allies "; but they treated it as a piece of almost prohibitive protection. The *Observer*, a strong supporter of the Government, denounced " its follies and futilities." The *Times* and the *Manchester Guardian* condemned it as cumbrous, exasperating, imbecile. And one Coalitionist Member of Parliament soon found himself voicing the general conclusion when he declared that " a more foolish proposal never entered the mind of man."

But a franker, and from the Conservative standpoint a more satisfactory, form of Protection appeared in the proposals for Safeguarding Industries introduced into Parliament in May 1921. The arguments about reparations were dropped : they had not proved brilliantly successful. But a new theory was developed, as an excuse for Free Traders who found themselves obliged to vote for tariffs—the necessity of guarding British industries against the depreciation of exchanges abroad. How foreign exchanges were going to be benefited by our imposing duties on foreign goods was not made evident. The proposal to put a duty on the exports of countries with depreciated currencies—a fixed duty in all cases whatever the depreciations of currency might be—was the very

way, one leading business man from Lancashire protested, " to prevent the exchanges improving." But
to some of Mr. Lloyd George's followers the blessed
word exchange was like the blessed word Mesopotamia, sufficient to dispose of a multitude of doubts.
Safeguarding and anti-dumping could only result in
checking or stopping cheap imports and in raising
the prices of production in this country. No worse
blow, in the view of Free Traders, could have been
struck at our struggling export interests, no worse
difficulties put in the way of a return to normal business here. If Mr. Lloyd George had ever believed
very seriously in Free Trade—Protectionists naturally
took leave to doubt this—he could hardly have sanctioned legislation of this kind. But he has too often
allowed himself to think that statesmanship consists
in fusing incompatible policies and interests, and
that with sufficient skill in bargaining and dealing it
is possible to get round economic laws. His position
in May 1921 was summed up by one acute Free
Trader in the House of Commons:

" We have for the present year the 100 per cent. duty under
the Reparation Act, the McKenna duties, the preference to the
Colonies, the Colonial reciprocity, the Palm Kernel's duty, the
Dye Industry Act, and now we are to have this safeguarding of
Key Industries Bill and this legislation for collapsed ex-
changes. . . .

"As the Prime Minister himself said, ' Protection is a quick-
sand.' Once you get your feet in it you cannot get out of
it."[1]

---

[1] See Captain Wedgwood Benn's speech in the House of
Commons, May 9, 1921.

There is no profit in following the story further. The policy of safeguarding industries was soon recognised by Tariff Reformers as promising them, if persisted in, all that they desired. The plan was to introduce Protection unostentatiously by administrative action, to limit it to certain scheduled industries at first, and then to extend it to such other industries as could convince a Board of Trade Committee appointed under Protectionist influence that they were suffering from unfair competition. What unfair competition meant nobody was ever able to define. But an elaborate apparatus for the creation of tariffs was set up, with such possibilities of wire-pulling and lobbying as that involved. Weak Free Traders, nervous Coalitionists, discovered that safeguarding was like strychnine, lethal in large doses but a useful tonic if the doses were small enough. The little doses of poison were quietly increased. In 1922 the Act was extended. The Conservatives insisted: the Prime Minister could not refuse. So far as he was a Free Trader, he must have realised that he was sacrificing the commercial interests of the country to the demands of his political allies. Mr. Lloyd George has since swung back to Free Trade, and is well able, of course, when circumstances require, to defend it eloquently on any platform. But it is difficult for men who value sincerity in politics to forget how deliberately he set himself to undermine it, to suit the necessities of his position, in his day of power.

VI

Free Trade, unhappily, is a matter of controversy with us still. But there is another subject in which Liberals and Conservatives must alike be interested, if there be any truth in doctrines which men like Peel and Gladstone, Cobden and Disraeli, Hicks-Beach and Goschen taught. Excessive expenditure and excessive taxation lie at the root of our economic troubles to-day. It is only by saving money for investment and by removing burdens and restrictions upon trade that the recovery of our business can be stimulated and workers in need of employment absorbed. If Liberalism is ever again to be a power in this country, its first duty will be to enforce economy with unsparing hands. What did Mr. Lloyd George do, in his hour of opportunity, to insist on this essential doctrine? What reason is there to believe that he has ever realised its importance, or would seek to establish it if returned to office? It is profitless now to consider how many hundred millions of debt might have been saved by a firmer and wiser administration of finance during the War. Fearlessness in necessary expenditure is one thing: reckless disregard of public money is another. Mr. Lloyd George, unhappily, never understood the difference, or saw where patriotism ended and prodigality began. And even when the War was over he found too many of his followers and assistants ready to identify activity with waste. To call a halt to expenditure then was the first of public duties.

Never was a strong Chancellor of the Exchequer more needed. But that might not have suited Mr. Lloyd George's views. He has often, of course, paid lip-service to economy, as to other Liberal ideas. He fought for it, indeed, in speeches frequently in his earlier days. But his real indifference on the subject was soon revealed in an illuminating phrase. When the Liberal Party were labouring to check the wanton expenditure of the Coalition in the worst period of swollen-headed administration after the War, the Prime Minister angrily denounced as " epileptic screaming " criticisms to which his followers could not shut their ears. And the outbreak illustrated only too clearly the value of the appeals for " relentless economy " which within a short time he substituted for his foolish taunt.

On one point in particular Mr. Lloyd George has always been at the mercy of temptation. He has a passion for appointing new assistants at the public cost. Under his Premiership the Cabinet Secretariat in Downing Street, his own Department, grew from nothing at all to ridiculous proportions. Its Secretary was assisted by one Principal Assistant Secretary, three Assistant Secretaries, three Principals, one Assistant Principal, one Editor—a curious feature in a Cabinet Secretariat—one Assistant for the Editor, two Administrative Assistants, four Clerks of one grade, twenty-two Clerks of another grade, thirty-nine Clerks and Typists of a third grade, eighteen Temporary Messengers and Porters, fourteen Charwomen and others. In 1917 this singular confidential apparatus, which, the Prime Minister explained, was not exactly " a constitutional departure," but the functions of which no one could clearly understand, cost the State under £4,000. In 1922, years after the War was over, when Mr. Lloyd George was busy promising that expenditure should be " ruthlessly " cut down, it cost the State over £32,000. It became, on a small scale of course, a significant example of the Prime Minister's administrative and economical ideas.

But the Cabinet Secretariat by no means stood alone. Mr. Lloyd George's advent to power was marked by the creation of two other new Departments on a much larger scale, a Ministry of Labour and a Ministry of Pensions. By 1921 each of these Departments employed over 26,000 persons. The vote for the Ministry of Labour in 1921–22 was £22 millions; the net estimate for the Ministry of Pensions was £111 millions; [1] and the cost of administration only was for each Department nearer six million pounds than five. After the War, when the call to save public money was imperative, more new Ministries leaped into existence. The first step in Mr. Lloyd George's schemes of reconstruction was always to construct new staffs. Early in 1919 Bills were introduced for a Ministry of Health and a Ministry of Ways and Communications. [2] Both soon became by-words for expense. Dr. Addison's enthu-

---

[1] But there was a little blunder, an over-estimate of £10½ millions, that year.

[2] But the Ministry of Health took over the duties of the Local Government Board and the Insurance Commission.

14

siasm for State-aided philanthropy soon made the Ministry of Health conspicuous, while the Ministry of Ways or Transport swelled larger and larger in its grandiose ambitions, and the Government showed a notable reluctanceto subject its expenditure to Parliamentary control. Meanwhile the War Controls still flourished gaily, spending public money right and left. In April 1919 the Government's proposal for a fresh Department of valuers in connection with their Bill for the Acquisition of Land—in addition to the special Valuation Department set up by Mr. Lloyd George in 1910—roused strong protest in the House of Commons. In June 1920 a new Ministry of Mines was recommended; the cost was not fixed—to an impressionist Minister such details do not matter— but it was not to exceed " a few thousand pounds." [1] In August men and women of all parties joined in protesting against the extravagant departmental schemes launched almost daily, and urged that the Ministries of Munitions, Food, Shipping, Labour and Transport should be abolished without delay. Public indignation was rising. Mr. Lloyd George, whose generalities about saving money had had no visible effect on his subordinates, was at last forced to declare that all expenditure not indispensable must be ruthlessly cut down.

But Mr. Lloyd George's easy liberality was known to his supporters. And his perfunctory exhortations

[1] The House of Lords compelled the Government to reduce the proposed new Minister of Mines to the position of a Secretary of the Board of Trade.

to economy were treated by his Departments as a matter of form. Three years after the War the expenses of the Army and Navy were practically double, the staffs of the War Office and Admiralty more than double, those of pre-war years. Little incidents like the Army's astonishing supply of motors [1]—between 9,000 and 10,000—or the charge for naval officers' servants—which had risen from £255,000 in 1914 to £733,000 in 1921—showed how much attention the Prime Minister's colleagues, naval and military, were paying to his economical talk. In the little matter of motor-cars the State was wonderfully generous. Even the Air Ministry in 1919 had forty-eight, thirty-three being kept for thirty-three officials. Mr. Winston Churchill had one kept by the Air Ministry and another obligingly kept by the War Office for him; and when he suggested that two were not needed, his suggestion was overlooked by the officer in charge. One is not surprised to hear of the Air Ministry presenting its estimates to Parliament before the consent of the Treasury had been obtained. Civilian Departments emulated this liberality of mind. The Treasury had once been the watch-dog of finance. The War had altered that. But after the War the cost of the

[1] Many illuminating details on these and other points will be found in the Report of the (Geddes) Committee on National Expenditure published in February 1922. It may be added that even in 1929, in spite of large reductions in the Army, the number of men employed both in the Military and in the Civil Department of the War Office, is far larger than in 1914 (see the *Times* of November 15, 1929).

Treasury went up in an alarming way. The meagre but adequate staff of pre-war days—one or two Secretaries at £2,000 a year,[1] five Principal Clerks and twelve First-Class Clerks, costing altogether some £19,000 a year—was, under Mr. Lloyd George's Administration, increased out of all knowledge. The nation in 1921 had the privilege of paying one Permanent Secretary at £4,000 a year, three Controllers at £3,500 a year each, three Departmental Controllers at £2,700 a year each, one Principal Assistant Secretary at £1,950 (rising to £2,250), one Director of Women's Establishments at £1,950, eleven Heads of Divisions at salaries from £1,690 to £1,950, one Temporary Representative in the Ministry of Transport at £5,000 a year, and others, costing together more than £50,000 a year.[2] Yet over the expenses of government there was no obvious increase of Treasury control. Indeed the Financial Department of the War Office, created to save public money, was stated to be costing about £962,400 a year.[3]

With the Treasury setting this example, other Departments of course followed suit. The Ministry of Agriculture's administrative expenditure, £168,000 in 1913–14, rose to £956,000 in 1921–22. The Stationery Office ran up its estimates to about

[1] In 1914 there were two Permanent Secretaries at £2,000 a year, in place of the one Secretary of older days.

[2] See the *Report from the Select Committee on Estimates*, 1921 (203). These salaries included bonuses. I have given details of the higher officials only. But the increase of Treasury officials and salaries is still very difficult to defend.

[3] *Ibid*. But this included the Pay Offices, and of course included also some abnormal expenditure due to the War.

four times the figure of pre-war days. The Ministry of Labour and the Ministry of Pensions thought in tens of millions. The Ministry of Munitions two years after the War was still employing thousands of people, and the disputed estimates of its expenditure varied from £19 millions to something like three times that sum. The Ministry of Shipping was still said to be costing over £20 millions. Even when these two Ministries ceased to exist, over 9,000 of their employees had to be provided for elsewhere. The Ministry of Health was not to be outdone by others. Its provisional estimates for 1922–23, towards the end of the Coalition's prodigal existence, were £22½ millions for net ordinary services, with an additional £2¾ millions for non-recurrent housing charges.[1] Mr. Asquith, commenting good-humouredly in November 1920 on the exuberance and costliness of the new bureaucracy—Captain Guest, Mr. Lloyd George's Chief Whip, had recently declared that the Government's expenditure could not be reduced— noted that the Ministry of Health required six superintending charwomen and seven deputy superintendent charwomen, who, " from their position of relative superiority," supervised the labour of 122 charwomen of a humbler grade.

But the Ministry of Transport rivalled in the scale of its magnificence all the creations of Mr. Lloyd George's bureaucratic art. No niggard spirit presided at its birth. Road-making was to reconstruct

[1] See the *First Report of the Select Committee on National Expenditure*, 1922 (137).

our England, and incidentally—though that appears to have been an after-thought—to sweep the perils of unemployment away. This Department began to operate in 1919. In 1920 it controlled expenditure amounting to some £27 millions, of which railway agreements were the principal item. The staff, described as "grandiose," included several hundred persons. Thirty officials received salaries ranging from £5,000 to £1,000 a year. One Director-General received £2,070, besides £922 of naval pay, another Director-General £3,000, another £2,500. A Chief Mechanical Engineer received £2,500 and a Consulting Mechanical Engineer the same. A Deputy Director General received £2,500 and two Chief Civil Engineers £2,000 each. A Director of Plants and a Director of Intelligence began at £1,669; an Assistant Director of Plants drew only from £1,203 to £1,436. But the Finance Department of the Ministry had three Directors of its own, besides its Director-General and its Assistant Secretary; each of these three Directors drew from £1,669 to £1,950, and one required also a personal allowance of £300. A fourth Director in this Department and four Assistant Directors were content with rather less. It is an expensive thing even to superintend Lloyd-Georgian finance. The Mechanical Engineering Department had five Directors, with three Assistants, on the same high scale, besides its Director-General, its Principal and its two highly-paid Engineers. One gentleman was good enough to duplicate the offices of secretary and solicitor—no doubt with the object of saving public money—for a fee of £4,250 a year. And this list is only a part of the tale. Five or six hundred other officials at more modest emoluments —the number is not exhaustive—contributed handsomely to the task of making work for the rest. No explanation was given of their functions, " actual, prospective or potential." Had there ever, asked one patient critic, been a new Department manned on such a scale before? In all, the salaries of a Ministry whose main function, we were informed, was to think, were estimated in one year at £352,000, in another at £416,000. To assist the processes of thought twenty-seven motor-cars were provided by the tax-payer, including two Rolls-Royce cars which cost £5,500.[1] And all this in years of grave national impoverishment, when saving was the first duty of the State! To complete the story, the new Department had not been three years in existence, when its head, Sir Eric Geddes, admitted that he could not justify its existence any more.[2] The new Ministry was sentenced to extinction, and some at least of its wasteful expenditure saved. The Coalition Government and the Conservative Government successively promised that it should disappear. But to this day the Department goes merrily on. In March 1929 the Minister in charge was taking credit for the fact that it had spent since 1920 some £57

[1] For the details of this expenditure see the *Second Report of the Select Committee on National Expenditure* for 1920 (118), and the *Report from the Select Committee on Estimates*, 1921 (203).

[2] In November 1921. The railways were restored to private ownership that year.

millions on road-work and bridge-work in relief of unemployment—though with comparatively little advantage to our unemployed. Can any man who values economy read the story of Mr. Lloyd George's Administration, with its large and ill-considered schemes, its slipshod ways, its inexcusable extravagance, and maintain the theory that he ever seriously cares to save? Public economy, it was said, with Mr. Cobden was " nothing less than a moral principle." Public economy with Mr. Lloyd George in power was little more than a belated expedient, to disguise the growing demoralisation of the system of which the Prime Minister was the responsible head.

This reckless multiplication of officials, combined with a habit of tiding over difficulties by new and heavy grants from the Exchequer, told seriously on the Budget. In 1919 the average expenditure from April to July was close upon £4½ millions a day.[1] The subsidies for 1919–20 included votes of £26 millions for coal-mines, £60 millions for railways and £50 millions for bread.[2] Under pressure of Parliamentary inquiries the revelations of mismanagement grew, revelations too of grave carelessness in permitting individuals to make large profits by doing business with the State. Taxes rose high. But the Government refused to levy a special contribution from wealth made out of the War; though many

---

[1] £4,442,000 was the average daily expenditure from April 1 to July 26. (See Parliamentary Debates, July 31, 1919.)
[2] Ibid., July 22, 1919.

thought that such a tax, imposed in 1919 or even in 1920, would have been both fair and practicable, would have given wide satisfaction, and would have appreciably diminished the burden of debt. The Prime Minister fluctuated between vehement denials of extravagance in practice and equally vehement insistence on economy in theory. The " epileptic screamers " of the Opposition found their epilepsy execrated one day, but echoed the next. Mr. Lloyd George's methods were freely criticised even by Coalition Members.

" The Prime Minister is at Deauville for a well-earned rest," wrote one on September 4, 1919,[1] " and there he has been strongly convicted of sin—in others. The result is a peremptory letter to his colleagues ordering them ruthlessly to cut down expenditure in Government Departments, although only a few days before in the House of Commons he had deprecated attack on those Departments, and praised the super-men who had saved the country hundreds of millions. One is entitled to ask whether the Budget and the estimates were not submitted for his approval, and did they not receive his imprimatur ? The epistle from Deauville will not do, and suggests the proverbial pill to cure the earthquake. It is useless and mean to attack Government Departments who are simply carrying out the settled policy of the Government, and doing work which the Government itself has created."

At last, however, necessity compelled the Government to act as well as talk. In 1921 they discovered that their expenditure was mounting to a figure between £1,000 and £1,100 millions, and that only £950 millions were forthcoming to meet the demand. The Chancellor of the Exchequer, Sir Robert Horne, was of opinion that no Government could spend less

[1] Mr. J. Wallace, M.P. for Dunfermline.

than £950 millions a year. But still a Treasury circular went out insisting on imperative reductions. The Departments discovered that they could with no undue effort save £75 millions almost at once. And the Geddes Committee followed up this discovery by suggesting reductions of nearly £100 millions more. These admissions by the Government's servants and by the Committee which the Government appointed speak for themselves. No other evidence is really needed to prove the reckless prodigality of Mr. Lloyd George's Administration and the startling inefficiency of the financial methods he pursued.

VII

But is there any other branch of that strange Administration to which one can look back with more comfort, or in which many serious indications of competent statesmanship are found? Mr. Lloyd George's foreign policy, when studied, reveals itself as little more than a series of failures. His Irish policy reached perhaps the lowest level that he ever touched. His economic expedients almost invariably ended in confusion. His incursions into personal controversy few will wish to remember. His incursions into Labour problems were often democratic in their sympathies, often nimble-witted and resourceful. But they were chiefly remarkable for their adroitness in discovering the conditions for a bargain, and they failed too often to inspire the confidence required. Since Mr. Lloyd George ceased to be Prime Minister he has not always been proof against the temptation to make party capital out of the coal question. Yet his own Government's handling of that perplexing problem was not only open to attack. It left the industry in a most unsatisfactory condition. The Coal Control fixed wages on so high a scale, and paid so highly for the Government's requirements, that the collieries were tempted to run prices up to extravagant heights. And the sale of bad coal to our Allies at exorbitant prices, when we had the opportunity, was afterwards partly responsible for the loss of our trade. Mr. Lloyd George's weakness for pursuing two incompatible policies together still further complicated a difficult position. Early in 1919 he was apparently thinking of nationalisation. To stave off a strike, he appointed the Sankey Commission, with the object, it was not unreasonably suspected, of finding a way by which nationalisation or something equivalent to it could be brought about. But when a bare majority of the Commission decided in favour of nationalising the collieries, Mr. Lloyd George, perhaps under pressure from his colleagues, drew back. He agreed to shorter hours and higher wages; and in July 1919, to pay, presumably, for these concessions, the price of coal to the consumer was raised by six shillings a ton. He agreed also to the State purchase of mineral rights, and was prepared to recommend to Parliament some scheme for reorganising the industry in convenient areas, which would reduce its expenses, maintain its exports, and secure the interests of miners and consumers alike.

But to taking over the management of the collieries the Government could not consent. The miners' representatives declined to accept this substitute for nationalisation. But as the discussion proceeded the Government discovered that their calculations had again been wrong. In November they suddenly lowered by ten shillings a ton the cost of domestic coal, which they had raised by six shillings a few months before! Industrial coal remained as dear as ever. The coal-owners turned naturally to the more lucrative trade. And for a time the country was threatened by a famine in domestic coal. Disagreeable comments in Parliament followed. The Government then brought in a Bill to regulate mining profits, which was to last for three months only: after that Government control was to cease. But against this plan even the " Coupon " majority revolted. Ministerialists described the condition of the industry as chaotic. The Labour Party protested against the virtual violation of a pledge. The second reading debate was adjourned, and the Government's Bill was heard of no more.

Still the policy of relying on temporary expedients, without frankly facing economic conditions, went on. In 1920 the Labour Party renewed the demand for nationalisation. The Government proposed a new Ministry of Mines, with new Boards and Committees, to control the industry and to regulate the remuneration of the workers. The Miners' Federation put forward repeated claims for an advance in wages, which, the President of the Board of Trade

pointed out, had already risen over 150 per cent.[1]
The miners believed that the Government were
making large profits out of the industry, and could
well afford to pay more wages and to reduce the
price of domestic coal. Negotiations, hardly inter-
rupted by a brief strike in October 1920, ended in
the Government yielding temporarily the advance
for which the men had asked. Fresh schemes for the
permanent regulation of the industry were en-
visaged. The war-control of coal-mining was to end
at any rate by August 1921. But suddenly the
Government, startled, as they so often were, by the
results of their own financial calculations, produced
and carried a proposal to end control on March 31.
This ill-considered action provoked a fresh conflict
over wages, and a serious strike in April 1921, which
resulted in a stoppage for almost three months.
Then the Government stepped in again and offered
£10 millions of public money; and the Government's
money and the Government's pressure gradually
prevailed. A National Wage Board and District
Boards were set up. A standard was fixed—twenty
per cent. above pre-war earnings—below which
wages were not to be allowed to fall. And the principle of profit-sharing was to some extent introduced. Mr. Lloyd George, optimistic as ever, was
sure that " peace for a very long period " had been
secured.[2] He did not realise that versatility alone
is not enough to make men trustful, or to solve a

[1] See the *Times*, July 27, 1920.
[2] See *Parliamentary Debates*, June 28, 1921.

problem aggravated for years past by the ill-judged interference of the State. His followers perhaps were quicker to see the justice of the criticism which described his coal policy as little more than " a humiliating series of ups and downs, chops and changes, advances and retreats." [1]

Other episodes in the history of Mr. Lloyd George's Government must be touched on lightly here. The same characteristics appear in them all—large ideas of progress and development, a genuine desire to improve the condition of the workers, a series of expensive expedients and improvisations for that and other objects, but too often, when it came to legislative or administrative action, a lack of efficiency in carrying difficult projects through. Interesting schemes of electrical development were propounded as early as 1917, and Acts to facilitate the supply of electricity were passed in 1919 and 1922. But the plans for development did not get much further while Mr. Lloyd George remained in power. It is fair to remember that he was overwhelmed with labours. But a competent administrator who meant business might have been expected to secure more satisfactory results. The railway dispute again, and the serious railway strike of September 1919, revealed once more the Prime Minister's activities, his

[1] No one will underrate the difficulties which Mr. Lloyd George and his successors had to deal with. But if it be correct, as stated on high authority, that the workmen engaged in getting coal now receive eighty-seven per cent. of the net proceeds, it is clear that the situation cannot be remedied by imposing fresh burdens on coal-owners.

ingenuity in negotiation, his energy in meeting threats. But the trouble in the railway world was largely due to the hasty, wholesale methods by which, under Mr. Lloyd George's Administration, assurances were given both to the Railway Companies and to the railway workers without realising fully what they involved. The Companies were promised revenue, the railway-men were promised wages, which the industry proved unable to supply. In the end Mr. Lloyd George got out of his difficulties— they were not slight—by an immense expenditure of money. The Government's offer, which became the basis of the settlement in 1919, " at least doubled the pre-war wages of railway workers," irrespective of the cost of living, and continued war allowances on a high scale as well. The Minister of Labour summed up the meaning of the Prime Minister's proposals. Before the War the Railway Companies paid in wages £47 millions a year. The Government's generosity increased this wages-bill by £67 millions a year.[1] The ultimate effects on the Railway Companies were never sufficiently considered. But the cost of Mr. Lloyd George's methods of government received significant illustration once more.

The same gifts of popular improvisation were relied on to meet other political and administrative problems. Public feeling rose against high prices and found indignant expression in the Press. Mr. Lloyd George immediately responded. A Committee was

[1] See Sir R. Horne's statement in the *Times* of September 27, 1919.

appointed to look into profiteering. In August 1919 a Profiteering Bill, characteristically hasty and inefficient, was brought in. The matter was so urgent that the Government refused to face the recess till the Bill was passed. But within three months Government spokesmen were admitting that the Profiteering Act had effected practically nothing. It met a " stunt " and stopped an outcry. And with those results the Prime Minister was content. Prejudice against foreign immigrants became active, and, this cause also received some stimulus from a section of the Press. The Prime Minister again responded. An Aliens Restriction Bill, so illiberal in character as to be shorn of some of its shabbiest features by a Conservative House of Lords, was introduced and passed.[1] Within a short time it proved to be a dead letter, like so many other of Mr. Lloyd George's legislative schemes. But again it had served its purpose: it had stopped an agitation in the Press. Unemployment was a graver problem. It soon grew to sinister proportions. In November 1918 the two Heads of the Coalition Government had declared that " active measures " to deal with it would be required. Power and light, railways and transport, new markets and increase of output were referred to, perhaps a little sketchily: more could hardly have been expected of an election address. In December Mr. Lloyd George had gone further. He had spoken

[1] It was read for a second time in the House of Commons on April 15, 1919. Genuine Liberals should note Lord Buckmaster's comments on this Act in a speech at the National Liberal Club, February 16, 1921.

of more detailed schemes. There were to be rural developments, which would " take the population back to the land." A canal system fitted for modern mechanical transport might be opened up. Hundreds " if not thousands " of miles of light railways might be laid down—all in addition to a vast increase in roads and a heavily increased burden upon Railway Companies. But these schemes, the thousands of miles of light railways in particular, do not seem to have yielded much result.

It was a much easier matter to institute a dole. On the eve of the General Election of 1918 weekly payments of twenty-nine and twenty-five shillings respectively were awarded to all men and women thrown out of work by the stoppage of war industries.[1] It was another hasty, ill-considered proposal —Ministers bent upon electioneering have not always time to think—and it was attended by many abuses from the first. The grants made were sometimes indiscriminate and careless. In the eighteen months which followed, when unemployment was comparatively low, over £60 millions were distributed to men and women demobilised from the war factories or the Forces, and a good deal of this money probably got into the wrong hands. The best feature in an ill-managed business was the provision of Juvenile Unemployment Centres to train young people who received the donation. The worst

---

[1] There were allowances for children also. Besides this Civilian scheme a similar scheme for men demobilised from the Forces was launched at the same time.

15

feature—and for this Mr. Lloyd George must be held responsible—was the introduction of the demoralising dole.

> " Governments," said Mr. Clynes, " so dreaded the effects of unemployment on a large scale that they had been driven to keep the workers in a state of order, and more or less in a degree of contentment, by paying them week by week large sums of money for doing nothing at all. He was not in favour of a policy which meant leaving 800,000 persons idle, tramping the streets and wasting their time, and yet paying them £1,200,000 a week. It was neither policy nor statesmanship, and was not what they meant by reconstruction."

After a few months the donation was found to be too costly to continue at the original rate. In May 1919 the civilian grants were reduced in amount. In November of that year they were suddenly stopped. But the Government's schemes to replace them were not ready. The problem had not yet been thoroughly examined, and the temporary makeshifts suggested with the best intentions broke down. There was a Land Settlement Scheme. It cost some £12½ millions to provide 16,000 men with small holdings. But bad years followed, and the small men with no free capital were forced in many cases to give up their holdings and to fall back into the ranks of labourers or unemployed. There was a Civil Liabilities Grants scheme. Over a 100,000 people were set up with small grants as small farmers, shopkeepers or carters—a scheme pre-doomed to fail. £3½ millions were spent, and most of the money was thrown away. There was an Over-seas Settlement Scheme. Mr. Lloyd George seemed

ERRATA

On pages 227 and 229 (footnotes)
for Davidson *read* Davison.

at one time to realise that emigration was a wiser expedient than any plans for artificial work. But the want of care and discrimination shown in selecting men on this side, and in securing them a fair start on the other, resulted in a stream of failures, and served to discredit an expedient which has never had the fair trial it deserves.[1] Of Mr. Lloyd George's genuine desire to deal with the Unemployment difficulty there can be no question. But the whole story is characteristic of his weakness as a public man. Few politicians are quicker in devising schemes or in supplying public money to pay for them. But ingenious improvisation is a different thing from statesmanship. And few politicians seem to have less serious understanding of the complicated nature of the social problems they assail.

VIII

More hopeful and important was the work done by the Coalition Government in extending Unemployment Insurance. That policy owed much already to Mr. Lloyd George's energy and courage. But it was not carried through after the War as promptly as might have been expected; and it was more than once diluted by expedients introduced to tide over temporary difficulties without regard to

[1] For all these schemes Mr. Lloyd George claimed credit in his election speeches of 1929. He seems to have forgotten the results. See Mr. R. C. Davidson's book on *The Unemployed*, pp. 92–4. But it is fair to add that officialism or policy in the Dominions has sometimes made emigration more difficult than it ought to be.

ultimate results. The new Bill, brought in at the end of 1919, was not passed till August 1920, and did not come into operation until November of that year. How much more rapidly these difficult problems can be settled by pamphleteers in opposition than by Ministers in power! The new Act covered 11 million persons. It has been enlarged in various directions by no less than twelve amending Acts since. That is not perhaps a sign of very efficient legislation. But it is satisfactory to note that the demands for Unemployment benefit made under it have been by no means alarming in recent years.

" Over a period of 2½ years, from October 1923 to April 1926 —years that were by no means free from serious hindrance to industry, both internally and externally—out of 11½ million work-people insured under the Unemployment Insurance Acts, nearly 8 million drew no unemployment benefit at all, and of the remaining 3½ million, the benefit drawn by 2½ million in no single case exceeded 100 days in all." [1]

The unsatisfactory feature of these Acts has been the constant demand for their alteration and expansion, caused first by the stoppage of the out-of-work donation at a time when unemployment was really becoming severe, and next by the changes thought necessary in the forms and rates of benefit, and the partial failure of the calculations on which the Acts were based. Hand-to-mouth legislation is rarely a success. The confusion resulting from the changes of policy initiated by Mr. Lloyd George's Government in 1921, and accepted perhaps inevitably as a basis for further changes by later Governments down to

[1] See the *Industrial Transference Board Report* (1928), p. 4.

1927, is only too evident to any student of the Acts.[1] The arbitrary improvisations resorted to, whenever fresh difficulties arose, have seriously weakened their economic framework. The scheme of 1920 has, in the words of no unkindly critic, been " distorted almost out of knowledge." And it cannot be said that any Government has succeeded in introducing elements of principle or permanence into the legislation which at present exists.

Yet, unsatisfactory as their development has been, the Unemployment Insurance Acts were a new and important departure in the treatment of a difficult problem. So much cannot be said of the proposals for Government works, to which, when in office, Mr. Lloyd George had recourse. In the autumn of 1920 the grave increase in unemployment caused alarm, and Ministers could think of no better way of meeting it than to fall back on projects of relief-works, now dignified as reconstruction or development, but often tried with miserable results before. An Unemployment Grants Committee, to consist this time of business men, was set up, with Lord St. Davids as its chairman. Its duty was to make grants to Local Authorities who would start public works in areas of serious distress. As time passed a great deal of money was spent by the Committee, first on schemes not intended to bring in revenue, then on revenue-producing schemes as well; and the more reluctant Local Authorities were to undertake them, the larger

---

[1] See Mr. Davidson's careful study of these Acts (*The Unemployed*, Chaps. III, IV and V).

were the grants which the Government had to offer to set them afloat. As in all previous experiences, the work proved in many cases unsatisfactory and expensive. Where competent labourers were used, little help was given to the problem of unemployment. Where short terms of casual labour were provided for less competent workers, the results were often very disappointing. A statement published in the *Manchester Guardian* from official sources on August 14, 1922, claimed that in two years the Government might—judging by confessedly inexact statistics—have found direct employment for some 130,000 men, and indirect employment for an equal number, at a cost of £41 millions. The work in this calculation included not only that provided by the Unemployment Grants Committee, but work on roads, railways, land and forests provided by various Government departments. The statement added:

" With regard to the Ministry of Transport, it is important to note that out of a total of £85,000,000 expended on roads during the past two years, no more than £12,500,000 has any relation whatever to unemployment, the difference being in the nature of normal expenditure."

Later on, in 1928, the Seventh Report of Lord St. Davids' Committee, analysing perhaps with more exactness a sum of £78 millions spent on Loan Schemes since 1921, showed that £21 millions of this total had been expended on roads and footpaths, £16 millions on sewage schemes, £10 millions on docks, nearly £7 millions on electricity, and the rest on tramways, parks, gas and water schemes, sea defence, land development, cemeteries, and so forth. The idea of anticipating normal work which would some day be really needed, and of making the jobs as business-like and as unlike relief-works as possible, was kept constantly in view. Yet, after seven years of such large, well-meant, expensive efforts, the Committee found that the figures of unemployment were " still unfortunately high "; that in the year under review (July 1927 to June 1928) these figures had actually gone up from 1,069,000 to 1,273,000; that the Local Authorities showed a growing disinclination to anticipate or accelerate work; and that the new schemes approved by the Committee during the year were " less than fifty per cent. of the value of those approved last year, and but two per cent. of the value of those approved the year before." The Local Authorities had clearly lost confidence in them, and had in some cases incurred very serious commitments with very little benefit to the localities concerned. If this is the considered verdict, after seven years' experience, of the Unemployment Grants Committee appointed by Mr. Lloyd George when in power, it is difficult to understand why sudden and glowing success should be expected from the public works, so strikingly similar in character, which he propounded as an electioneering programme in 1929. The Report of the Industrial Transference Board in 1928, a thoughtful State paper, issued under the orders of the Ministry of Labour by three distinguished public servants who will not be accused of party feeling,[1] adds a grave warning as to the results of such schemes:

"When we consider that since the Armistice under the varied and comprehensive programmes of works in relief of unemployment (not including Trade Facilities guaranteed schemes) works of the total estimated value of slightly under £190 millions have been approved, and that, notwithstanding the magnitude of the undertakings, there have been at no one date more than 75,000 men employed on such works and of these many for short spells only, and that we have still to face a heavy volume of unemployment, we believe it would clearly be contrary to public policy to begin another cycle of such works."

The weakness of these programmes is that, however well-intended, they only touch the superficial aspects of the problem and distract attention from the real difficulties, the underlying facts. And if it be true that an expenditure of £190 millions has only been able to supply work for 75,000 men at a time—or even for double that number—it is certainly hard to see how a temporary loan of £200 millions could supply for hundreds of thousands of workers work which they would be able or willing to do, which would prove so productive as not only to pay for itself but to increase the resources of the nation, and so prompt and benevolent in its operation that it would within a year sweep abnormal unemployment away.

It will be admitted, however, that the schemes for relieving unemployment which Mr. Lloyd George set on foot when in office, were marked by great activity, variety and cost. Did they even materially

[1] Sir W. Fisher, Sir J. Cadman and Sir D. Shackleton.

reduce the numbers of the unemployed? The figures speak for themselves. In 1919 Mr. Lloyd George admitted that it was " almost impossible " to prevent unemployment, because nobody could command the fluctuations of trade. But industrious people must be saved from suffering under it—an unanswerable demand. In 1920 Cabinet Committees examined the problem. But little came of these Committees except schemes for road improvement, for absorbing ex-service men into the building trade, for acquiring land for works of public utility, and for promoting relief works as described. In May 1921, after two and a half years of Mr. Lloyd George's peace administration, the official figures of Unemployment were 2,558,000, higher than any recorded before or since.[1] Another Cabinet Committee to examine the problem was announced. Ambitious projects for beautifying England—by something else, it may be hoped, than arterial roads—were said to be taking shape in the Prime Minister's mind. In August 1921, the figures of unemployment were still alarmingly high. But Dr. Macnamara confessed that the Government's schemes had only found work for about 100,000 men.[2] In September there was fresh, even feverish, activity. The Cabinet, summoned to meet at Inverness— Lord Curzon, who slept badly in trains resented these inconsiderate Northern meetings—decided again to examine the subject, and proposals for schemes of

[1] See the *Industrial Transference Board Report* (1928), p. 3.

[2] See *Parliamentary Debates*, August 17, 1921. Dr. Macnamara put the figures at 2,170,397 totally unemployed, besides 988,394 on short time.

utility to be undertaken by Local Authorities emerged. Eight London Labour Mayors arrived at Inverness in quest of the Prime Minister, while the police tried to cope with Unemployed demonstrations in London and elsewhere. Mr. Lloyd George, tracked to Gairloch by the Mayors, assured them that their views would have his earnest consideration. Before September ended new schemes by the Government were announced. Sir Alfred Mond, after three Cabinet meetings in a day, declined to be either " pessimistic or desponding."   On October 1 Mr. Lloyd George received at Gairloch financial and industrial " experts " on the subject. And on his way back to London he made an eloquent speech at Inverness on the need of " marching side by side " —Gairloch possibly suggested Harlech—" not in sections, not in tribes, marching as a nation, marching as a people."

In October the Government's new plans were presented to the House of Commons. They included a grant to assist the emigration of ex-service men, an extension of the scheme for export credits, aids for the development of public enterprises, for relief works, forestry and land drainage, and for the dependents of the unemployed. But all these projects were marked by the same weakness. They were hasty improvisations, produced under the pressure of agitation, to show that the Government were doing something. And their authors rarely seemed to realise that the first step to make such projects answer, was not merely to go marching side by side, but to ascertain facts in detail, to analyse the material they had to deal with, to find out not the numbers only but the qualities and circumstances of the unemployed. Doctors called in to deal with human maladies at least attempt to diagnose them. Political practitioners are sometimes tempted first to advertise their cures. The results of such methods were what one might expect. In January 1922 Mr. Lloyd George declared that we had still nearly two million unemployed.[1] In September of that year his Chief Whip announced that measures to banish unemployment and doles would be the principal task of the next Administration. A month later the Coalition Government fell. It would not be fair to blame Mr. Lloyd George for the very serious industrial situation of those years, nor to deny his fertility in devising temporary expedients to amend it. But when seven years later he suddenly proclaimed that he could conquer unemployment in a twelvemonth, it was inevitable that men should wonder why he had failed so conspicuously to do so in four years of great activity and undisputed power.

[1] See Mr. Lloyd George's Memorandum for the French Government printed in the *Westminster Gazette* of January 12, and quoted in the *Liberal Magazine* of February, 1922.

CHAPTER VI

MR. LLOYD GEORGE, POLITICAL FUSION AND POLITICAL FUNDS

There is only one other topic in the history of the Coalition Government which needs consideration here; and that is Mr. Lloyd George's relation to political parties, his endeavours, with the help of Mr. Churchill, to re-organise them in his own interest, and his efforts to provide himself with finances for that purpose. Many Liberals cannot help regarding it as one of the least satisfactory chapters in his career.

I

Early in 1919 some well-meant efforts were made to reconcile Coalition Liberals with genuine Liberals—if I may be allowed to distinguish them so. But the Coalitionists declined to pledge themselves not to oppose Liberal candidates selected by properly constituted Liberal Associations, and Mr. Lloyd George promptly killed the suggestion by supporting a strong Conservative against the Liberal candidate at the West Leyton bye-election. The result of that election did not appear to encourage the Coalitionist idea.[1] Schemes, nevertheless, for a new birth in politics went on. In July 1919 Mr. Churchill, after a significant visit to Criccieth, announced that the democratic forces in Conservatism and the patriotic forces in Liberalism could no longer be kept apart, and heralded the formation of a Central Combination in which Party and its evils would be for evermore unknown. In the following winter another pioneering spirit, Lord Birkenhead, discovered that the Coalition was "invertebrate," with no clear policy on which its members were agreed. Fusion became a popular term—more popular than reunion. A National Party was suggested; but it appeared that there was a Grand Council somewhere already in possession of that patriotic name. The new Combination had a bad Press; but its advocates continued to recommend it. In March 1920 Mr. Lloyd George convened the Coalition Liberals and invited discussion on projects of fusion. National Democratic would perhaps do for a title, as the simple term National was already engaged. A Liberal National Democratic Wing and a Unionist National Democratic Wing might enfold all nationally-minded people. A "thorough and efficient organisation" was somehow or other to be created. Closer co-operation was essential among the followers of the Government, or else anarchy would submerge the world.

[1] In spite of the "coupon" Mr. Newbould converted a Coalition majority of 5,668 into a Liberal majority of 2,019.

These suggestions were not altogether well received, even by Mr. Lloyd George's supporters. Mr. Asquith was perhaps pardonably distrustful. There was some talk about fusion " with a very big capital F." There was even some talk about " organised insincerity," which the Prime Minister could not understand. The *Times* doubted whether Mr. Lloyd George had ever been a genuine Liberal, and pointed out that many Liberals were turning towards Labour, simply because they could not find in Mr. Lloyd George and his associates the clear principles or the straightforward honesty which they desired. Mr. Bonar Law more cautiously confined himself to saying that something must be done. In May 1920 the General Committee of the National Liberal Federation pointedly declined Mr. Lloyd George's invitation to co-operate more closely with the Conservative Party, after an unfortunate attempt by certain Coalitionists to make disunion and disorder there. Lord Birkenhead was hurt that his views should not prevail in the National Liberal Federation, and Mr. Lloyd George grieved audibly over dissensions which he had done more than any man knew to avert. Dr. Macnamara, with less restraint but possibly more candour, denounced Liberals who rejected Mr. Lloyd George's scheme of fusion with Conservatives, as " utterly narrow, bitter, disgruntled partisans . . . nagging, carping, gibeing, booing," while the tide of human affairs passed them by. Meanwhile, as the *Observer* noted, Mr. Lloyd George had crossed the Rubicon.

In December 1920 he was the guest of the Constitutional Club, and spoke to them as the Constitutional Club would desire. Conservative Members —one in particular, who had been an Assistant Director of the Propellant Branch of the Ministry of Munitions and afterwards a Controller of Oils and Fats—began to see that Mr. Lloyd George was very close to them in sympathy, " although he still felt a kind of necessity to call himself a Liberal." Sir William Joynson-Hicks declared that, passing up and down the country, he could discover practically no trace of the Coalition Liberal Party. Early in 1921 Captain Guest, a Coalition Liberal Whip who had already announced that he had " burnt his boats," appeared with a fresh plan— Consultative Councils—for getting Liberals to vote for Tories. In March Mr. Lloyd George delivered a fierce attack on Socialism. It meant " the overthrow of everything." It would tear up the orchard, " to plant the wild and poisonous berries of Karl Marxism." [1] The Independent Liberals represented nothing. The only hope for the country was to close the ranks of the anti-revolutionary party. The *Observer* unkindly remarked that, if Mr. Lloyd George was to secure any Liberal support in the constituencies, he must prove his Liberalism as well as assert it. But Mr. Lloyd George was just then more bent on securing support from the Conservative Party. Lord Derby, with an almost embarrassing wealth of metaphor, welcomed him

[1] See the *Times* of March 24, 1921.

publicly as their " newest recruit." He had found
the right haven at last. " A reformed poacher
made the best gamekeeper." And Mr. Lloyd
George explained, with unusual coyness, that co-
operation rather than conversion was the more
convenient term to use. One prominent Coalition
Liberal was unable to discover in Liberal principles
anything beyond a question of personal ascendency
and party funds. Another could not understand
why genuine Liberals could not love their neigh-
bours as themselves. But clearer-headed politicians
fixed their eyes on Mr. Lloyd George's actions and
bluntly refused to put their trust in him.

For a year or two the fusionist farce went on.
The Prime Minister, speaking to a Welsh audience
in July 1921, explained that it was only because he
wanted to save Liberalism that he had become a
recruit to the Conservative Party. The old party
system was passing away: only the Coalition on
one side and Labour on the other side would
survive.[1]

" Away with faction," cried one of his followers, " away
with sectionalism, away with the self-centred demands of
groups, and inscribe upon your banners the welfare of the
whole people! Is that possible? Is it practicable? Well if it
is practicable, it is—Coalition."

Unhappily, as the last year of Mr. Lloyd George's
Government proceeded, it became clearer every
day that these ideals were not practicable at all.

[1] This utterance caused comment, and the *Daily Chronicle*
was employed to explain it away (July 7, 1921).

Deeper and deeper murmurs arose from the Conservative Party. The *Morning Post* found that the Coalition had all the vicious elements of partisanship without its compensating advantages. Sir George Younger, the chief representative of the Conservative organisation, was credited with sentiments which no well-disciplined Coalitionist could repeat. At the end of 1921 the " inner Cabinet," a body unknown except in Mr. Lloyd George's singular Administration, a little group of political augurs—one might almost say, with respect, political conspirators—among whom the Prime Minister, Lord Birkenhead and Mr. Churchill had come to play the leading parts, decided to precipitate a General Election.[1] The Coalition was evidently drifting on the rocks. And then Sir George Younger boldly came out with the surprising declaration that a sudden Election would be not only pure opportunism, but a complete betrayal of Conservative interests. He refused to take any responsibility for an appeal to the country at a time when industry was gravely depressed, when unemployment was alarmingly high, economy still uneffected, and the promises of the Coalition Government still unredeemed.

Sir George Younger's defiance was a political event. It was the first open check given to the

---

[1] It is impossible to doubt this in view of the statements made on January 3, 5, 11 and 16, 1922, by the *Daily Chronicle*. See also the *Times* of December 30, 1921, and January 12 and 23, 1922.

16

dictatorship of Mr. Lloyd George. And its importance was emphasised when, after angry protests
from Coalition Liberals, the Prime Minister surrendered to it. He too had burnt his boats, and
knew he could not live without Conservative support. He suddenly discovered that the talk about a
General Election had all been a mistake.

"Who started it ? I did not. I never started the idea."

The statement was curious, as Mr. Lloyd George's
principal organ had announced the idea in large
type. The plan for an immediate Dissolution
was abandoned. But the rift in the Coalition
widened every day. While Mr. Lloyd George still
assured his special following that it would be
"fatal" to return to the old party conflicts, Sir
George Younger talked of "a bill of divorcement"
between Liberals and Tories with a familiarity
which shocked Lord Birkenhead. There were re-
marks about the Cabin Boy seizing the helm. The
helm itself wobbled in an alarming manner. There
were threats of resignation from Mr. Lloyd George
and assurances of devotion from the Unionist
leaders. There was a diplomatic retirement to the
hills of Criccieth while the friends of the Coalition
laboured to avert a split. Mr. Lloyd George, who
had entertained the idea of drawing after him the
greater part of the Conservative Party and leaving
the rest to shift for themselves, was compelled to
realise that, if he resigned, the Conservative leaders
would make up their minds to do without him, and

that the Conservatives as a whole would not allow him to break up their party as he had broken up his own.

II

While the fortunes of the Coalition were in this delicate condition, one curious episode threw a strong light on the system of Cabinet Government which Mr. Lloyd George had set up. Mr. Montagu, the Secretary for India, had thought it his duty to take steps of an unusual nature to thwart the policy of some of his own colleagues upon Eastern questions, and Mr. Lloyd George had been compelled to ask for Mr. Montagu's resignation. The latter retorted by publicly pouring scorn on the Prime Minister's " grotesque " pretence that in the Coalition Government any such thing as collective Cabinet responsibility existed.

" The head of our Government at the present moment is a Prime Minister of great if eccentric genius, whose contributions to the well-being of his country and of the world have been so well advertised as to require no stress from me, whose achievements are so well known, but who has demanded the price which it is within the power of every genius to demand—and that price has been the total, complete, absolute disappearance of the doctrine of Cabinet responsibility ever since he formed his Government." [1]

It is not perhaps a very clear indication of genius to destroy the Cabinet system in this country. But Mr. Montagu's singular comments on his leader did not add to the credit which the Cabinet retained.

[1] See the *Manchester Guardian* of March 13, 1922.

From such perplexing questions Mr. Lloyd George escaped in April 1922 to the Conference at Genoa, carrying with him some rather tepid encouragements from the House of Commons. Mr. Bonar Law, who was no longer in office, took occasion to observe that some people were inclined to " overdeify " the Prime Minister as an electioneering agent. Lord Hugh Cecil went even further in candour :

" I am quite sure that no Prime Minister could be so bad as the present Prime Minister, and that so long as he is Prime Minister the condition of the country will go on getting worse and worse, as it has gone on getting worse and worse ever since the Armistice." [1]

It was evident that the Coalition's life was ebbing out. Mr. Lloyd George brought back no triumphs from abroad, and the *Manchester Guardian's* singular efforts to defend him produced a remarkable protest from Mr. Ramsay Muir :

" During the last two years Mr. Lloyd George has been trying to wriggle out of the consequences of his election promises and of the action which followed from them. But he has never frankly confessed that a disastrous blunder was made, which has to be repaired. He has gone on assuming that the treaty must be maintained, but has tried, with immense ingenuity, in a long series of futile secret conclaves, to manœuvre France into accepting less than she believes to be her right. The result is that France has been more and more alienated. . . . There is only one way of escaping from this terrible *impasse*. It is by substituting plain dealing for slimness." [2]

---

[1] See *Parliamentary Debates*, April 3 and 5, 1922.

[2] See the *Manchester Guardian*, May 24, 1922. A valuable letter from Mr. Ramsay Muir, protesting against the *Guardian's* attacks upon Lord Grey and its attempts to force Mr. Lloyd George into the position of Liberal leader, will be found in the *Manchester Guardian* of February 16, 1922.

Mr. Lloyd George was losing caste all round. The Conservative murmurings grew still louder. In June a large group of Conservative Peers and Members of Parliament published their opinion that " to drift further with ever-changing policies must quickly produce chaos, disaster and ruin." In September Mr. Lloyd George's deplorable blunders in Eastern policy made the crisis among his followers acute. The *Spectator* begged responsible men to " get together " and to convince the Prime Minister of the need of resignation. The *Observer*, which had often defended him, declared that the Prime Minister had " hopelessly outstayed his luck." Mr. Lloyd George still relied on his personal influence with the Conservative leaders. But the foundations of his power were slipping away. His inefficiency as a Minister was now widely admitted. His untrustworthiness as a leader only a few of his followers would deny. The vast Parliamentary majority whom he had nominated would no longer support him. Conservative Under-Secretaries rebelled and resigned. Mr. Baldwin confessed that the " dynamic force " which had smashed the Liberal Party to pieces, would certainly, unless someone restrained it, smash the Conservative Party also. Mr. Bonar Law, returning to active politics after some months of absence, was persuaded to support Mr. Baldwin's view. And, in spite of Mr. Chamberlain's efforts to dissuade them, the Conservative Party decided to part company with Mr. Lloyd George. A few distinguished and typical Tories, Lord Balfour, Lord Birkenhead, Lord Lee and Lord Crawford, were among those who protested against the decision. Their loyalty to a falling leader was honourable and kindly.[1] But if a man is to be judged by the company he keeps, it was hardly a proof that Mr. Lloyd George was entitled to the confidence of the Liberal Party. The *Morning Post* represented more faithfully the bulk of Conservative opinion. It had deplored the " complacency " of Mr. Bonar Law. And it had no hesitation in welcoming the change: [2]

"Now that the chains of the Coalition are broken, we might pause, at least, to draw a deep breath of relief and thankfulness."

The *Times* declared that never in living memory had the fall of a British Government evoked less public regret. Journalists indeed of all opinions testified that Mr. Lloyd George's Government fell unhonoured and unwept. No Minister had ever set himself so steadily to court the influence of newspapers. No Minister perhaps, by the end of his Administration, ever forfeited more completely even newspaper support.

III

One last point in the Coalition Government's history attracted and requires attention—its method

[1] This of course was equally true of Mr. Austen Chamberlain, one of the most loyal and scrupulous of public men.
[2] See the *Morning Post* of October 9 and 20, 1922.

of collecting party funds. But it would not be fair to hold the Conservatives responsible for the steps taken, by the Coalition Liberal Whips with the Prime Minister's authority, to build up a political fund, apparently neither Liberal nor Conservative, but wholly under Mr. Lloyd George's personal control. This is a disturbing incident, not honourable to Liberal traditions, and no man who values clean-handed politics ought to shut his eyes and pass it by. The whole question of the collection of money for party purposes is a difficult problem. Political organisation involves expense, though much more might still be done to limit it. So long as political parties exist, party managers will have to find means to maintain them, to organise their forces and their propaganda, to contribute to the cost of fighting expensive and unpromising contests. With the vast increase of the electorate the need of money for these purposes increases also, and it would not be fair to blame either those who give or those who take it, provided that public motives and decent standards are maintained. It is, as matters stand, both reasonable and necessary that money should be subscribed by men who can afford it, to support the party to which they belong. And it is inevitable that gifts of this kind should establish some claim on those who dispense the honours of the State. Money contributions, after all, are sometimes the only form of effective service which men of sincere and genuine convictions can contribute to the cause which they espouse.

But while this system is at present difficult to get rid of, it is obviously open to abuse. And the more it is wrapped up in secrecy, the more unsatisfactory it becomes. It would be a long step towards purity in politics if every contribution made to party funds had to be acknowledged in published and audited accounts; and there is no reason except a bad tradition why that should not be done. To administer such a system well Party Whips with a strong sense of fitness and of character are needed, and Prime Ministers with high standards and stiff backs. In Mr. Gladstone's day there was still a tradition of dignity and discrimination. Merit and service still counted for much in the award of political honours. Since then the practice has been laxer. Rich men with few qualifications except riches have found it easier to secure distinctions— Baronies no longer rare, Privy Councillorships unillumined by counsel, Baronetcies and Knighthoods only less numerous than the sands on the sea-shore. Under Mr. Asquith this laxity to some extent increased. The Master of Elibank, for instance, was hard pressed for funds to popularise Mr. Lloyd George's Budget. He had to provide in 1910 for two General Elections in quick succession, to fight the expenditure of the Tariff Reform League and the powerful resources of a Landed and a Liquor interest both highly alarmed by Liberal finance. And it is possible that in his hours of anguish he anticipated too exuberantly the favours of the Crown. That example Mr. Lloyd George was only

too ready to follow and to carry to lengths un-
dreamed of yet. But between the two cases there
was this difference. The Master of Elibank was
working single-heartedly for the interests of his
party. Mr. Lloyd George in this matter was working
for his own.

In considering Mr. Lloyd George's action, however, one point should not be forgotten. He has
never sought or accepted distinctions of this nature
for himself. It was no desire for rank or gain which
brought him into politics or kept him in the public
service. Power and political fame have been his
objects. His ambitions have been often large and
not ignoble in conception, if woefully disappointing
when he came to work them out. And there is this
further point to be remembered also, that for many
years in Parliament he was a poor man. It is only
poor men who fully realise—taught sometimes by
a hard experience—the great advantages which in
politics the command of money can confer. These
considerations should have their weight. But they
cannot, after all, excuse the methods by which
Mr. Lloyd George, when Prime Minister, set to
work to accumulate the largest political fund on
record, not for the benefit of any definite principles
or party, but to secure his own position in public
life. The methods of collection were sometimes
astonishingly crude. The end of the War offered
of course an exceptional opportunity for a shower
of honours, whether earned or purchased, deserved
or undeserved. There were not only very many

men who had richly merited the distinctions given them. There were many who, by no fault but the chance of circumstance, had made great fortunes out of the public needs. Their purses were full. Their political principles perhaps were fluid. Their desire for social recognition may have been easy to arouse. And it is clear that Mr. Lloyd George's agents set to work to stimulate and to reward it with a systematic cynicism never practised to the same extent before. The Conservatives had apparently no part in the transactions which followed—transactions at times almost incredible even to those who know something of the weaker sides of public life. The Chief Coalition Liberal Whips, Captain Guest and his successor Mr. McCurdy, must, it seems, share the main responsibility between them.[1] They had junior Whips in their offices, and the junior Whips had their correspondents or agents, and the agents had—it is difficult to choose the term exactly, but something analogous to travellers or touts. At each stage of the proceedings, no doubt, there were details left to the subordinates to deal with, details on which a Chief Whip would not ask for information, and with which a Prime Minister could have no concern. It is always easier to disavow what one has not been told. But the money came to the Chief Whip, and the Chief Whip presented his list to the Prime Minister, and the Prime Minister recommended

---

[1] Captain Guest was Mr. Lloyd George's Chief Whip from 1917 to 1921; Mr. McCurdy succeeded him in the post.

the applicants for honours and took undisputed control of the fund which accrued.

Some light has already been thrown by the Press upon the methods adopted. I will confine myself to facts already published, and not apparently disputed. But they must be taken as samples only of what was widely going on. A systematic search, it seems, began for gentlemen who would pay handsomely for " honours." Names were collected of men known to have made fortunes in war-time: in most busy industrial centres there were such men to be found. Relations were gradually established with them, through friends or acquaintances or local lawyers, or by visits from the travellers of the Ministerial firm. Sometimes the travellers were tactful, the feelers put forth comparatively delicate:

> " DEAR SIR,
> " I am requested to place before you a social matter of a very confidential nature which it is thought may be of interest to you. Will you kindly let me know whether you can suggest a meeting within the next few days in London or elsewhere ? "

Sometimes they went to work more briskly:

> " A Mr. —— came to see me at my office and inquired whether I would contribute the sum of £14,000 to a Party Fund raised to combat Bolshevism and receive a Knighthood."

Sometimes, it seems, a Cabinet Minister was good enough to say a word to stimulate the traffic.

> " On the 13th of May, 1922," writes a well-known Dublin gentleman, " I received a letter, dated the 12th, from a Cabinet Minister, asking me to come and see him in London

on the 15th. I went to London and saw him in the House of Commons.

"He informed me I was being recommended by him for a Knighthood at the Birthday Honours, and to make certain of it I would require to put £5,000 to a certain fund." [1]

One gentleman was given to understand that the price for a Knighthood was £5,000 with merit, but without merit double that or more. Baronetcies ranged in price from £20,000 to £40,000. Merit might reduce the price perhaps; but for profiteers as a whole no "nonsense about merit" was permitted to interfere with trade. Peerages were naturally dearer. But the number offered was not on that account restricted, nor was there any censorious sifting of candidates willing to subscribe. In 1922 Sir William Vestey was recommended for a Barony. He had removed his very lucrative business from this country during the War, and had domiciled himself in the Argentine Republic, to avoid paying British taxation.[2] That seemed an inadequate reason for his passing, on Mr. Lloyd George's recommendation, into the House of Lords. In the same year a peerage was awarded to Sir Joseph Robinson, a gentleman known in connection with South African mines. There were sharp and repeated protests from men familiar with Sir Joseph Robinson's record. One of them, Lord Buxton, made a statement in the House of Lords which may suffice:

[1] For the letters noted here, see the *Morning Post* of August 28 and 29, September 6, 11 and 18, 1922.

[2] See Lord Banbury's letter in the *Morning Post* of June 17, 1922.

" I will undertake to say that no single person in the Union, white or black, considered that either by his services or by his record he deserved this honour. When it was announced in the Press, so far as I can learn, it was received with universal astonishment and mystification; I will not use a stronger or uglier word." [1]

In the end Sir Joseph Robinson wrote to the Prime Minister that he would rather not have the peerage if there was so much feeling about it. He denied that he had paid for the offer; there were cases apparently of payment by results. Lord Carson, on the evidence of papers seen by him in Chambers, spoke of " a regular brokerage " for honours. Other men of standing have spoken from personal knowledge of the traffic which went on. There is little doubt that it was both unblushing and widespread. In June 1922 Mr. Lloyd George refused to allow an inquiry into the subject. In July, under pressure, he agreed to the appointment of a Royal Commission, to inquire, not into the scandals revealed, but into " the procedure to be adopted in future." It was the best way of stopping inquiry into the scandals of the past. All that summer he must have been well aware that Coalition support was slipping from him, and that the contributions which his agents were busily collecting were being given for no particular principle or party, but simply for the Prime Minister to deal with as he pleased. Before the Coalition ended, it is understood that a fund not far short of £1½ million had

[1] See *Parliamentary Debates* (Lords) June 22 and 29, 1922. Lord Harris' observations also should be noted.

been secured.[1] It is not true to say that in this matter Mr. Lloyd George and his Whips acted only as their predecessors had acted before. The methods employed were quite unprecedented. So were the uses to which the money has been put. No party which allows a single politician to use a fund collected in this fashion to purchase personal support for himself, to pay for candidates who will advocate his leadership, and for agencies and publications to advance his interests, can hope to escape some loss of popular esteem. Is it for the honour of British politics that such methods should be condoned or repeated, or that men who so exploit the trust reposed in them by Crown and nation should again occupy a high place in public life?

IV

On the sudden collapse of the Coalition Mr. Lloyd George found himself uncomfortably lonely. Six years of unequalled power and opportunity had left him distrusted on all sides, without a Government, a majority or a party at his back. He had deserted and proscribed his old colleagues. He had succeeded in dividing his new ones. He had done his best to form a new party out of a small number of Liberals attached to his fortunes and a large number of Conservatives and colourless

---

[1] It is now known that within a few years the fund had grown by fortunate investment to a total of nearly £3 millions. (See later, p. 286.)

cross-bench-men, who were persuaded that his political acuteness would help them into Parliament or establish them in power. But, though some distinguished individuals held by him, it was plain that the great bulk of the Conservatives were weary of Mr. Lloyd George's rule, and it was equally plain that the great bulk of Liberals would have nothing to say to Coalitionist schemes. For some months the ex-Prime Minister had no choice beyond a doubtful isolation. The change in his position was extraordinary. His hold on Parliament had gone. He had been almost omnipotent in the House of Commons: he could now almost be ignored. And while Conservatives and Liberals rejected him, the Labour Party, reinforced by many a young Liberal idealist whom he had disillusioned, were not prepared to accept him as an ally. But some of them could not quite resist the temptation to glance over their shoulders at the best-advertised politician of the day, who was always putting out feelers in the direction of Socialist experiments, and always as ready as any Socialist to deal royally with public funds.

There must have been some serious self-examination in the little group of Parliamentary followers whom the General Election of 1922 had left to Mr. Lloyd George. They had returned only fifty-five strong—to such a figure had four years of their leader's administration reduced the most overwhelming majority of modern times. There were among them men of Liberal instincts and traditions, who had been drawn half-unwillingly into compromising schemes, who had never liked, though they had supported, a foreign policy of bluster and intrigue, the re-establishment of Protection in trade, and violent measures of coercion in Ireland. There were others who for years past had been drifting away from Liberal opinions, who depended on Conservative support in their constituencies, and had been confidently expecting to find their future in a fusion with the Conservative Party. It was inevitable, as Mr. Lloyd George confided to a newspaper, that they should feel themselves in an " embarrassing and even desperate situation." For they did not all share their leader's adroitness in adapting themselves to the vicissitudes of public life.

It may be allowable to mention one or two names. Captain Guest had been a Chief Whip and a Secretary of State in Mr. Lloyd George's Administration. In 1923 he was still sighing for " a coalition of all moderate-minded men," and regarding Liberalism as " a political expression " best fitted for " the left wing of a great national party." In 1924 he felt himself obliged to support the " stable and orderly progress " of Mr. Baldwin's Government, and to that obligation he has since consistently adhered. No one will question Captain Guest's right to support the Conservative Administration. But to Liberals of an older school it seemed inappropriate that he should at the same time help to vote Mr. Lloyd George into the Chairmanship of the Liberal Parliamentary Party. As time passed and Captain Guest voted steadily in the Conservative lobby, his devotion to Mr. Lloyd George as Liberal leader became embarrassing even to Mr. Lloyd George himself. And the Election of 1929 revealed the painful spectacle of Captain Guest standing as a Liberal candidate in Bristol, supported apparently by Mr. Lloyd George's Chief Whip, but thrown over at the last moment by a leader for whose advancement he had sacrificed a good deal that Liberals respect. His plaint, indeed, must touch our hearts:

" On April 19 Sir Robert Hutchison wrote to me, presumably with Mr. Lloyd George's approval, ' I look on you as the Liberal member for North Bristol.' On May 13 Mr. Lloyd George writes to my opponent, ' I and my colleagues will welcome you to our counsels.' If Mr. Lloyd George had desired to make Liberalism ridiculous in Bristol he could not have taken a better course."

Possibly in rendering Liberalism ridiculous Captain Guest must share the responsibility with his chief. But in a world where it is never too late to find salvation, he has drawn at last, from his special experience, two conclusions which few politicians will dispute—first, that Mr. Lloyd George's fund is not a source of strength to the Liberal Party, and secondly, that Mr. Lloyd George's leadership inspires no confidence in Liberals or in anybody else.[1]

Sir Robert Hutchison is another Liberal whose relations to his Conservative constituents illustrate

[1] See his letter in the *Times*, of June 4 1929.

17

the embarrassments in which Mr. Lloyd George's leadership is apt to land his friends. In March 1927 Sir Robert Hutchison was heckled by Conservative supporters at Montrose. He explained that as Liberal Whip he had voted for " about seventy per cent." of the Conservative Government's measures. And when asked whether he was " a Constitutionalist really or a Liberal "—Constitutionalist is a polite term for Conservative—he escaped from the dilemma by bravely answering " Both." [1] Mr. Winston Churchill, one of Mr. Lloyd George's principal lieutenants, has now definitely returned to older attachments, but over the anti-Socialist wing of Mr. Lloyd George's following he long exercised a fascination which occasions no surprise. Sir Edward Hilton Young and Sir Hamar Greenwood, both Coalition Ministers, the latter closely associated with the triumphs of the Black-and-Tans,[2] have both found salvation and advancement in the same capacious camp. Lord Melchett,[3] an active adherent once of Mr. Asquith, then an active supporter of Mr. Lloyd George, then an active reconciler of Liberal differences, to whose good offices Mr. Lloyd George at one time owed much, has been led to the fold of the Conservative Party by considerations which

[1] See the *Montrose Review* for March 25, 1927.

[2] Sir H. Greenwood was in 1929 recommended for a Peerage by the Conservative leader.

[3] An old colleague of Sir A. Mond at the Free Trade Union may be permitted to regret, with more courtesy than Mr. Lloyd George, the vicissitudes which his views have undergone.

Mr. Lloyd George has described in a fashion of his own. Dr. Addison, another Coalition Minister, has passed into the ranks of Labour. And of others it is here unnecessary to speak. These men, it would seem, had no reason for holding together in politics except their attachment to the fortunes of their leader; and when those fortunes failed to prosper, their faith in their leader had perhaps already disappeared. Mr. Lloyd George's comments when deserted by these colleagues at different moments need not be repeated. But it is at times a little melancholy to ponder on the sacrifices required of one's friends by their careers.

There is more interest and more humour to be found in Mr. Lloyd George's efforts, when the Conservatives threw him over, to secure again a place as leader in the Liberal ranks. For a time, it is clear, he was a little uncertain whether that course would appeal to him or not. In November 1922 he was still asserting that Coalition Liberals and Coalition Tories stood " for the clear-headed vision of the morning "—whatever that eloquent phrase might mean. Even after the General Election of 1922 he was still hoping that " moderate men of progressive outlook in all parties " would see the wisdom of acting together. For such men, it was inferred, a leader, equally fit for all moderate parties, would be forthcoming when the call arose. But the call was long in coming. Moderate men, and immoderate men also, had the bad taste to look for a leader elsewhere. In March 1923 Mr.

Lloyd George was talking tentatively about Liberal unity, but not in the mood of " suppliants for shelter or beggars for alms." He was still harping on the Coalition's merits. And he was prepared to place the National Liberal record—threats and bluff in Turkey, Black-and-Tans in Ireland, Safeguarding and all the rest—" side by side with that of any Liberal Government that ever existed," and to be " proud of the comparison " too. There was evidently still room for some change of heart. But as time passed it became apparent that this tone of self-righteous defiance would not do. Those of Mr. Lloyd George's followers who did not wish to join the Conservative Party realised the need of getting back into the ranks of Liberalism if they were to remain in public life at all. A very natural desire for unity made itself felt among Liberals in the country, especially among Liberals who had not studied very closely the peculiar methods of Mr. Lloyd George. Prominent Coalitionists began to develop the theory that only petty and personal jealousies could prevent the reunion of ancient friends. Mr. Lloyd George, yielding to pressure, lowered his note. He took to appealing to Liberals not to sling " poisoned arrows " at each other: the poisoned arrows were the recollection of the Coalition's ways. He found he had no personal aims, no thought of seeking leadership. All he wanted was a programme to unite them: the passion for programmes not even adversity could quench.

There was an interlude of doubt. Fusion as a watchword had given place to reunion. But men of experience pointed out that, where people differed deeply on questions which went to the root of policy and conduct, unity could not be manufactured in a moment by gestures or phrases or secret agreements. Some felt that real unity depended upon confidence, and that confidence, in view of Mr. Lloyd George's record, must be a plant of slow and tender growth. There were disconcerting episodes in the summer of 1923. On one vital Liberal issue in Parliament it was found that half the National Liberals present, on another that all the National Liberals present, preferred to vote in the Tory lobby. A National Liberal was unseated at Berwick. His wife came forward as a Conservative, to hold the seat till a National Liberal could be returned again. There were still grounds for suspecting that the ex-Prime Minister regarded reunion chiefly as a stepping-stone to some fresh orientation of parties under his own control. Sir John Simon pointed out with fairness and courtesy two serious difficulties in the way of cordial co-operation: first, the existence side by side with Liberalism of a separate National Liberal Organisation with a separate fighting fund, and secondly, the elements of instability and uncertainty in the political genius of Mr. Lloyd George. But before the year 1923 was over doubting Liberals were drawn together by the mistakes of their political opponents. Mr. Baldwin suddenly resolved to plunge into Protection. Mr. Lloyd George, uncomfortably committed to schemes of Safeguarding and Imperial Preference, may have had some anxious moments in balancing interests. But he decided to come down upon the Free Trade side. And on that issue the Liberals returned to Parliament, not strong enough, indeed, to form a Government themselves, but strong enough to decide the destinies of any Government formed by other parties in the House of Commons.

CHAPTER VII

MR. LLOYD GEORGE AND THE LIBERAL PARTY

With the year 1924 the latest chapter opened in Mr. Lloyd George's varied career. The Prodigal had at last returned. He brought a subdued and half-hearted following with him. And it is to be feared that, in place of the husks of repentance, he brought an undue consciousness of ill-gotten wealth. Still once again in 1924 it seemed as if Liberal unity might be re-established. And once again Mr. Lloyd George destroyed that prospect by his incurable habit of intrigue. He was now in partnership again with his old colleagues, men whom, all the world knows, he could trust. They were men, their leaders especially, conspicuously free from personal rancours. Mr. Asquith's magnanimity was admittedly one of his greatest qualities. And Lord Grey's single-minded indifference to every kind of personal ambition is a commonplace of our public life. Their principal colleagues were men of the same stamp. And the suggestion, so often repeated in Mr. Lloyd George's interest, that the only consideration which prevents Liberals from accepting his leadership is a morbid love for venomous vendettas, must be known,

263

even to those who make it, to be as foolish as it is insincere.

" We differed very deeply," Lord Grey has said, " from those Liberals who were in the Coalition Government. They were not mere differences of policy, they were differences which concerned the honour and reputation of the British Government both at home and abroad. They were differences which affected the standard of public life in this country." [1]

But when Mr. Lloyd George returned to the Liberals on the Free Trade issue, a determined effort was made by the Party leaders to lay aside differences and to start afresh. They were always ready to work with Mr. Lloyd George if they found he could be trusted. But unhappily a very short experience showed once more that that condition could not be attained.

I

As early as April 1924 there was a talk of revolt against Mr. Asquith's leadership. Mr. Lloyd George then would not hear the word revolt mentioned. It was " absolutely untrue." Differences were merely signs of vigour, proofs that Liberals were human beings. But in spite of such assurances it soon became clear that Mr. Lloyd George was as determined as ever to play for his own hand. The first and most obvious source of trouble was the continuance of his separate political fund, worked by his personal agents to promote his individual interests. For the General Election of 1923 Mr. Lloyd George, anxious

[1] See the *Times* of December 14, 1926.

to be re-admitted to the Liberal Party, had supplied
some £100,000,[1] and the Liberal organisers, of
whom Lord Gladstone was the chief, had placed all
the resources they had at the disposal of the united
party. But the following year found the Liberal
finances seriously reduced. The Parliamentary position was precarious. It was necessary to prepare for
another Election. And at this juncture Mr. Lloyd
George showed a strange unreadiness to help. He
had secured his reunion with the party. He would
only finance it now on his own terms. From
January to October 1924 the Liberal organisers and
Liberal leaders pressed upon him the urgency of the
situation, the vital need of securing Liberal candidates and the means to enable them to fight. Month
after month Mr. Lloyd George procrastinated. He
said the Liberal organisation was bad. So Sir Alfred
Mond was called in to examine it in his interests, and
Sir Alfred recommended that Liberal candidates
should be got into the field without delay. Still Mr.
Lloyd George held back. He even expressed the
view that too many Liberal candidates were not desirable: three hundred, for six hundred seats, would
be enough. It was not till the Dissolution was announced that he was prevailed on to contribute to
the needs of the party. He then agreed to give
£50,000, but no more, out of the very large funds at
his disposal. His tactics had gone far to ruin the

[1] £90,000 was paid to Liberal Headquarters, and it is understood that £10,000 more was spent in Wales. These figures are
sometimes given incorrectly still.

chances of his friends. Lord Gladstone, whose fairness and sincerity are as undeniable as his knowledge of the circumstances, summed the position up:

" We had loyally and consistently consulted Mr. Lloyd George. We did everything we could to meet his wishes and suggestions as regards his own position in the party, some awkward difficulties in Wales, disputes about ' sectional ' rival candidatures in certain constituencies, and the condition of the party organisation. We were acting under and for reunion in the fullest sense of the word. We gave everything we had to the united party. We told him all the facts in the electoral position. Mr. Lloyd George for nine precious months withheld the necessary guarantee." [1]

It may be argued that a man with a million or two to dispose of is entitled to study his own interests. But Mr. Lloyd George's conduct inevitably weakened the confidence of the colleagues whom he had rejoined.

Disputes about money always seem undignified. Yet in politics, as in all campaigning, money means the sinews of war. And the experience of 1924 convinced many responsible Liberals that Mr. Lloyd George's aim was not so much to reunite the Liberal Party, as to make himself, with his fund and his agents, an independent political force. He would work with the Liberals if they accepted his dictation. But he was equally ready to work, it was shrewdly suspected, with any other party which would bring him back to power. The election of Mr. Lloyd George in Mr. Asquith's absence to lead the Liberals in the House of Commons—an election effected

[1] See Lord Gladstone's letter in the *Times* of June 11, 1926.

largely by ex-Coalitionist votes—did not tend to ease a difficult situation. A Radical Group was formed, to maintain the old traditions of Liberalism and perhaps to watch the new leader.

" The distinctive characteristic of the Radical Group," said their Chairman, Mr. Runciman, " was that they were not embarrassed by compromise in any direction, either right or left. They did not regard politics as a game, and they did not wish to arrive at understandings with their opponents for the compromise of their principles."

Mr. Lloyd George still protested his unreserved loyalty to Mr. Asquith. But his action during the session of 1924 had not been calculated to win the confidence of Mr. Asquith's followers and friends.

II

To re-establish himself in the favour of Liberals, Mr. Lloyd George fell back on his favourite resource —programmes. Apart from his duties as Parliamentary leader, he was known to be developing new policies of his own. In 1924 he presided over a Committee on the Coal question, and his Committee produced an interesting and valuable report on *Coal and Power*, with a view to providing the Liberal Party with a definite policy on that difficult subject. In 1925 another Committee, under his presidency— treated with equal friendliness by Lord Oxford [1]— published a large and elaborate scheme for rural land reform, which again showed a great deal of

[1] Mr. Asquith's acceptance of an Earldom was announced in January 1925.

work and contained valuable information and suggestions. Before the end of the year this was followed by a further Report, the Urban Report of the Land Inquiry Committee, also designed to provide the Liberal Party with a policy prepared under Mr. Lloyd George's auspices and financed by his fund. But interesting and useful as in many respects these land schemes were, they contained some doubtful and controversial features. And Liberals as a whole could not help feeling that definite plans on matters of importance, intended to be adopted as the policy of the party, ought not to be framed by independent Committees appointed and subsidised by a single man, and then imposed—it might almost be said foisted—on other Liberals who had not been consulted. It looked inevitably as if Mr. Lloyd George, while careful perhaps to secure some general assent from Lord Oxford, was working behind the backs of most of his colleagues, and trying to commit them to policies of his own.

Moreover, Liberal unity was the last thing which these new policies seemed likely to achieve. Certain features of the new land schemes bore a rather close resemblance to proposals put forward by the Socialist Party. And these features so alarmed some of Mr. Lloyd George's Coalitionist followers, that one of them, not the least valued, felt compelled to turn his back for ever on his Liberal friends.

" The position of the Liberal Party," wrote Sir Alfred Mond to Lord Oxford in January 1926, " has been steadily drifting from bad to worse. The unity which we have striven for, and which I did my best to promote, has, in fact, never been achieved, and all efforts to revivify and re-organise the Liberal forces have been rendered hopeless by the introduction by Mr. Lloyd George of a land policy which has produced a new profound cleavage and embarrassment in the Liberal ranks."

Other Liberals, of a stauncher breed and perhaps of steadier judgment, found grounds for criticism in the rural land report, in its sensational tone, its ill-considered finance, its pathetic belief in State interference, its needless multiplication of public officials— seven new authorities were to be created—a feature almost inseparable from Mr. Lloyd George's political panaceas.[1] Other Liberal critics again, while approving generally of the various projects which Mr. Lloyd George "sent whirling through the air," lamented the perilous economic doctrines which he seemed anxious to associate with his new crusade.

"There are disconcerting signs," wrote the *Nation*, " that the land question has become an obsession with him ; and he persists in giving his agitation the most eccentric and *bizarre* of turns, a turn, incidentally, in violent conflict with Liberal tradition. The keynote of every speech he makes is that we now import some £400 millions of foodstuffs, the greater part of which we ought to grow at home. . . . Indeed the gist of his message seems to be that to increase the size of the agricultural population and to free ourselves from dependence on imported food should be the supreme objectives of British statesmanship to-day."

The *Nation* was not alone in thinking it " appalling " that these loose and reactionary doctrines should be regarded as the authoritative expression of the

[1] Criticisms of this kind were made with great force and knowledge in a speech by Mr. Runciman at Devizes on November 21, 1925, and were widely repeated by other Liberals.

Liberal faith.[1] Many Liberals disliked Mr. Lloyd George's proposals and resented his attempts to "jump a claim." But again Lord Oxford and his colleagues did their best to prevent these methods from breaking up the party. They tried to compose the differences created, and to bring Mr. Lloyd George's schemes into line with Liberal ideas. The Liberal Candidates' Association, led by Mr. Pringle, a Liberal who had stood by his principles and worked strenuously for them all through the dark days when Mr. Lloyd George was trampling Liberalism underfoot, set itself to work out a land policy on which Liberals could agree. Mr. Lloyd George, who is quick to realise when opinion is turning against him, showed a readiness for compromise and consideration which he would have done better to show before. And a Land Conference called in London in February 1926 was able to arrive at some useful conclusions, and to outline a policy which Liberals who were neither Land Nationalisers nor Protectionists could reasonably combine to accept.

Meanwhile Mr. Lloyd George proceeded on his way. A special Land Campaign was launched on his initiative. Agents and advertisers in profusion were enlisted. The personal fund put forth its strength. Demonstrations were organised regardless of expense wherever Mr. Lloyd George went to speak upon the subject. Liberals making speeches on land reform,

[1] See *The Nation and the Athenæum* for February 20, 1926. I understand that the *Nation*, like other Liberal newspapers, has now passed under the influence of Mr. Lloyd George.

which had for years past been an object of Liberal policy, suddenly received unsolicited cheques from Mr. Lloyd George's fund,[1] intended perhaps to intimate that all land reformers were to enjoy his special patronage in future. But Liberals who remembered the recent history of Mr. Lloyd George's land taxes were inclined to deprecate and even to resent this ostentatious appropriation of the topic. Enterprising efforts were made by the Land and Nation League " to create an effective public opinion," with a view to removing injustices and anomalies in our land system. The *Times* printed one example of invitations sent to firms and individuals by the Press Department of the League:

" I write to ask your co-operation in this effort. Will you be good enough to write, for circulation to the newspapers, a short letter dealing if possible with one or more concrete cases of injustice within your knowledge? Alternatively, if you cannot find time for this, would you be prepared to sign a letter, drafted in this office and based upon information in our possession, to the same purpose? "

Yet even in these highly-modernised activities some old-fashioned Liberals found matter for complaint. The *Nation* committed itself to the opinion that " there could be no more wretched fate for the historic Liberal Party than that it should perish as the personal bodyguard of Mr. Lloyd George and as the publicity agent of his more esoteric doctrines." The land crusade, regarded as electioneering, did not

[1] In one case brought to the knowledge of the writer—there may well have been others—the unsolicited cheque was returned.

altogether prosper. There were indications that, considering the lavish expenditure, it was not found to pay. Mr. Lloyd George is not always very patient. Like other speculators, he seeks quick returns. The land revolution was presently allowed to fall into a secondary place among his programmes. New experts were called into consultation. A new panacea was prepared. And the whole apparatus of agents and advertisement, rendered possible by the resources of Mr. Lloyd George's fund, was switched on to another project, well worthy of study and attention, worthy indeed of something better than to be exploited for electioneering ends.

III

Mr. Lloyd George's fund had proved, since " reunion " was achieved, to be a fruitful source of trouble. His land schemes had been hardly more productive of peace. The third conspicuous example of his intention to pursue his own interests in politics, with little regard for the feelings of his colleagues, was his action at the time of the General Strike. It has become the custom for leading politicians who have served in Cabinets together, and who wish to guide their followers on points of difficulty when out of office, to meet in " Shadow Cabinets " or " Skeleton Cabinets " and to discuss the policy of their disembodied parties. Of the Liberal Shadow Cabinet Mr. Lloyd George was after 1923 a very prominent member, and if real unity were to be attained it was important that he should loyally support its collective opinion. He had ample opportunities of influencing that opinion from inside. But unhappily he can rarely be depended on to play the game. The great Strike of 1926, arising out of the trouble in the Coal-Mining industry, was the gravest crisis which this country had faced since the War. On May 1 the General Council of the Trades Union Congress decided to call a strike of vital services affecting some millions of workers, to hold up transport and supplies, and to dislocate the whole life of the nation. It was an attempt to coerce the community in the supposed interests of one great group of men. The Labour leaders, it is now widely admitted, showed themselves, in face of a dangerous situation, irresolute and ill-advised. The Government, whatever their previous errors, met a far-reaching threat with steadiness and patience. And most responsible Liberals felt bound to strengthen the Government's hands in resisting so serious a challenge to the State. " If it had succeeded," said Lord Oxford later, " Parliamentary Government would have been at an end."

" It was, as it seemed to me, the first duty of Liberalism not to parley and falter, not to wait upon events, but to condemn it root and branch with promptitude and with no uncertain voice."

At a meeting of the Liberal Shadow Cabinet held on May 3, in which Mr. Lloyd George took part, it was agreed that, however critical they might be of some

18

of the Government's actions during the Coal Dispute,
they must throw all their influence into resisting the anti-social pressure of a General Strike. Mr.
Lloyd George was believed to be a party to this decision, but he preferred to play a separate hand. On
the same day he made a curiously hesitating speech
in the House of Commons. He admitted, indeed,
that a General Strike was something very different
from an ordinary trade dispute. He agreed that it
struck " at the very root of democratic government."
But he then proceeded to qualify these opinions and
to divide the blame impartially between the Government and the strikers :

" I am not, therefore, going to express any opinion as to
whether under any given conditions you may have a general
strike, but I think it is a mistake at the present moment. I say
also that I think it was a very serious mistake on the part of
the Government to announce this morning that they would not
negotiate. They will be forced out of that position by circumstances. It is a mistake."

Lord Oxford and Lord Grey spoke out in clearer
tones. They both pleaded as strongly as Mr. Lloyd
George for a return at the first possible moment to
methods of negotiation and counsels of peace. But
they both declared in unmistakable language that
the General Strike must be ended first.

" We should have lost all sense of self-respect," said Lord
Oxford, " if we were to allow any section of the community at
its own will, and for whatever motives, to bring to a standstill
the industrial and social life of the whole nation."
" The issue now," said Lord Grey, " is not what the wages
of miners should be, but whether democratic Parliamentary
Government is to be overthrown."

Few Liberals were willing to exploit for party purposes the grave situation in which the country stood.

A few days later, on May 10, Lord Oxford called the Liberal Shadow Cabinet together, expecting the cordial co-operation of its members on a matter of principle which seemed beyond dispute. But Mr. Lloyd George, in a letter to the Liberal Whip, pointedly refused to attend the meeting, and dissociated himself in strong terms from the action of his colleagues. He attacked the Government in vehement language for "precipitate, unwarrantable and mischievous" action, and declared that he could not condemn the General Strike without condemning the Government, who were "equally, if not more, responsible."[1] It was not a letter designed to calm or help a dangerous situation. Its breach with the policy of the responsible Liberal leaders was deliberate and complete.

"We felt at the time," said Lord Grey, "that Mr. Lloyd George thought that the General Strike was going to last some time, that it was going to produce a great political upheaval, throwing everything into the melting-pot, and that he wanted to have his hands completely free, and thought it desirable that he should not be politically associated with us any more."

Was this view either mistaken or unfair? It was clear that Mr. Lloyd George was fishing already in

[1] See Mr. Lloyd George's letter to Sir Godfrey Collins dated May 10, 1926. He afterwards told the Manchester Reform Club (June 5) that he had been refused an opportunity of placing his views before his colleagues.

troubled waters. The General Strike was at its
height. The nation, though quite ready to be generous to the miners, was determined not to surrender to
the threat of force. Yet at that moment he not only
separated himself ostentatiously from his colleagues, but he published broadcast in the United
States an alarmist and sensational message, dwelling
on the faults of the British Government and the
black outlook for British trade. The article was not
without balancing and qualifying phrases, suggesting some uncertainty of mind or aim. But the tone
was on the whole as discouraging as it well could be.
No one could say how long the strike would go on.
If all the trade unions joined in, God only knew what
would happen. If the Government surrendered to
force, not even God knew what would follow. The
Government must preserve order and maintain
essential services. But the unions were strong and
well-disciplined, and Mr. Lloyd George at any rate
did not believe that they would readily desert their
leaders. The strikers could not win if the nation
held out; but the nation would soon become worried
about its vanishing trade:

" If the Government adheres to its resolve not to enter into
any further discussions for settlement unless the strike is first of
all called off, the conflict will inevitably go on, day after day,
week after week, until some unforeseen event happens."

For all that, there had been so far no bloodshed.
And Mr. Lloyd George had faith in British coolness
and in the British Parliament. But his article, it
must be admitted, showed very little of the one

and betrayed a complete misunderstanding of the other.[1]

To most people Mr. Lloyd George's tactics came as a shock. One veteran journalist, indeed, whose warm attachment to an idealised leader no pressure of evidence or experience could alter, hastened, as usual, to make excuses for him. The *Manchester Guardian* discovered in these American Press confidences just what a sensible man would have written, and just what the Archbishop of Canterbury would have approved. But thoughtful people as a whole regretted that an ex-Prime Minister of England should have stepped in to stimulate panic and to damage the credit of the British Government, at a moment when the great majority of Englishmen felt it a duty to give the Government support. The responsible leaders of the Liberal Party agreed that these mystifying manœuvres could not be overlooked. On May 20 Lord Oxford, after consultation with his colleagues, wrote to Mr. Lloyd George expressing the feeling which his action had aroused. He recalled the circumstances. He commented gravely but not unkindly on Mr. Lloyd George's separation of himself from his colleagues during the most critical days of the General Strike:

" It was, in my judgment, the primary duty of all who were responsible for Liberal policy, and certainly not least of the

[1] It is interesting to compare Mr. Lloyd George's account of this article, in his letter to Lord Oxford dated May 24, with the extracts from it printed in the English papers, *e.g.* in the *Evening Standard* of May 20, 1926.

Chairman of the Parliamentary Party in the House of Commons, at such a time to meet together for free and full discussion, and to contribute their counsels to the common stock Your refusal to do so I find impossible to reconcile with my conception of the obligations of political comradeship."

He could not but deplore the article—" a desponding, though highly-coloured, picture of our national straits "—which Mr. Lloyd George had thought it right to contribute to the American Press, at a time " when it was above all things necessary to demonstrate the essential unity of the country." Mr. Lloyd George endeavoured to justify himself in a long and rambling answer, dated May 24, which is open to the public judgment. Into most of his excuses we need not go. One sentence in the letter explains his action more fully perhaps than he was aware:

" It is true I assumed that the Trade Union Council would stand by the miners to the end. There I miscalculated."

Mr. Lloyd George in fact had calculated that the strikers would win. He had separated himself from his colleagues, in order to be free to take his own line if the Government and those backing it went under, hoping perhaps to find in the confusion new possibilities of power.

But even the astutest calculators sometimes make mistakes. When the strike failed and the result upset his calculations, Mr. Lloyd George swung back quickly to an earlier mood. His first step was to deny that he had ever intended to desert his colleagues. His refusal to attend the Shadow Cabinet had meant nothing at all. He had merely wished to avoid friction. He could not understand what the trouble was about. His next step—a favourite resource during the days of the Coalition—was to appeal to the Manchester Reform Club in the guise of a man much misunderstood, the innocent victim of obscure cabals. His speech there—one of the worst examples of his method—was full of angry defiance, of open sneers at his old colleagues, of attempts to shift the issue and confuse the facts. The Liberal leaders—conspirators all—were trying to " drum " him out of the party, because he was " on the side of conciliation " in a dispute where millions of British workmen were concerned :

> " I was walking peaceably along my path when suddenly I was assailed by an angry Bull of excommunication."

He had not had a square deal. He had been condemned unheard :

> " They would not make allowance for the fact that I was living in a remote part of Wales." [1]

His treatment had been a ghastly blunder. He would not be driven from Liberal platforms. But the only thing in the world which he really cared for was to regenerate this beautiful and bountiful land. The guests at the lunch, we are told, cheered wildly, for every art of elocution, every artifice of emotion, was

---

[1] Yet Wales is served with telegraphs and telephones, and Mr. Lloyd George is credited with houses not at Criccieth only but in London and in Surrey. His speech to the Manchester Reform Club on June 5, 1926, is worth study as an example of his tactics.

employed. But on the value of these apologetics two brief comments may suffice. One is by Lord Oxford, not a man who allowed public principles to be sacrificed to personal rancour:

" Mr. Lloyd George, in the exercise of his own judgment, and for reasons of which I am the last to question the gravity, chose to separate himself, in the most formal manner, from our deliberations in a moment of great emergency. He was not driven out; he refused to come in."

The other is a statement sent to Lord Oxford by twelve staunch and valued members of the Liberal Party, who had again and again tried to work with Mr. Lloyd George and to trust him, and had been driven to admit that their trust was not deserved— Lord Grey of Fallodon, Sir John Simon, Mr. Walter Runciman, Lord Lincolnshire, Lord Buckmaster, Lord Buxton, Sir Donald Maclean, Lord Cowdray, Mr. Vivian Phillipps, Mr. Geoffrey Howard, Mr. W. M. R. Pringle and Sir Godfrey Collins:

" We have done our best in the interests of Liberalism to work with Mr. Lloyd George in the councils of the party, but we cannot feel surprised at your feeling that confidential relations are impossible with one whose instability destroys confidence."

No doubt, Mr. Lloyd George persuaded himself, here as always, that public motives of some sort had influenced his action. He was confident that he was better qualified than any other politician to settle an industrial struggle, and that, if the failure of others gave him the opportunity, he could seize a dominating position in politics again. But it is just this facility of self-persuasion, combined with a restless and calculating opportunism, which has caused him again and again to forfeit the respect of many who wished to be his friends.

IV

After the General Strike Mr Lloyd George's tone altered. The affection of humility, never very convincing, was dropped. He had, indeed, made Lord Oxford's position as difficult as anyone could make it. And he had started a fresh feud, on which he counted to transfer to him the leadership for which Lord Oxford had little inclination to fight. Reunion as a cry disappeared. Mr. Lloyd George rejoiced in the prospect.

" The forces that are now rallying to my side," he declared, " contain the most thoughtful personalities in the party—men who have fretted for years over the lost opportunity of Liberalism."

He did not explain what had become of that opportunity while he was in power :

" This split has opened a new vision and started a new era in British politics. Liberalism may soon again take the lead in the march of progress."

He had now become one of the rank and file, " one of the common soldiers in the battle." [1] But this particular common soldier was determined not to be a common soldier long, and he had very substantial

[1] See Mr. Lloyd George's article in the *Sunday News* of June 13, and his speech at the National Liberal Club on June 23, 1926.

resources to help him in improving his position. The National Liberal Federation, the party machine, had still to be secured. Mr. Lloyd George of course controlled the majority of the small Liberal Party in the House of Commons—though the votes of that party upon public questions showed how frequently they were divided—and in July 1926 steps were taken to replace the Chief Liberal Whip, Sir Godfrey Collins, by Sir Robert Hutchison, a National Liberal readier to accept Mr. Lloyd George's instructions. In October Lord Oxford was driven to resign. He had done, he might well claim, as much as any man for Liberal unity. But he was convinced that real unity was impossible under a system of rival authorities, with separate organisations and separate funds. Mr. Lloyd George was still busy with his journalism, working hard to get control of Liberal newspapers, to popularise, one might not unfairly say to advertise, his objects and his personality at home. And for advertisement abroad—popularity there was less important—he had syndicated articles, appearing in newspapers all the world over and paid for on a very generous scale.

On this point Mr. Lloyd George has been good enough to volunteer some interesting information. He has told us that, working hard as a journalist " to earn his livelihood," he secured in four years emoluments much greater than the aggregate of his salaries during seventeen years of office.[1] But while we re-

[1] See his letter in the *Times* of December 3, 1927. If those aggregate salaries considerably exceeded £70,000, Mr. Lloyd George's journalistic earnings must have been in the region of

joice in his profitable penmanship, and even permit ourselves to hope that the livelihood sufficed, no man who values the reputation of British statesmen can help regretting some of the articles he wrote. It is evident from specimens seen here that they were largely devoted, in Mr. Churchill's phrase, to " vilifying his successor in office " : Mr. Lloyd George had not forgiven Mr. Baldwin for breaking up the Coalition and driving him from power. It may well be that it galled him to find Mr. Baldwin's finely-tempered patience during the General Strike contrasted with his own restless self-seeking. And the surprising statements made in these articles on foreign policy and foreign Ministers were on a par with the petulant and undignified criticism which he sometimes applied to the action of the Government at home.

" We can only marvel," wrote the *Review of the River Plate*, "at what appears to be the ex-Premier's blind disregard of what, to one with Britain's welfare at heart, might seem to be a golden opportunity. Here is Mr. Lloyd George with a chance to say at least an occasional good word for his country in the leading newspaper of South America—a paper read by the most critical and intelligent leaders of public opinion in Argentina. And what is the result? The best he can do is to indulge in a flow of bitter party diatribe and to embark upon odious comparisons between the respective personal characteristics of Mr. Baldwin and President Coolidge." [1]

£20,000 a year. Specimens of his writings and his defence of them will be found in the *Times* of May 19 and June 30, 1927, November 14 and 24, 1928, etc.

[1] In a letter to the *Times* of May 20, 1927, Mr. Lloyd George denied that he had described President Coolidge as " malleable and garrulous." The *Times* in reply quoted the words used in Mr. George's article in the Argentine Press.

Apart from the mischief which such utterances may do, one does not like to see the Argentine Press holding up to reprobation the newspaper performances of a man who has been Prime Minister of this country.

Many men have to earn their livelihood. Mr. Lloyd George has always found time for other activities as well. Even before Lord Oxford's withdrawal, it was clear that Mr. Lloyd George was busily employing his agents and resources to recover ascendency in the Liberal Party. The Land Crusade and the differences over the General Strike, the latter much misrepresented, had drawn to him certain adherents. Lord Oxford's retirement brought in others, well-meaning Liberals, who in their desire to see the party re-established, getting back to Parliament and getting back to power, were tempted perhaps to slur over too lightly the value of loyalty and principle in public life. Mr. Lloyd George was quick to note and to exploit this feeling. He redoubled his efforts to win these waverers, and his overtures lacked nothing of the persuasive, flattering geniality which has won the heart of many a kindly journalist, and even turned the heads of some. Cabinet Ministers are admittedly human, ex-Cabinet Ministers more human still. Two or three, who had served under Lord Oxford, and who indulged in no illusions as to the reliability of Mr. Lloyd George, began to think it might be advisable to make terms with him, to try, perhaps a little shamefacedly, to make use of him for party ends. " He is a rascal, but we've got to use him," argued one of them with surprising candour. It did not probably occur to the speaker that " the rascal " might all the time be making use of him. Other Liberals of less experience and shorter memories were drawn into the current. Mr. Lloyd George had such " dynamic " force. He was so clever at electioneering, so successful in getting hold of the Press. He had such conquering qualities in party management, oddly enough, almost all mono-syllabic—such push, drive, urge, pep, vim and snap.[1] He had such powers too of speech, lyrical, eloquent, persuasive, or, if need be, vehement and fierce. He was so ready to laugh at his own in-sincerities when hard pressed.

" For the unreflecting portion of mankind the spectacle of energy on a large scale has always irresistible attractions; vigour becomes an end in itself and an object of admiration for its own sake." [2]

Sir John Simon and others might plead for a little more political consistency, might remind us that it was " no good acting one day as though you very nearly agreed with the Duke of Northumberland and the next day very nearly agreed with Mr. Cook." But criticism of this kind was voted out of fashion, wanting in movement, urge and pep and vim. Was it not necessary somehow or other to get Liberals back into Parliament? Was there not, above all, one

[1] The monosyllables here mentioned are all taken from writers who advocate Mr. George's interests.

[2] See Mr. John Morley on Lord Palmerston's policy (*Life of Cobden*, 1881, Vol. II, 64).

over-mastering necessity, the want of money, and were not Mr. Lloyd George's pockets over-flowing with resources of which he and he only could dispose?

V

Mr. Lloyd George's agents lost no opportunity of pressing these considerations. And with many the money argument had irresistible power. The two or three millions of " loot " or " swag," as Mr. Birrell cheerfully described it, was as fascinating to some political schemers as it was humiliating to oversensitive politicians. Mr. Lloyd George was often questioned about his fund, and was obviously always unwilling to answer. For months, for years indeed, he refused to give any information about its management. On its origin he could hardly be expected to dilate. It was admitted that under Mr. Lloyd George's " close attention " its value had enormously increased. But the sale in July 1927 of *United Newspapers Ltd.* to the *Daily Chronicle Investment Corporation*, a new Company formed to acquire control of the *Daily Chronicle, Sunday News, Edinburgh Evening News, Yorkshire Evening News* and *Doncaster Gazette*, revealed the fact that Mr. Lloyd George was the owner of at least 610,000 shares in *United Newspapers, Ltd.*,[1] and that he had arranged to sell his holding for

[1] Apparently 614,003 shares were sold. The facts are set out in the *Times* of July 21, 1927, p. 19. I have quoted round figures above. Mr. Lloyd George's long-awaited defence of his action, in the *Times* of December 3, 1927, did not meet the points raised by his critics.

£2,888,000 to the new Company, and to receive in exchange £1,743,000 in cash and £1,145,000 in fully paid ordinary shares of £1 each. The advertisement treated Mr. Lloyd George as sole vendor: there was no mention of any trustee. His close attention to business had resulted in a very handsome profit, and he very properly called in a few friends to help him in his responsibilities without limiting his own freedom. It is not a matter of much concern whether he described these friends as his trustees or his committee, or what proportion of the loot he " advised " them from time to time to spend on his behalf. Nobody supposes that Mr. Lloyd George has surrendered control of the money.[1] Nobody supposes that he would use it for anything but what he conceives to be public objects. But he is always too ready to assume that these are identical with his own political ambitions. It is a matter of more concern to those who are jealous of the influence of money in politics, and who think that the danger of political corruption cannot be too closely watched, that a fund of two or three million pounds should be attached to the fortunes of a single politician, used steadily to advance his personal interests, and employed to bring into the House of Commons candidates who depend on his financial support. That still seems to many Liberals to be a new and sinister thing in English politics, and it is trivial to allege that all who

---

[1] It is quite clear from his negotiations with the National Liberal Federation that he has always regarded and treated the fund as his own.

object to such transactions are moved only by a personal animus against the opulent possessor of the fund.

It is difficult for any man to resist temptation. It is doubly difficult for politicians with an empty chest. And no Liberals will wish to dwell on the protracted and painful negotiations which occupied the Executive of the National Liberal Federation from October 1926 to January 1927. They ended in securing a substantial share of Mr. Lloyd George's " loot " for Liberal necessities, and in making Mr. Lloyd George for the time the paymaster of the Liberal Party. The figures of the deal are even now a little misty.[1] The conditions imposed are mistier still. One fact alone emerges clearly. Mr. Lloyd George insisted on securing control of the Party machine in return for his gifts, and drove some of the most loyal and representative of Liberals out of the executive and councils of the Party. Those compelled to retire or to protest included not only one or two Liberals like Mr. Vivian Phillipps, who were closely attached to Lord Oxford—though that is hardly a proof that they were unfitted to serve the Liberal cause. They included men like Lord Grey of Fallodon, who is not moved by shabby motives, Sir Donald Maclean, who had led the Party with rare courage in days, not very distant, when Mr. Lloyd George was doing his best to destroy it, Mr. J. A. Spender, the most dis-

---

[1] But it is understood that £300,000 was supplied for Election purposes, and some £35,000 a year secured to Liberal Headquarters till the Election took place.

tinguished and conciliatory of Liberal journalists, and Sir Robert Hudson, who for thirty-two years had presided with unfailing fidelity over the central organisation. Let Liberals who wish to judge fairly ask themselves whether a party is likely to prosper when, for the sake of the resources offered it, it discards leaders and servants such as these. Sir John Simon and Mr. Walter Runciman were other conspicuous figures at the dinner in December 1926, at which Lord Grey voiced the deep regret of many Liberals at the humiliating bargain made:

" The existence of the fund has brought more blight than blessing to the Liberal Party. . . . I feel that we will serve the Party better by continuing our Liberal work without being a party to these particular negotiations or responsible for the proceedings at headquarters."

Sir Robert Hudson's comments have interest, because few men knew more of the inner history of Liberalism, or had done more for years past to serve, to unite and to finance the party. He resented " the slur deliberately cast," at Mr. Lloyd George's instigation, on men and women who had devoted themselves to Liberal work under conditions of unparalleled difficulty. And he was not alone in wondering whether such action would not at an early date be regretted by many who had been persuaded to give it their assent. Since then a General Election has been fought. Much of the loot, it seems, has been expended.[1] It is said that Mr. Lloyd George is now

[1] It appeared in October 1929 that the £300,000 had been expended, and that only an inadequate income would be available for Liberal Headquarters in future from the fund.

19

strongly of opinion that the results have not justified the outlay to which he has been put. More loot— and where is it to come from?—more bargaining, more surrender of friends may be needed. Faust, we must remember, had to face his day of reckoning. Dare we hope that Sir Charles Hobhouse, or even Sir Herbert Samuel, will escape?

VI

Since Mr. Lloyd George succeeded in securing control of the Party organisation he has not ceased to press his claims to leadership with all the re- sources he commands. His energy and eloquence are very great. His physical vitality is still remark- able. His speeches are as full of liveliness as ever. One especially, in January 1927, where he took as his text a subject on which his authority cannot be disputed—" waste everywhere, everyhow, and all the time "—showed characteristic freshness in draw- ing attention to social and political problems which Liberalism might set itself to solve. His hold on the Liberal Press has increased. By his personal influ- ence with newspaper proprietors he has been able to reduce to docility or silence almost all independent criticism there. His influence in the selection of Liberal candidates has been pushed as far as possible. It is the old story of the paymaster calling the tune. In 1927 and 1928 his agents showed remarkable activity, especially at bye-elections, where they descended in great strength on the constituencies with demands that Mr. Lloyd George's leadership should be acknowledged and Mr. Lloyd George invited to speak. No pretence was made in such cases of encouraging Liberal unity: the object of Mr. Lloyd George's agents was, naturally enough, to serve Mr. Lloyd George. When Mr. Holt in September 1926 had fought with great credit a hard battle in North Cumberland, the *Daily Chronicle*, one of Mr. Lloyd George's organs, made an attack on the Liberal candidate as " out of touch with live Liberalism "—that is, with Mr. Lloyd George; and these things are rarely done without hints from above. When Mrs. Runciman in 1928 fought and won a hard fight in the St. Ives Division, the *Manchester Guardian* published statements obviously intended to depreciate a candidate who would not accept Mr. Lloyd George as leader, and the action of one of the *Guardian's* correspondents was disavowed at Liberal headquarters by fairer-minded men.[1] When the Tavistock Liberals in 1928 unanimously invited Mrs. Runciman to contest that Division—an invitation accepted with the happiest results—Mr. Lloyd George tried, through one of his most important agents, to insist on the invitation being withdrawn. The constituency's freedom of choice went for nothing. No Liberal who would not capitulate to Mr. Lloyd George's leadership should, if he could prevent it, enter the House of Commons. This surprising intrigue was defeated by the firmness of the

[1] See the *Manchester Guardian* for February 22, 23, 24, etc. 1928.

Tavistock Liberals and by the respect for independence which Liberal Headquarters still retained.

It is not agreeable to dwell upon such episodes. But it is necessary to note them, because Liberals as a whole are not aware of the devices which, to secure his own ascendency, Mr. Lloyd George encourages and employs. I have before me at this moment a group of pamphlets published in his interest, all unsolicited gifts from his friends. One is a bitter attack on certain independent Liberals. Another is an illnatured biography of Mr. Baldwin. A third is a dithyrambic panegyric, beginning with a portrait of Mr. Lloyd George at his astutest, and ending with the quotation " I have made thee a little lower than the angels and crowned thee with glory and honour." A fourth is an appeal from a Liberal candidate to be allowed to launch upon me a hundred copies of a work to illustrate the " outstanding public services " of his leader. It may well be that Mr. Lloyd George knows nothing of these particular pamphlets. It may even be that the famous fund does not in all cases pay the bills. But Mr. Lloyd George and his agents are unquestionably the chief promoters of this whole system of personal advertisement. And it will be a melancholy thing for the independence and the character of Liberalism if it allows its leaders to be foisted on it in this way.

Other incidents, less personal but not less significant, have illustrated the quality of Mr. Lloyd George's leadership in recent years. His incursions into questions of foreign policy have been sometimes so capricious, as to indicate rather a desire to damage the Government at home than any clear plan for serving British interests abroad. To fish in troubled waters is always to Mr. Lloyd George a delight. And the contrast between his irresponsible proceedings and the quiet simple dignity which we are accustomed to associate with Lord Grey, helps to explain why all the world distrusts Mr. Lloyd George's diplomacy, while all the world, in England and outside it, trusts Lord Grey's. Free Trade again is a subject which most Liberals regard as vital. But the inventor of Safeguarding has obvious reasons for deprecating too much discussion on that head. It interferes with his schemes for a land crusade. It interferes with election campaigns on unemployment. And before the Election of 1929 intimations went forth from Mr. Lloyd George's agents and organs, in which genuine Free Traders found it difficult to acquiesce, to the effect that Liberal activities must not be concentrated too closely or exclusively upon questions of Free Trade. In 1928, indeed, the Carmarthen bye-election saw a Liberal candidate in Wales, under Mr. Lloyd George's ægis, apparently outdoing even the Safeguarders and committing himself to the idea of Protection for food.[1] These aberrations cause distrust among those to whom Free Trade means something more than opportunism; and it cannot be denied that Mr. Lloyd George's vagaries in regard to both agricul-

[1] See the statements of Colonel W. N. Jones as reported in the *Western Mail* for June 23, 1928.

tural and manufacturing Protection have made him the sport of the Tariff Reformers and the worst possible leader for a Free Trade campaign. On the question of Imperial Preference his attitude has been characteristically uncertain. He has been against it. He has been for it. He has thrown his influence both ways, as his political necessities required. No one can say how he will vote on the question to-morrow. What is leadership of that kind worth? And on yet another Free Trade issue, the possibility of inducing Continental States to reduce the mischievous tariffs which have multiplied so freely since 1918, Mr. Lloyd George's attitude has been curiously disappointing. He has not only done nothing to help. He has, for reasons quite incomprehensible, depreciated and even mocked at some of the efforts made by Free Traders. When the bankers of this country published in November 1926 a Plea for the removal or reduction of restrictions upon European trade—a document remarkable because it was signed both by leaders of British commerce and by some of the most representative figures in banking, trade and industry abroad—Mr. Lloyd George sneered at it in public as a " money-lenders' circular," and appeared to be wholly blind to the value of the movement of which it was an important part. Money-lenders, no doubt, bankers are. But it might almost have been expected that the great financial interests which had done so much to save Europe from starvation, would have been described by some term more courteous by an English political leader. The fact is that on all questions of taxation and economy, and on almost all questions involving serious economic study, it is impossible for Liberals to feel certain what at any given moment Mr. Lloyd George may do or say.

VII

One other issue only of importance in Mr. Lloyd George's leadership remains to be touched on here. His proposals to conquer Unemployment, published on the eve of the General Election of 1929, raised high expectations, not in the world of electioneering only, but in many who cared little for electoral success. The methods adopted were not unfamiliar. An Orange Book replaced the Green Book and the Yellow Book. A deluge of pamphlets, adorned by Mr. Lloyd George's portrait and financed by his fund, was poured out. We were informed that a group of " experts," working under Mr. Lloyd George's direction, had discovered a complete remedy for the most serious social evil of the day. We were assured by Mr. Lloyd George himself that he had drawn into this service " some of the greatest economic thinkers not merely in this nation, but in the world." But his reluctance to disclose the names or qualifications of his thinkers, and the exaggerations of which the Orange Book was full, discounted even this glowing testimonial. Liberal Members of Parliament were not consulted on the subject. The National Liberal Federation was not invited to consider the plan. But a scheme drawn up by these anonymous celebrities was suddenly produced at a Liberal luncheon, and flung upon the table as the latest Liberal programme. It was accompanied by an astonishing pledge. The Liberal Party, if entrusted with power, was affirmed to be ready with schemes of work which could be " put immediately into operation." The work would " reduce the terrible figures of the workless in the course of a single year to normal proportions." And the plans proposed—though it soon crept out that some £200 millions would be needed—would " not add one penny to national or local taxation." It was obvious that many of those present at the luncheon—men of experience who could remember the history of the last ten years—were taken aback by this amazing declaration. It was impossible not to recall the warning given by Sir John Simon to his fellow-Liberals a few months before :

" Do not let us, whatever party we belong to, go forward at the next Election, like a cheap-jack in the fair, and announce that we have some patent remedy that will sweep unemployment away without question and without delay."

And yet, so weak are logic and electioneering human nature, and so credulous are political agents when they set themselves to forecast political results, that it was widely thought that this preposterous pledge would " catch on." Politicians who cared for sincerity were quick to dissociate themselves from it. But the Stock Exchange—possibly not the best representative of Liberalism—was said to be greatly impressed. In speculative circles Mr. Lloyd George's stock went up. Liberals of weight and character, while avoiding a pledge which they did not believe in, thought that something might be made of Mr. Lloyd George's proposals, and were anxious to give his objects at any rate all the support which they could. For they felt that he had at least rendered a public service in concentrating attention once again on the urgent problem to be solved. Advertisements drawn upon the largest scale, and rendered exquisite by portraits dear to every shade of Liberal opinion, filled the pages of many newspapers, and incidentally served to dispose of a good deal of Mr. Lloyd George's objectionable fund. His advisers were confident that the latest prescription was one which no reasonable patient could resist. Mr. Lloyd George, one of his admirers has told us, likes Parliamentary followers " compounded from his own prescription." But in 1929 the electorate appeared to know the veteran practitioner too well. The apothecaries in the background might remain invisible : the patients were unhappily familiar with the drugs. The pledge to conquer unemployment at once without adding a penny to taxation was condemned as neither specious nor sincere. The programme suffered from its methods of advertisement. The trail of electioneering was over it all. And not even the intrepid efforts of Sir Herbert Samuel to light once more the Liberal beacons from Land's End to John o' Groats, could disguise from the more clear-sighted of the watchers the will-o'-the-wisp which danced within the flames.

It is not necessary to examine in detail the programme which the Orange Book put forward, because it only recapitulated, with curious calculations, crisp rhetoric and lively partisanship, a large number of proposals for increasing houses, roads, bridges, telephones, electricity-schemes,[1] drainage-schemes and so forth, which had occupied the attention of various Governments for several years past. Mr. Lloyd George's experts, with the best possible intentions, seem in fact to have discovered little except a way of making party capital out of these ideas. As party men they have, no doubt, a right to do this. But it is not reasonable to represent their efforts as a profoundly fresh and philosophic contribution to the most difficult social problem of our time. That is not to be solved by merely manipulating figures, and the problem of Unemployment stands exactly where it stood before the Orange Book appeared. The Government had no difficulty in showing that many or most of the plans there sketched were already in active operation; that since 1920 successive programmes for roads and bridges had been expedited, with a view to providing work, at a cost of many millions to the State; that 350,000 men could not be put on the roads, as the Orange Book suggested, with any real advantage to the country, to the roads or to themselves; that large contracts for electricity, afforestation and land

[1] I find it hard to reconcile the statements made and the advice given on this point in the Orange Book, on the one hand, and in the Liberal Industrial Inquiry of 1928, on the o ther.

drainage were already in hand; that over 120 schemes of slum clearance had been already sanctioned; and that the difficult problem of housing had advanced so well, since Mr. Lloyd George retired from office, that 800,000 houses had been built within four years. Other critics, with no interest in defending the Government, pointed out that the unemployed were a large and miscellaneous body, that 243,000 of them were women, that thousands of others were ill-suited by age or physical strength or training for heavy labour of any kind, that some were skilled and many unskilled, some steady, some unreliable, many merely casual labourers, many in a real sense unemployable, many also seasonal workers always out of occupation at certain seasons of the year; and that to employ on tasks where strength and special training were needed, labour so varied and so often inefficient, would add inevitably to the cost and lower the quality of the work done.

It was asked how housing accommodation was suddenly to be provided for the 350,000 new labourers on the roads. It was asked what effect this abnormal development of road transport would have upon the railways, on the decreasing traffic and the unemployment there.

" With 110,000 transport workers unemployed," wrote one caustic but competent critic, " of whom 28,000 are road vehicle workers, and 55,000 canal and dock workers on ' the dole,' it is plain that one difficulty is not lack of roads but lack of goods to be carried." [1]

[1] Most of these criticisms, and the figures quoted in them, dated from March 1929.

It was asked how long it would take, in the twelve months allotted to the miracle, to survey the new highways, to manufacture the material for them, and to secure the necessary Parliamentary powers. It was asked what was to be done with the workers with special trades or characteristics, men with fine hands or inherited training, printers, pottery workers, textile workers—there alone the unemployment was estimated at 143,000—or again with clerks and shopmen, travellers and waiters, men obviously ill-fitted for hard outdoor toil. It was asked what, at the end of the twelve months or the two years or the five years of the experiment—whatever the period during which the Government went on offering work and borrowing money—was to become of the army of workers then enlisted, who had been taught to look to the State for support. It was asked how any schemes of work artificially provided, however large or costly, could reasonably hope to escape from the fate which for generations had attended almost every species of relief-works tried. It was asked how such benevolent but inefficient make-shifts could possibly touch the root of the evil, stimulate the great staple industries we principally depend on, find us the additional markets we are needing, or fail to divert our capital and credit from a wiser and more productive economic use.

To none of these serious questions, on the answers to which the whole project depended, did Mr. Lloyd George or his experts in the background find it possible to give adequate replies. Indeed, with a political pusillanimity rare in so inveterate a fighter, Mr. Lloyd George absented himself noticeably from debates on the subject in the House of Commons, and failed to offer any answer to the challenging questions which his proposals had provoked. It is much easier to fling down an electioneering manifesto, making large and indefinite promises, than to face in Parliament the economic difficulties which such rash promises involve. The juggle about expenditure was particularly difficult to explain, because it very soon became apparent that Mr. Lloyd George, while pledging himself not to add a penny to taxation, intended to borrow at the first opportunity scores of millions for his grandiose designs. Men familiar with his methods prophesied that the State might whistle for the repayment of these loans. And Liberals, who had for years been insisting on the need of reducing debt and taxation, could not face with equanimity proposals which made fresh borrowings of public money the first step in their return to power. The truth is, Mr. Lloyd George's whole scheme, however sincere the philanthropy behind it, revealed once again his characteristic inability to grasp anything beyond the electioneering aspects of the problem to be solved. The only permanent cure for Unemployment is to restore credit, to expand and to enfranchise trade. But when temporary palliatives are needed, statesmanship can surely offer something better worth consideration than Mr. Lloyd George's Election programme. What we need is, not a repetition of old errors, but a fresh and close examination of the social, moral and economic forces involved. For that end impressionist pictures and airy calculations are equally useless. Without discrimination, analysis, patience, the study of individual conditions and the understanding of individual needs, public money may be poured out like water, but most of it will go in waste. But with those qualities the State may yet do much to mitigate the fluctuations of employment which every industrial country has to face, to build up and strengthen the system of insurance, to increase the fluidity and the migration of labour, to organise training for the unskilled and untrained, to encourage within closely-guarded limits necessary works of national improvement—the supply of water to cottages which have none is not less needed than orbital or arterial roads —to establish conditions which may make emigration possible and popular, to turn to account, in spite of economic jealousies, the large opportunities which our Dominions could offer for the employment of labour and the production of wealth.

VIII

Judged by the results of the General Election Mr. Lloyd George's effort to make Unemployment a party issue was not a success. Many Liberals, indeed, did splendid work in that campaign. And the rally of voters in many districts showed the depth and strength of the old Liberal ideas. But the great bulk of the industrial voters, once the vanguard of the Liberal army, again made it clear that they had completely lost confidence in the promises of the ex-Premier; and the Orange Book proved no more helpful than the Green Book or the Yellow in re-establishing the Liberals in power. All Mr. Lloyd George's expenditure, all his publications, all his advertisements, all his agents—and all the efforts, let it be added, of thousands of Liberals far more serious and single-hearted than he—only resulted in the return of fifty-nine Liberal Members to the House of Commons, of whom one promptly deserted to the Labour camp. And it is significant that the one quarter of the country where the Liberals secured their most notable triumph,[1] was the quarter where the Liberal candidates had been least identified with a leadership which they did not desire. It is a mistake, said Mr. Bonar Law once with cruel candour, to " over-deify " Mr. Lloyd George as an electioneering force. Character and consistency still count with British voters; and for the lack of them no cleverness in programme-spinning can atone.

I do not propose to continue this study beyond the General Election of 1929. But I would ask my fellow Liberals to consider whether Mr. Lloyd George's claims to lead us ought to be decided without examining closely, as I have tried to examine in this essay, the circumstances of his political career. To sum up, what does it all come to? Why do men who begin as his admirers so often come to doubt

---

[1] Liberal candidates of an independent character won all five Cornish seats.

and to distrust him? It is not a matter of agreeing or disagreeing with his political opinions, for Mr. Lloyd George will work with any party, and there are few phases of political opinion with which he has not professed himself in sympathy at different times. It is not a matter of personal liking or disliking, for there are few critics who do not acknowledge Mr. Lloyd George's personal charm. It is something more. It is a question whether behind that charm he has the character and judgment which entitle him to be accepted as a leader by men with whom sincerity and conviction count. Mr. Lloyd George's remarkable qualities no one will deny. The romantic story of the young Welshman, humbly born and bravely nurtured, fighting his way to influence and power, revealing early his industry, his intrepidity, his large ambition, his genius for handling a popular audience, his strong sympathy with the democracy from which he sprang; passing into Parliament, and rapidly acquiring there, by his nimble wits and his persuasive speeches, a reputation hardly second to the reputation he had won at home; passing on to Ministerial office, and showing there again the same genial and resourceful shrewdness, the same quick eye for a bargain, the same fearlessness in fighting, if fighting seemed likely to bring advantage or renown—that story is long since familiar to the world. Often in those early days he won admiration both from friends and from opponents. Once he rose to a high level, when in the Boer War he imperilled his popularity and future for the sake of a great public cause. But more than once it seemed to his friends that he was capable of sinking to a lower level also, and was a little too anxious, when opportunity offered, to push his own fortunes, to play for his own hand. As time went on, observers noted a growing facility in political manœuvre, in compromise, in " gammon," in intrigue. All humour, no doubt, has in it possibilities of humbug, and all finesse possibilities of fraud. As power came to him, his natural self-assertiveness increased. His restless ambition grew with it, his scheming became more determined and persistent. He meant well by his friends. But he never perhaps felt much compunction in pushing aside any who stood between him and his objects. In 1916 he probably comforted himself with the illusion that his supremacy was essential for his country's good. And his success was rendered easier by the fact that the colleagues whom he then threw over— men of far finer quality and temper—did not, as it happened, care to push themselves.

The Great War brought to Mr. Lloyd George a great personal triumph. Whatever his merits, he reaped also a full harvest from the labours of other men. But success did not strengthen his character. It brought into prominence its weaker sides—the passion for self-assertion and intrigue, the headstrong, dominating temper, the easy indifference to principle, the conviction that a gift for managing men and manipulating opinion, the control of the Press and the control of money, were the things that really counted for leadership in public life. The

20

simplicity, which had once been his charm, became more and more overlaid with assurance, genial assurance when not thwarted, but less agreeable when it did not get its way. The purer aims of youth perhaps had vanished. But much of its vitality and restlessness remained. And even the restlessness was to some extent a sign of force. The Liberal Party must always be a party of movement, and in all parties there is a natural temptation to identify movement with programmes. Mr. Lloyd George has utilised this instinct to the full; and his large resources have enabled him to create a factory of everfresh proposals, which have undoubtedly interested, occupied, propitiated—dare I add, bamboozled?—a large number of able Liberals who liked neither his record nor his ways. Some of these proposals are of real value, and admirable work has been done in threshing them out. Some are more open to criticism. Some are too obviously mere electioneering. But they all have served their purpose in drawing adherents to Mr. Lloyd George's standard, and in diverting to new issues, or at least to new discussions, the thoughts and doubts of candidates whom Mr. Lloyd George desired to have under his control.

And yet with Liberals whose faith is something more than opportunism considerations of a different kind will tell. Men of experience have learned to wonder whether programmes help political parties so much as some anxious politicians suppose. Now and again a great issue like Reform or Free Trade will stir and sweep the country. But in the last sixty years how often has it happened that any party has got into power on the strength of its electoral programme? It is, no doubt, true that General Elections in 1885 and in 1910 were fought to some extent on definite programmes, the first on the illusive formula " three acres and a cow," the latter upon the famous land taxes for which their author has since shown so little respect. But the chief feature of the Election of 1885, apart from the new interest of the rural voters, was the failure of Mr. Chamberlain's unauthorised programme to appeal to the industrial workers; and at least one of the Elections of 1910 was decided not by the new land taxes but by the old issue between Lords and Commons. With these two possible exceptions there is no case in the last sixty years of a General Election being won on a definite programme. Normally British Elections are decided by the failings of the Government in power. Mr. Disraeli's victory in 1874 was due to the unpopularity earned by Mr. Gladstone's first Administration. Mr. Gladstone's victory in 1880 was due to distrust of the foreign policy of Mr. Disraeli. In 1886 we had a strong protest against Home Rule. In 1892 we had a weak reaction against Lord Salisbury's Administration. In 1895 we had a stronger reaction against a Liberal Government which had not power enough to carry its measures. In 1900 we had a War Election. In 1906 we had a protest against Mr. Chamberlain's plunge into Protection and Mr. Balfour's singular determination to shut his eyes to the inconveniences involved. In 1918, again, we had a War Election; it will hardly be suggested that anyone troubled his head much about Mr. Lloyd George's or Mr. Bonar Law's programme. In 1922 we had a revolt of the Conservative Party against the leadership of Mr. Lloyd George, and in 1923 Mr. Baldwin's lapse into Protection, which at once knocked his Government on the head. In 1924 we had a collapse without a programme; no programme could have done so much for the Conservative Party. And the Election of 1929 has taught us how little the most elaborate programmes can help the Liberal cause. It may be added that it has given us a Government which can exist only by shelving all the most distinctive features of the programme which it has been offering the electorate for a generation past. Is it, on these facts, worth while for Liberals to sacrifice the ideals and character of their party, merely for the sake of securing a leader who is thought to be unrivalled in the preparation and production of programmes?

A graver question follows. Suppose that Mr. Lloyd George succeeded one day in securing a majority in Parliament, or effected a combination which put him into office, what kind of leadership might Liberals expect? Is the past no clue to future actions? Could we altogether close our eyes to our experience in order to give him a fresh trial, a clean sheet? In Foreign Affairs alone his accession to power might prove embarrassing. No British Minister of modern times has made himself so generally

distrusted: and the distrust is not personal rancour;
it is based on a vivid recollection of his ways. The
politician who was as much responsible as any man
for the Treaty of Versailles, but who, before the ink
was dry upon the paper, began his schemes to alter
and upset it, who was so deep in the intrigues which
followed that our Allies in France, in Italy, in
Greece, and even in America, became hardly less
suspicious of him than our enemies elsewhere, and
whose passion for abortive conferences made our
Foreign Office helpless and our diplomacy absurd,
may have had some excuses for his bewildering vacillations, but his troubles arose too often from his
curious reluctance to avow the truth. In the end he
lost the esteem of every country, and his return to
power might shake the confidence of all. The politician who in the dangerous Turkish crisis of 1922
was ready to plunge us back into war, and who
rejected with contempt proposals to resort to the
" wheezy harmonium " of the League of Nations, is
not the man to inspire respect for ideals of arbitration, if he takes up the cause of disarmament again.
No Foreign Office in the world would wish to see
Mr. Lloyd George's methods of bluff and manœuvre
substituted for the safer and more honourable in-
fluences which since his day have worked for European peace.

In Home Affairs the prospect of Mr. Lloyd
George's return to office would be as serious for
Liberals who still place some value on principle in
public life. What does genuine Liberalism stand for?

What ideals distinguish it from Conservatism upon
the one hand and Socialism upon the other? It has
something in common, no doubt, with both. The
wisest Conservatives have begun to admit the force
of the Liberal tradition. The wisest of the Labour
leaders are men trained in Liberal ideas. But
Liberalism has still a mission, distinct from Conservatism, Socialism or opportunist "stunts." It
stands for soberness and equity in politics, for individual and public freedom. It stands for fair dealing and friendliness with foreign nations : that is the
basis of its doctrine of Free Trade. It stands for
social independence, against the demoralisation
which dependence on the State entails : that is the
basis of its doctrine of economy, the meaning of
personal and public thrift. It stands for liberty in the
fullest sense, but a liberty conditioned by reason, and
deep-rooted in convictions of duty, sacrifice and self-
restraint. It is, no doubt, true that there are elements of priggishness in these opinions, and Mr.
Lloyd George, whatever his failings, has never been
a prig. But still some tincture of serious and unself-
ish purpose is of the very essence of Liberalism, and
without that quality—though Heaven forbid that
we should talk about it—no Liberal is worth his salt
in public life. Mr. Lloyd George has seen the light,
but he has let it fall behind him. It glints even now
at times across his speeches, and renders transparent
the expedients and excuses they contain. But one
cannot set oneself to become the most successful
opportunist in Europe and trail the clouds of glory

with one still. The truth is that there is hardly any direction in which Mr. Lloyd George, since he deserted his early traditions, has not sacrificed the interests and beliefs of Liberals, and rendered doubly difficult their re-establishment in future. It is comparatively easy for a leader of note to break up and demoralise a party. It is a harder task to rebuild what he has broken, to restore the confidence which he has destroyed.

I do not doubt that I shall be accused of many rancours in thus examining without fear or favour the political record of Mr. Lloyd George. But impartial minds will know that I have written from no private motive, but simply from a desire to see sincerity and loyalty prevail in public life. I have been Mr. Lloyd George's follower. I have parted unwillingly from him. I have never ceased to recognise his better qualities, so far as in later years he has allowed them to appear. I have fought a good many elections now for what I believe to be Liberal principles. And I claim with other Liberals the right to say frankly why we can no longer tolerate Mr. Lloyd George as a leader or trust him as a public man. One of the finest spirits that ever entered English politics found himself, many years ago, compelled to confess to a veteran statesman why he could not help attacking the policies which that statesman had pursued. Mr. Cobden had come to regard Lord Palmerston as an " incorrigible old dodger." He could not refrain from expressing his opinions. And he was met with a generous candour equal to his own. " A public man," Lord Palmerston told him, " is right in attacking persons." If his motives are public motives, they do not need excuse.

Is sincerity, or is it not, a part of statesmanship? Is it necessary, in following a political leader, to be able to trust the individual who leads? That is the plain issue between those who share the views expressed in this essay, and those who are content to accept Mr. Lloyd's George's domination on the ground that in modern politics money matters more than principle and forcefulness pays better than good faith. The years ahead may prove to be an ordeal alike for statesmen and for nations. There is a vast new electorate, awaking slowly to the powers which it possesses, and little trained to use them yet. There is an unexampled opportunity to lead or to mislead opinion. There is a perilous temptation for political rivals to outbid each other in material appeals. Never did we need more to find in the leaders of the people a sense of deep responsibility, restraint, nobility of mind. It is said that some of Mr. Lloyd George's younger followers have begun to scoff at the ideals of Mr. Gladstone. And yet in moments of doubt or tribulation it is to the moral power of Mr. Gladstone that the memory of genuine Liberals returns. We cannot hope to reproduce in every generation that matchless union of qualities and training, genius and industry, passion and judgment, strength and self-control. But the character which Mr. Gladstone bore, and the standards of conduct which he left us, have won the homage of the world. The Liberal Party can still give us leaders in whom that great tradition lingers; and to men in that line of succession only can they with confidence entrust their fate.

PRINTED IN GREAT BRITAIN BY R. CLAY & SONS LIMITED
Bungay, Suffolk

A History of the
University of Oxford.

By Sir Charles Mallet.

In three volumes. Illustrated. Demy 8vo. **21s. each, net.**

Volume I, THE MEDIÆVAL UNIVERSITY AND THE COLLEGES FOUNDED IN THE MIDDLE AGES.

Volume II, OXFORD IN THE SIXTEENTH AND SEVENTEENTH CENTURIES.

Volume III, MODERN OXFORD, 1689–1927.

" It is indeed both a learned and a delightful history."—*Times Literary Supplement.*

" A fascinating story, fascinatingly told."—*Morning Post.*

" A monument of solid industry . . . a great book."—Sir CHARLES OMAN in the *Edinburgh Review.*

"Immense difficulties . . . have been triumphantly overcome, and the book is altogether worthy of its inspiring title."—*Outlook.*

"Every Oxford man worth calling such will feel that Sir Charles Mallet has bankrupted him in gratitude twice over. First, by telling in such faithful and delicate detail the history of each man's own College . . . and secondly, by setting out with such a wealth of learning and understanding the great pageant of Oxford in history."—*New Statesman.*

"This work is a great achievement, and all Oxford men will add Sir Charles Mallet to their list of benefactors. Learning, judgment, and humour all distinguish it, and it is safe to predict for it generations of readers. . . . Sir Charles Mallet's task was heroic, almost invincible. But, in our judgement, he has triumphed."—Mr. KEITH FEILING, in the *Observer.*